Part I
Introduction

City, State, and Market

City, State, and Market

The Political Economy of Urban Society

MICHAEL PETER SMITH

Basil Blackwell

Copyright © Michael Peter Smith 1988

First published 1988

Basil Blackwell Inc.
432 Park Avenue South, Suite 1503
New York, NY 10016, USA

Basil Blackwell Ltd
108 Cowley Road, Oxford, OX4 1JF, UK

Library of Congress Cataloging in Publication Data

Smith, Michael P.
    City, state, and market : the political economy of
    urban society / Michael Peter Smith.
        p.   cm.
    ISBN 0–631–15848–0
    1. Urban policy—United States. 2. Cities and towns—
United States. 3. Capitalism—United States.
    I. Title.
    HT167.S55 1988   88–5090
    330.973'0927'091—dc19   CIP

British Library Cataloguing in Publication Data

Smith, Michael Peter, 1942–
    City, state, and market : the political
    economy of urban society.
    1. United States. urban regions. Social
    conditions. Effects of economic planning
    I. Title
    307.7'6'0973

    ISBN 0–631–15848–0

Typeset in Linotron Sabon
by Photo·Graphics, Honiton, Devon, Great Britain
Printed in the United States of America

Contents

Foreword

When the stranger says "What is the meaning of the city?
Do you huddle close together because you love one another?"
What will you answer? "We all dwell together to make
money from each other." or "This is a community."?
                                        T. S. Eliot, "The Rock"

In the case of the social production of cities, the realist's answer
to the existential question raised by Eliot is, not surprisingly,
"both" rather than "either/or." In the case of the social production
of ideas, a realist can be more optimistic. Ideas are not created
in abstract time and space but developed through the process of
communication. Throughout the course of writing this book, I
have, of course, been informed by the current intellectual debates
in urban and state theory and research, and by my own efforts
to shape the terms of discourse in these debates. More concretely,
and more importantly, I have benefited from the helpful comments
of a community of scholars who have read all or part of this
manuscript as it was being written. My greatest debt is owed to
my colleague Bernadette Tarallo, whose careful reading and
insightful comments on the entire manuscript have immeasurably
improved the final product. I also wish to thank several persons
who have offered thoughtful comments on various parts of the
manuscript. These include Richard Tardanico, Joe R. Feagin,
Dennis Judd, David Perry, Joel Devine, Ray Taras, William Canak,
and Mickey Luria. Thanks are due as well to the students in
seminars I have taught in recent years at the University of
California at Davis and Tulane University, and as a Visiting
Professor at the University of California at Berkeley. My editorial
assistant Evelyn Harris has been exceptionally helpful in easing

the process of final revision and copy-editing. My American and British editors at Basil Blackwell, Peter Dougherty and Sean Magee, are acknowledged not only for their grace and good cheer, but for their intellectual understanding of this project and its purpose.

My wife Pat, to whom this book is dedicated, deserves the final thanks for the depth of her love and support, which have kept me sane enough to keep going. In this, she has been helped in basic ways by Felix, Daphne, and Imre, and by the coast of Maine.

Michael Peter Smith
Davis, California

ACKNOWLEDGEMENTS

Chapter 3, "Structural Marxist Urban Theory" has been substantially revised from an article which first appeared in *Comparative Urban Research*, Vol. VII No. 3 (1980) under the title "Critical Theory and Urban Political Theory." The section of Chapter 7 on minimum wage legislation was drawn from an op-ed column, "Maintaining a Minimum" originally written for the *New York Times* (December 1, 1980, p. A19). Copyright © 1980 by the New York Times Company. Reprinted by permission. Portions of Chapters 8 and 9 first appeared in my article, "Global Restructuring and Local Political Crises in U.S. Cities," in *Global Restructuring and Territorial Development*, edited by Jeffery Henderson and Manuel Castells and published by Sage Publications, London, 1987. I thank the editors and publishers of these works for permission to use parts of them in this book.

1
Urban Development: Why Politics Matters

In all social systems, politics, public policies, and state power shape economic activity, employment patterns, population migration, and urban development in complex ways. In the US political economy, local, regional, national, and transnational business interests, as well as the professional segments of labor, have been especially successful in capturing access to different parts of a highly fragmented state structure to protect and promote their interests, power, and privilege. The use of the authority of national, state, and local governments to serve particularistic ends, in turn, has been a major theme in American political discourse, frequently politicizing issues of social and spatial inequality. This has produced, in its turn, a concentrated effort by dominant interests to mask the political dimension of their power. Ruling economic and political elites have treated the uneven distributional consequences of their actions as unfortunate but necessary side-effects of purely technical and economic processes of growth and change. Current ruling elites have insisted that the social and geographic inequalities so produced will even out in the long run if those best able to manage "the economy" (i.e., business interests) are allowed the freedom to produce sustained economic growth. In this book I will show that there are no separate containers called "the polity" and "the economy." In actually existing societies economic activities are necessarily embedded in culturally specific social processes and political relations. In the last instance, technical and economic development have no imminent logic apart from their relationship to politics and society.

POLITICIZING THE URBAN ECONOMY

Three major theoretical approaches have been used to explain the uneven development of urban America, the rise of the welfare state as a response to that unevenness, and the contemporary fiscal crises of US cities and the American welfare state. These are the market capitalist perspective, welfare state liberalism, and structural Marxism. In this book I will argue that each of these approaches misinterprets the role of politics, markets, and the state in shaping urban form and the opportunity structure of US cities.

According to the proponents of market capitalism, the production of unevenly developed cities and regions is viewed as the inevitable outcome of technological change within a market capitalist economic system that readily adapts to innovation (Gottdiener, 1985: ch. 7). This rationalization for uneven development implies that no political or policy choices could have avoided the inevitable adaptation of the economic system to more efficient forms of spatial use and economic development. Politics and society are reduced to "bearers" of inexorable economic and technological forces. The implication of this view is to treat as natural and immutable, processes that have been established and maintained by politics and are subject to modification by human will. As Ryan (1981) has said, this amounts to regarding "as timeless and 'natural' what were actually the expressions of quite specific and changeable social relationships."

The market capitalist view of urban growth and decline is that these restructurings of the form and functions of our cities are healthy adaptations to new market conditions and to technological change. Locational choices are viewed as individual decisions by people and firms, premised on short-term gain. In the long run, these choices are seen as ultimately beneficial to society as a whole because of the greater efficiency that they are assumed to bring to the economy. Because "free market forces" are seen as the most efficient allocators of capital and labor, government interventions either to buffer or to facilitate market forces are seen as unnecessary, wasteful, and possibly even harmful to the general welfare (Kasarda, 1980, 1981:340). Thus, for example, proponents of market capitalism argue against social welfare expenditures as well as against federal government financial aid to declining cities. They contend that such policies of public support for needy people and places are actually harmful because they "anchor low wage workers to sites of low employment opportunity, discourage labor force participation, and inhibit labor mobility" (Yago, 1983:120).

Welfare state liberals also accept the assumption that free markets maximize efficiency. Nevertheless, they acknowledge that institutional and cyclical "market imperfections" have left certain places and people in prolonged economic distress. In this view, the greater-long run efficiency of the national economy necessarily produces short-term local, regional, and sectoral decline and disinvestment which must be rectified by compensatory government policies. Thus, for instance, in the name of fairness to losing people and places in the "market struggle" for greater efficiency, the Carter administration's urban policies offered tax incentives to create jobs, special revenue sharing to localities with high unemployment rates, job retraining programs, and various other intergovernmental transfers to people and places left behind in the market search for higher profits.

Despite their policy differences, both market capitalists and welfare state liberals share the assumption that the current economic restructuring, population redistribution, and uneven pattern of urban growth and decline taking place in contemporary America are products of economic processes operating in an autonomous sphere called "the economy."

Structural Marxists, particularly those subscribing to the "capital logic" school of urban political economy, also see technical and economic processes, and the structural logic of their development under the laws of motion of capitalism, as the basic engines of urban change and uneven development (for discussion see Jessop, 1982; Feagin, 1984). Thus, according to "capital logic" analysts the capitalistic world economy periodically requires global economic restructuring, usually in response to new international competition and crises of overproduction and falling profitability of firms. This restructuring in turn has immediate effects on any city's built environment, as when entire cities experience rapid economic decline (see Hill, 1983; Hill and Feagin, 1987). Other cities or other parts of the same city which are tied into new global investment patterns may flourish, resulting in uneven development both among and within major metropolitan areas.

Although structural Marxists do assign a role to the state and to urban politics in shaping urban form, this role is viewed as only "relatively autonomous" (Poulantzas, 1978). By this is meant that state policies and local political life are viewed largely as reactive to the "structured coherence" of the "laws of motion" of capitalist economic development (see especially Harvey, 1982, 1985: ch. 6). In this respect, paradoxically, structural Marxism resembles the economistic thinking of the New Right devotees of market capitalism. Both attribute too much historical significance to the material forces of production, i.e., to technical and economic processes, while failing to acknowledge how deeply these processes are embedded in historically specific national and local social and political processes.

The social actions producing uneven urban and regional development, the social and fiscal problems of our cities, and the crisis of the US welfare state are not mechanical reflections of the productive system. Cities change not only as a result of the requirements of economic logic but also as a result of changing social and political relations at the local, national, and international scales (Smith and Tardanico, 1985, 1987). The political organization of any society and of its cities, for example, is an especially important factor mediating processes of economic growth and decline and shaping elite and popular perceptions of the point at which given levels of national or local public expenditure constitute "fiscal crises" (see Marcuse, 1981).

In this book I argue that changing urban and regional development patterns, and their attendant social and fiscal consequences, are best understood as the long-term outcomes of social actions taken by both economic and political actors operating within a complex and changing matrix of relations between global and national political-economic forces and national and local social and political processes. It is the historically specific social and political processes through which economic forces must work rather than general laws of capitalist economic development which best account for the uneven pattern of urban development in the United States.

This is why the particular forms of uneven development – sprawling suburban development, widespread urban fiscal stress, extreme class segregation of residential communities, and pronounced population deconcentration of affluent communities to the hinterlands – are not found in this same form in other advanced capitalist states. In Europe, for instance, suburban sprawl is less pronounced; centralized state structures finance a larger share of local government budgets, thereby mediating local fiscal stress; uneven development tends to be more pronounced within central cities than between cities and suburbs; and the upper strata are less anti-urban in lifestyle and residential location.

In the US political economy, several interrelated social and political processes have been especially important in producing the historically specific American pattern of uneven urban and regional development. Taken collectively, these processes highlight the uniqueness of the US state and underline the importance of political variables in explaining uneven development. The operation of these socio-political processes forms the subject matter of *City, State, and Market*.

To illustrate the scope of the argument developed in this book these social and political processes may be arrayed from the most local to the most global level of analysis. They include:

1 the political sociology of suburban exclusion, including the use of the zoning and land use controls of the "local state" (Cockburn, 1977) by professional working strata to maintain their ability to reproduce privilege (chapter 1);

2 the social production of an ideology of housing market dynamics among private interests and public policy-makers in the housing supply network which legitimates unequal access to housing market opportunities by race, ethnicity, and class (chapter 1);

3 the political relations between local economic development interests and federal and state "infrastructure" development bureaucracies (chapters 2–4);

4 the urban and regional impacts of the rise of the "tax state" or "Fiscal Keynesianism" as a key driving force in public policy-making, especially the tax treatment of economic growth inducing business production and housing consumption activities (chapters 1–4, 7 and 9);

5 the struggle between segments of capital and labor at all government levels to affect the distribution of the costs of government between businesses and households (chapters 2–9);

6 the role of the military industrial complex or "Military Keynesianism" in channeling interregional investment patterns which create new patterns of regional growth and new settlement spaces (chapters 2, 4, and 7);

7 the role of national Republican party officials in transferring public resources to supportive Sunbelt and suburban constituencies; as well as the backlash effect occasioned by national Democratic party officials' efforts to integrate urban blacks into the mainstream of society, the economy, and the polity (chapters 1–2, 4, 7 and 9);

8 the role of the proponents of market capitalism as a socially produced ideology which has shifted the center of gravity of US welfare capitalism increasingly rightward and masked new uses of state power under the guise of a return to the free market (chapters 5–7);

9 the political strategies of multinational firms for shifting investment globally to the most manageable political jurisdictions and labor forces (chapters 8–9); and

10 the demographic movement of economic and political migrants as survival strategies on a global scale in the international political economy (chapter 9).

These last two global processes, political as well as economic in nature, in turn, feed back into the politics of local government. Because capital and people moving globally must locate locally we must include as a final political process the local political struggles occasioned by the mounting social costs of rapid investment, disinvestment, population change and restructuring of the built environment in *both* growing and declining cities, and the consequences these struggles have for the future economic development of cities and regions (chapters 4, 8 and 9).

In this book the interplay among these key dimensions of the political economy of uneven urban and regional development in the US urban system will be examined. To illustrate the central themes of the book this chapter will now focus upon the issues of uneven development between central cities and their suburbs and uneven development among US cities and regions. This focus was chosen to specify concretely the intellectual vantage point forming the basis of my subsequent assessment of the crisis of US welfare capitalism and my critique of the structural Marxist and market capitalist responses to the urban dimension of that crisis. Once this is accomplished, the final section of this chapter spells out the structure of the rest of the book.

THE POLITICS OF SUBURBAN EXCLUSION

Three major dimensions of uneven development within metropolitan areas in the United States may be distinguished. These include unequal access to housing stock; race and class segregation; and unequal access to housing credit, popularly known as "redlining." Each of these is best viewed as a result of neither economic nor technological inevitability but as a deliberate outcome of public policies enacted by political processes and sustained by social forces. Taken together, these phenomena constitute a public policy of "suburban exclusion," the roots of which are not difficult to discern.

Suburban exclusion is a social product of three interacting forces: public policies of local governments in affluent suburban communities responsive to the demands of professional segments of labor; national tax and mortgage subsidy policies and their use by competitive segments of capital and broader segments of the working population; and the social practices of private lending institutions and their public regulators. Let us consider each of these dimensions of suburban exclusion.

Suburban Exclusion and the Local State

US local governmental structure is highly fragmented, a condition which opens up multitudinous possibilities for the capture of pieces of public power by private interests. The historical pattern of incorporation of affluent, middle, upper-middle, and upper class enclaves is a case in point. Affluent professional strata have either used existing suburban local governments or created new municipal government jurisdictions out of previously unincorporated areas to insulate themselves from central city social problems and to consolidate their own material and cultural resources for the reproduction of their preferred life-style as well as their social power and privilege (see Newton, 1975; Neiman, 1975). The result, now common in all metropolitan regions of the United States (see Abbott, 1981 on the growing fragmentation of Sunbelt metropolitan areas), has been a class structured hierarchy of settlement spaces. The socio-political logic which underlies this organization of space has been nicely expressed by Ken Newton (1975:251–2):

There is a vicious circle entailed in urban fragmentation in that to keep taxes and expenditures down, the wealthiest suburbs must use their powers to keep in their own money and to keep other people's problems out. . . . Because of this imperative, the wealthiest suburb must protect itself against the slightly less wealthy, which is forced to defend its borders from invasion by the still less wealthy, and so on down the line until the working class suburb is forced to use its powers against the block-busting tactics of nonwhites or white ethnics. At each boundary, the more affluent have better weapons than the less affluent to protect their interests.

Thus, far from being an expression of rationally calculated economic choices by individual consumers for different housing and amenities bundles, the race and class segregation of metropolitan areas in the United States is a byproduct of the social actions of political actors in various local jurisdictions pursuing a conscious policy of local protectionism. In this way, the managerial and professional strata erect significant barriers to residential and social mobility: zoning laws, restrictive building codes, property tax differentials and the like, which stratify metropolitan communities by income, race and class, thereby preventing free mobility of individuals. Only the top strata, as Newton (1975: 254) has observed, have sufficient slack resources "to survey the full range of packages of goods and services produced in different jurisdictions and to choose freely the combination they prefer." Having done so, they are in a position to use exclusionary public policies like large lot zoning to limit the choices available to the slightly less wealthy. These, in their turn, follow suit, until the bottom of the social structure is reached. In this position "market choice" is virtually non-existent.

National Policies and Residential Inequality

National public policies to promote housing production also have contributed to the unequal distribution of settlement space within metropolitan areas. Until quite recently, for example, Federal Housing Administration (FHA) loan guarantee policies to enable middle income working strata to obtain credit to buy homes and thereby to subsidize the decentralized homebuilding industry, were restricted to newly constructed homes. This public policy was intended to stimulate economic growth (Perry and Watkins, 1977; Stone, 1980), to subsidize the housing and mortgage lending industries, and to incorporate additional segments of labor into the status of home ownership. Because of the scarcity of land in many central cities, combined with the purposive use of racial criteria by lending institutions, the real estate industry, and their public regulators, such loan subsidies generally "trickled through," to housing consumers in ways that accelerated the race and class segregation of metropolitan America. This policy was a key factor which stimulated, subsidized, and channeled the suburbanization of more and more enclaves.

Once channeled in this way, however, those segments of the working class with enough savings and taxpaying ability to benefit from the policy then acted much as more affluent professional workers had done. They used the political power of local government to incorporate separately in order to protect their newly acquired status, at the expense of the revenue base of the deteriorating central cities. Both the larger policy structure and local political processes have thus contributed to the intractability of the current pattern of metropolitan residential inequality that is one of the central dimensions of uneven development and the current fiscal crisis of central cities.

The deductibility from federal income tax liabilities of both interest payments on home mortgages and local property taxes has been an even more significant national policy stimulating suburbanization and structuring the unequal distribution of settlement space within metropolitan areas. Even those who might have preferred central city amenities and life-styles have found it difficult to pass up the substantial home ownership subsidy contained in the federal tax code.

Gottdiener (1985) has nicely captured the scale and significance of public policy incentives in shaping the kind of world in which most Americans now live and work.

It has long been repeated . . . that suburban development has occurred because of an insatiable demand among Americans for the single family home. Clearly such massive growth would not have occurred after World War II were it not for the variety of government subsidies directed toward supporting the supply of that particular form of housing. In addition to the government programs . . . which propped up both a housing industry and a real estate financial framework, admissable tax deductions also worked specifically to reduce the burden of mortgage payments and local property taxes on homeowners. In 1974 the combined subsidies from tax benefits amounted to nine billion dollars of which the major portion was realized by those families making more than $20,000 a year. . . . In short, the reason why single family home ownership is so popular in the United States is because people are literally paid to purchase into this mode of housing.

By 1980, following a decade of high inflation in housing prices, the combined "tax expenditure" offered disproportionately to homeowners in suburban and nonmetropolitan areas by the tax deductibility of mortgage interest and property taxes had risen to over $30 billion per year (Cho and Puryear, 1980:208). This public subsidy to owner-occupied housing was a central engine of uneven investment between the core and periphery of metropolitan areas.

Understanding "Redlining"

David Harvey's case study (1975a) of changes in the urban spatial structure of Baltimore attempts to show the growing importance of finance capital in structuring the circulation of capital to modify land uses in decisive ways. Harvey focuses upon the key institutions of financial capital: commercial banks and savings institutions, life insurance companies, private pension funds, credit unions, and real estate investment trusts which establish the ground rules within which individual locational choices must be made. Harvey improves on the market capitalist view of housing supply by recognizing the structuring role played by institutions in constraining market choices. Nevertheless, he still regards the processes which produce uneven settlement space as largely economic. According to Harvey's "capital logic" view, various fractions of finance capital have institutionally channeled investment and have organized local housing markets in the ways that have helped segregate metropolitan areas by race and class. Harvey traces the spatial patterning of housing markets, central city neighborhood decay, fiscal and educational disparities between cities and suburbs, and a host of related socio-spatial inequities that we have come to term "urban" problems directly to this structuring of uneven social access to resources by the residential and commercial banking system (see Harvey, 1975a and b, 1985: chs 4 and 5).

Having said this, and largely agreeing with Harvey that housing supply has been unevenly organized by these institutional forces, I must be clear about how I think these forces operate and why it is inappropriate to interpret them as "economic processes." To say that growth, decay and uneven development of residential neighborhoods is structurally channeled is *not* to say that this dimension of urban space is determined by any sort of *automatic economic process,* whether this is called the logic of the market or the "laws of motion" of capital. The practice of redlining well illustrates the limits of theories which rely on deductive, ahistorical explanations like "market logic" or the logic of "capital accumulation" to explain the behavior of economic institutions. These theories fail to consider historically specific social, political and organizational factors which shape the actual perceptions and actions of decision-makers who have social power.

For example, quite apart from purely economic criteria such as "rate of return," mortgage lenders in contemporary America are tied to a set of institutional supports which powerfully shape their perceptions of social reality, and hence their choices. Their choices, while real in their consequences, are not deducible from a simple calculation of profit rates. Rather, they are *socially produced* and *politically mediated* by the interactions of mortgage lenders in the institutional milieu which comprises their everyday social environment: real estate agencies, political regulators, appraisers, builders, and the other institutional bodies whose collective perceptions and actions set the patterns of residential land use in contemporary American society.

These socio-political institutions socialize their members in ways that transcend the capacity of actors within the institutional nexus to apply strictly the logic of capital accumulation to lending decisions.

The set of ideological beliefs which reinforces socially produced decisions to redline particular neighborhoods has been termed the "housing market ideology" (Tomer, 1980). The socially produced rationalization for lending decisions that reorganize local residential communities is a set of interrelated ideas, beliefs, and assumptions held by most actors managing the economic and political institutions that structure the housing market. Social pressures on lenders to conform to the shared assumptions held by real estate brokers and appraisers, home builders, life and fire insurance companies, and public regulatory agencies having a role in housing finance, are subtly reproduced by regular social interaction. In this way, a desire for attitudinal consistency with the "significant others" in the social network of private and public housing suppliers has created an ideology which incorrectly elevates to the status of "economic laws" the following premises: "Suburban housing is more desirable than urban housing and ... suburban growth is inevitable and desirable; older urban neighborhoods inevitably decline and die; and ... 'less desirable groups' and 'dissimilar land uses' [inevitably depress] housing values" (Tomer, 1980:210).

As Tomer (1980:210) has succinctly said, the influence of the social network of housing suppliers on its members and their influence, in turn, on policy-making "leads firms to adopt decision rules which are biased (in an economic sense) against lending in older urban areas, especially those whose residents are considered low in socioeconomic status." Therefore, if any logic at all is operating in this context, it is the logic of social, organizational, and political processes rather than the logic of accumulation or market efficiency. It is the former rather than the latter that shapes the unequal distribution of access to housing, housing credit, and residential neighborhoods. Socially or politically based exclusionary policies simply reduce the number of potential bidders on parcels of land and real property, thereby distorting the one universally recognized "economic" law: the law of supply and demand.

UNEVEN DEVELOPMENT AND URBAN FISCAL CRISIS:
BEYOND ECONOMISM

A second key dimension of uneven development in the US urban system is the widely diverse rates of growth and decline among large American cities and the general increase of investment in Sunbelt cities as compared to Snowbelt cities. Peter Marcuse (1981) has nicely summarized the basic empirical facts of these spatial changes in the United States about which urban analysts agree. These include: declining central city populations; sharp decline of older manufacturing cities; generally high suburban growth and metropolitan deconcentration; rapid growth in the South and West; rising state and local expenditures throughout the 1960s and 1970s accompanied by declining revenues; and a deterioration of urban public services and basic urban infrastructure, especially in declining older cities.

Both welfare state and market liberals treat these developments as inevitable by-products of basic economic and technological processes: the wearing out of past infrastructure, the emergence of new transportation and communication technologies, the changed "spatial needs" of an economy that has evolved from a manufacturing to a service base (see Kasarda, 1981). "Capital logic" exponents prefer to focus on the global concentration of capital and growing interdependence of production activities on the international scale to account for these developments.

From each of these basically economistic perspectives the fiscal crisis of older central cities in the United States is viewed as stemming from inevitable economic developments. Political factors accompanying the fiscal crisis – conflicting demands in declining cities from minority group service users, public service unions, and taxpaying households demanding fiscal austerity – are seen as the results of an unavoidable restructuring of economic investment away from older cities in the advanced societies. The regressive distributional consequences of these developments are seen as unfortunate but unavoidable byproducts of the logic of economic growth. Likewise, the rapid growth of Sunbelt cities and the attendant social benefits and costs of this growth are seen as driven entirely by "the economy."

This explanation of rapid urban growth and decline introduces politics only *after the fact* as a local reaction to forces and conditions set into motion by "the economy" and "its" inexorable demand for ever greater efficiency which may produce painful dislocations while expanding growth and capital accumulation. This way of interpreting events ignores the fact that several distinctively American political processes have entered the picture *before the fact*, contributing importantly to the current pattern of urban growth, decline, and local fiscal crises in both growing and declining cities.

The Exceptionalism of the Political State

In subsequent chapters of this book it will be shown that four central features of the uniqueness or "exceptionalism" of the US state structure and the American political process are important before-the-fact political elements in uneven development. For the sake of clarity I will briefly rehearse my argument at the outset. First, the fragmentation of governmental jurisdictions within the American federal system provides state and local governments with a greater degree of both autonomy in policy initiative and interdependence of policy impact than is true of more unitary and centralized state structures in other advanced capitalist societies such as Britain and France. This dispersal of state sovereignty creates a multiplicity of contradictory channels for the representation of political interests. As we shall see, this has produced contradictory state policies which shape as well as respond to changing political and economic conditions in urban America.

Second, the social base of support for American Keynesianism embodied in the US Democratic party has been a loosely structured urban, ethnic and regionally based coalition rather than a class-based political force. This has proven to be an insufficiently broad base of political support to sustain a redistributional political agenda to either needy people or needy places. Hence, despite much fanfare about "saving cities" and "ending poverty" the social crisis of central cities continues. The real agenda of both major political parties has been to stimulate economic growth through somewhat different combinations of public spending and taxation policies. These policies shape and exacerbate rather than resolve the urban crisis.

Third, the growing reliance on tax incentives rather than direct state intervention as a public policy tool used by all levels of government in the US has had important implications for urban fiscal stress and local politics. Despite continuing social distress in urban America, the role of the state in shaping these tax incentive policies (which I will term "fiscal welfare") has had a depoliticizing effect on grassroots community politics.

Fourth, the political leadership of the normally dominant wings of both major US political parties have favored high levels of national defense expenditure. This has virtually institutionalized what I will term "military Keynesianism." The massive deployment of public resources to the military industrial sector that military Keynesianism has entailed has been a major factor shaping the growth and decline of US cities and regions.

We have already illustrated an important reason why politics matters – socially and politically produced governmental forms, state policies, and ideologies have helped to sustain uneven development *within* metropolitan areas. Politics also matters because the unique combination of social forces underlying the rise of the "tax state," the transformation of national political party alliances, and the resilience of military Keynesianism have been central engines of uneven development *among* US cities and regions. Consider the following political dimensions of the shifting urban and regional investment pattern:

1 Political processes underlie the public policies by which the national government, through the federal tax code, has underwritten business and household locational shifts away from central cities (see Bradford and Rubinowitz, 1975).

2 The high level of public spending for national defense has had uneven regional consequences (see Abbott, 1981; Markusen, 1984, 1987). This inducement to invest in Southern and Sunbelt communities has been fostered by the concrete political power of the military-industrial complex rather than the abstract logic of efficient investment.

3 Republican party elites in the past three decades have purposively designed federal urban programs to shift resources away from predominantly Democratic urban constituencies in northeastern and midwestern cities and toward suburban constituencies and emergent, predominantly Republican, constituencies in urban areas of the Southwest (Mollenkopf, 1983).

4 The strategy of incorporating minority constituencies into traditionally Democratic urban coalitions by Great Society expansion of the welfare state was accelerated by the urban rebellions of the 1960s. The subsequent effort of Democratic politicians to hold together their party's contradictory coalition of segments of business, labor, and minority groups by expanding public spending in turn helps explain the timing of the effort by corporate interests to shift future investment to southern and southwestern locations, assumed

to be more politically quiescent (see Marcuse, 1981;
Mollenkopf, 1983; Smith and Judd, 1984).

The Politicized Economy

Having now clearly stated the central theme of this book, that
politics matters, it is equally important to realize that political
and economic processes are complexly intertwined. A second
major theme of this book is that "politics" and "economics" are
not separate terrains. Such public issues as national economic
policies, partisan alignments and strategies, patterns of defense
spending, the political forces supporting the tax laws, and the
public infrastructure investments that favor new construction in
suburban, rural fringe, and Sunbelt locations (Bluestone and
Harrison, 1982; Marcuse, 1981) cannot always be neatly divided
into separate containers labeled "political" versus "economic"
determinants of business investment shifts.

Public policies are *political-economic* products, which, in their
turn, affect the "economic" calculus of "efficient investment."
Thus, for example, the political economic alliances underlying the
US tax code have structured subsidies into federal tax laws which
favor investment and construction at new locations. By the early
1980s this tax subsidy was "more than twice the total budget of
the United States Department of Housing and Urban Development
per year, and almost three times the total federal expenditure on
community and regional development for the whole country"
(Marcuse, 1981:12). In this way, when a steel mill closes an old
facility, it gets to write off the closing as a loss, thus directly
allowing it to retain capital with which to make new investments
in new locations. In the absence of such provisions, or in the
presence of alternative provisions designed to achieve other
objectives, the rush to new, more geographically dispersed
locations, while still possible, would be far more costly, and hence
less likely. It is certainly not determined by any inevitable logic
of market efficiency.

To illustrate concretely, Barnekov, Rich and Warren (1981)
have nicely identified several significant dimensions of the structure
of incentives for capital investment in growing regions embedded
in existing federal taxing and spending policies. As these authors
indicate, the effectiveness of these incentives in restructuring

capital investment to the West, Southwest, and Southeast also profoundly challenge the simplistic assumption that technical or economic logic, unfiltered by politics and policy, has driven investment to more "efficient" locations in the South and West.

In pointed criticism of the recent controversial *President's Commission on the 1980s* report, these authors support the argument being developed here and amplify upon it in the following way:

> A central assumption of the New Privatism is the presence of technologically driven forces that will inevitably result in vast shifts in people and activities .... However, the assertion that the technological changes that are affecting the spatial structure of the nation are beyond the capacity of government to control or ameliorate cannot be accepted as fact. It may be embraced on faith or ideology, but the evidence runs in the opposite direction. The booming economies of the West, Southwest and Southeast are in large part the result of the cumulative effects of decades of federal subsidization of the physical and resource infrastructure and economic base of these areas. The flow of federal funds for rail, highway and air systems that link these regions with each other and the rest of the country and for resource development, particularly water, hardly reflect market responses to the intrinsic advantages of these regions. Similarly, the more recent infusion of Department of Defense dollars that serves to shore up if not dominate the economic base of these areas could not be explained as constituting or resulting from the natural expression of forces beyond government control.

The Social Costs

A third theme of this book is that because of these deliberately adopted public policies, uneven development and urban fiscal crisis are nurtured in several distinct ways. The pace of capital restructuring is accelerated by tax subsidies for modernization; the capacity of the public sector to respond to the crisis is weakened by the policies used to encourage business location, which invariably entail some combination of government expenditures and forgone tax revenues which drain the state's capacity to incorporate those dislocated by economic restructuring. The fragmentation of public authority, itself sustained by power, tradition, ideology and political interest, prevents the federal level of government from significantly transferring revenue from growing to declining areas.

Among the most obvious social costs to declining cities and to society stemming from this socially and politically produced unevenness are: (1) the waste of useful but unused and underused physical capital facilities – housing, schools, factory buildings, and hospitals, and mass transit operations, to mention just a few; (2) the decline of local fiscal capacities to maintain even basic fire and police services; (3) the hidden psychic costs that these engender. The latter cost is not restricted to particular distressed localities, as reflected in the striking national rise in the use of private police forces to protect those businesses, neighborhoods, and people who can afford the cost of this type of socially unproductive investment; (4) the excess waste of human resources as dislocated workers experience unemployment, loss of private health insurance, and the need to "reskill" at substantial personal cost if they are to secure a decent living standard (see Saks, 1983); and (5) the uneven distributional impacts of public service cutbacks which reflect the relative political weakness of low and moderate income constituencies in resisting the cuts. To add insult to injury, these have been accompanied by a spate of local tax breaks to prevent further relocation by those most able to do so: corporations, industry, financial and commercial institutions and people with high income (Marcuse, 1981: 22, 25–9).

Cities facing rapid growth as a result of the processes we have been discussing are not immune from social costs. The mismatch between their production and consumption capacities engenders housing shortages and drives up housing costs. Their inadequate basic infrastructure creates attendant problems of poor drainage, frequent flooding, and impure water supply (Feagin, 1983). An excess reliance on the automobile in sprawling growth centers creates congestion and environmental pollution. All of these reduce the quality of everyday life in America's most booming cities (see Feagin, 1984; Judd, 1983, 1984). In addition to these environmental costs, the rapidly transforming social structure of boomtowns has been associated with a variety of emergent indicators of social disorganization including high rates of violent crime, suicide, and divorce (Viviano, 1981). Everyday life for those at the bottom of the local social structures of booming cities in the Sunbelt has been especially difficult because of the lower wage structures, limited occupational benefits, and limited social welfare spending in many of these cities (Smith and Keller, 1983; Saks, 1983).

LOOKING FORWARD

The complex interplay among the forces producing the social problems, fiscal crises, and uneven development of US cities and the operation of US welfare capitalism is the subject of the remainder of this book. The second part of the book, "The State and the US Urban System," consists of chapters 2, 3 and 4. Chapter 2 discusses the form and content of the US welfare state, distinguishing it historically from the types of welfare states found in other advanced capitalist societies. The legitimation of both New Deal and Great Society welfare state liberalism and the urban policies which flowed from these initiatives rested squarely upon the expectation that unbridled economic growth could transcend social divisions, generate tax revenues, and finance social policies which would reduce economic and social inequalities. Chapter 2 shows not only that this was not the case but also that the overall effect of the taxing and spending policies of the US welfare state has been to generate new social divisions and new forms of social and spatial inequality. When combined with the declining performance of the US political economy, these new social divisions have produced a crisis of legitimacy which has created the political space for the development of new social forces on the left and right seeking to restructure welfare capitalism.

In chapter 3 the structural Marxist theoretical explanation of the crisis of welfare capitalism and the urban fiscal crisis are subjected to critical scrutiny. The argument advanced in chapter 3 is that structural Marxist urban political economy fails to adequately take into account the historically specific social and political structures through which different advanced capitalist societies operate and through which political-economic crisis tendencies are mediated. This leads proponents of this approach to predict the inevitable rise of insurgent urban social movements, which, in the American case, have not materialized as predicted. It is argued that the rise of the US "fiscal welfare" state is central to our understanding of why and how the urban crisis tendencies of the 1960s have been depoliticized.

Once this is accomplished, Chapter 4 examines the old and new meanings of "urban crisis" created by the political managers of the US urban system to mediate the changing economic and political conditions facing US cities from the 1960s to the 1980s. The chapter demonstrates that in the US case the national political crisis of welfare capitalism has been closely connected to fiscal, social, and economic crisis conditions found at the urban level.

The third part of this book, "Market Capitalism and Urban Development," is comprised of chapters 5, 6, and 7. This part focuses upon the market capitalist response to the crisis of welfare capitalism and its impact upon US cities. Chapter 5 spells out the basic theoretical premises of market capitalist social theory, challenging its biases and rebutting its utopian vision of a depoliticized society where "natural" economic processes can have free reign. Chapter 6 assesses the urban policy implications of the market capitalist approach. Moving once again from theoretical critique to historically grounded analysis, chapter 7 considers the impact of the Reagan administration's actual and proposed urban policies and the urban impacts of Reagan's more general attempts to enshrine market capitalism as a ruling ideology. The chapter separates the image of unbridled market capitalism from the real political power relations underlying Reagan's suburban and Sunbelt oriented military spending and pro-growth policies.

The final part of the book, "The Global Economy and Local Politics," is comprised of chapters 8 and 9. These chapters further develop the underlying argument that the political economy of American cities can best be understood by analyzing the historically particular social and political processes that interact with economic forces to produce socio-spatial inequalities. The argument is extended in these chapters to encompass the relationship between the changing nature of the global political-economy and the rise of new forms of urban politics in contemporary America. Local political actions are treated as real social forces, linked to global political-economic forces, in an open and contingent historical process, rather than as mere epiphenomena of the "needs" of transnational capital in a closed, deterministic world system.

Viewed in this light, *City State, and Market* represents an effort to bring the study of social power and political processes – local, regional, national, and global – to the center of the stage now called urban political economy and to show how power relations underlie the formation of dominant political-economic ideologies and the production of urban form.

Part II

The State and the US Urban System

2
Welfare State Capitalism in Crisis

Despite historically particular differences in the public policies of the advanced capitalist welfare states since World War II (Heidenheimer, Heclo, and Adams, 1975), each has relied upon three basic policy mechanisms: the use of macroeconomic monetary and fiscal policy to regulate the extremes of the cycle of unemployment and inflation; state provision of services which the private economy was deemed incapable of providing by means of profit incentives (e.g. urban mass transit, moderate income housing); and the use of transfer payments justified as a form of compensation for those adversely affected by the side-effects of capitalist production. These policies have been defended by welfare state liberals for "softening the harsh edges of capitalism" (Galbraith, 1981:30). This chapter will assess the validity of this claim in the case of US welfare capitalism. It will examine the character and distributional effects of the post war American welfare state to establish a factual basis for evaluating competing ideological claims concerning the current meanings of the legitim- ation crisis of welfare capitalism, the "urban crisis," and the fiscal crises of the city and the state. The central questions to be addressed are: What political interests and processes produced the US welfare state? What interests and processes have been produced and reproduced by its expansion? What difference has this made in the rise, fall, and restructuring of American cities?

Welfare state liberals have tended to blame "the market" for inequalities of income and opportunities. They have depicted the welfare state as the basic means for reducing inequalities produced by the economic process. In so doing they have focused upon direct social policies and have downplayed or ignored the question of who pays for welfare capitalism. Curiously, like welfare state liberals, market capitalist and neo-Marxist critics of welfare capitalism have paid little attention to the effects of "tax expenditures" as politically produced public policies which have created new social class divisions and new forms of inequality in American society. In their respective explanations of national and urban fiscal crises, both market capitalist and neo-Marxist critics focus upon the *output* side of the expenditure/revenue gap (see, for instance, Pickvance, 1980; Savas, 1982). For the former, the fiscal crisis is the result of excessive demands for services by relatively unproductive "service demanding" groups, producing a condition of "governmental overload" and fiscal insolvency. For the latter the objective contradictions of capitalist production create the problems which either "require" an expanded state sector to manage capital accumulation while promoting legitimation of the system to popular classes (the structural Marxist perspective) or "displace" class struggle from the workplace to the political state (the class struggle variant of Marxism). In either instance, the costs of financing "collectively consumed" (see Castells, 1977; Dunleavy, 1980) state services begin to drain the accumulative capacities of the economy and the ability of the state to promote accumulation. Rancorous political struggles ensue around efforts to reduce the visible outputs of the national and local welfare state. Thus both market liberals and neo-Marxists stress the expansion of state *expenditures* produced by highly visible political processes of demand making; neither has shed much light on the political interests and processes producing the drain on state *revenues* in the far less visible political arenas where growth-oriented tax policies and sectorally stabilizing occupational benefits have been produced.

In this chapter, Titmuss's (1958) important but neglected classification of general "welfare" into three types – public or social, fiscal, and occupational – forms the basis for my explanation of the legitimation, rationality, and fiscal crises of American welfare capitalism. An understanding of the social and political consequences of these three forms of "welfare" will help us to assess the following theoretical claims: (1) claims that the US welfare state has had little effect in reducing social inequality (Devine, 1983); (2) claims that "fiscal welfare" policies such as tax expenditures have grown to the point that they now offset the distributional effects of social welfare policies and have displaced social welfare as an urban policy tool (Smith and Judd,

1984; Smith, Ready, and Judd, 1985); and (3) claims that the distributional effects of the three systems of welfare provision have engendered new forms of inequality and new consumption-based interests around which new forms of social and political conflict have emerged (Smith, 1984b; Saunders, 1981; Kirby, 1985; Davis, 1986).

THE RISE AND FALL OF WELFARE CAPITALISM

For much of the booming 1960s and early 1970s the welfare state liberal policy agenda was buttressed by the ability of the American political economy to generate growth. In the context of an expanding pie, it was possible to build political support for a social wage, environmental protection, health and safety policies in the workplace, and even efforts to compensate society's losers by saving declining cities and declaring "war" on poverty. Yet even when the economy was rapidly expanding, American "exceptionalism" in the political sphere limited the scope of the redistributional effects of the New Frontier and Great Society initiatives. While support could be mobilized to help the "poor" to enter the ranks of wage labor, little political or ideological support developed for public policies to produce equality of outcome.

Welfare state liberal political economists like Arthur Okun, for instance, maintained that although society had an obligation to help its "losers," the forms of assistance to people in need ought to be structured to "rehabilitate and motivate the losers and even the slackers in the community" (Okun, 1977:30). If transfer payments to "the poor" were too generous, it was felt that they might undermine the material incentives for work, productivity, and economic growth. Welfare state liberals thus supported limited redistribution of the social surplus through a combination of progressive taxes and moderate transfer payments. They often explicitly rejected public policy proposals intended to achieve greater equality of outcome. As Okun (1977:31), expressed the issue:

If . . . full equality of income cost us a generation's worth of economic growth . . . four-fifths of our citizens would be made worse off by the trade. [Thus] we are better off living with some economic inequality . . . because it is the most practical route to greater economic benefits for the vast majority.

Because the legitimation of the American welfare state has rested squarely on the ability of the political economy to generate economic growth, the performance of the American economy from the mid-1970s through the early 1980s left the previous social basis of support for welfare capitalism vulnerable. Critics on the left began to discover fundamental contradictions in the very structural logic of welfare capitalism (see O'Connor, 1973; Gordon, 1977; Castells, 1978; chapter 3, this volume). They were joined by market capitalists and supply-side economists on the right who formed the ideological underpinning for Reaganomics. The assault against welfare state capitalism from the right challenged not only the effectiveness of US welfare capitalism but its very theoretical logic. The focus of the attack was the claim that economic growth had come to a standstill because public consumption was a drain on private production. The expansion of welfare state services in response to the political demands of the 1960s left the most redistributional programs of American welfare capitalism, the urban and anti-poverty programs of Lyndon Johnson's Great Society, especially vulnerable to the assault. Although less extensive than middle class tax subsidies, they were more visible, as was the political process of urban rebellion that had expanded them. They were thus challenged as ineffective and wasteful byproducts of an "overloaded" political process.

The erosion of confidence in the capacity of US welfare capitalism to deliver on its promise of endless growth undermined the credibility of Keynesian policies of macroeconomic "fine-tuning," as well as challenging the state's management of "overloaded" demands for public services. From the end of World War II until the late 1960s, objective conditions such as low interest rates, cheap energy supplies, easy lending conditions (and because of these, relatively stable prices and limited wage demands) enabled national political elites to implement a relatively painless set of monetary and fiscal policies. The federal government could spend and borrow liberally to cope with recessions and falling profit rates by stimulating aggregate demand. With easy access to credit on favorable terms, the state could simultaneously increase public services and cut taxes.

Throughout this period, global corporate concentration increased, as did the power of corporate capital to raise prices if circumstances in the political-economic environment such as collective bargaining agreements or energy shortages might change the costs or control of factors of production. Changing contextual realities – higher energy costs, the initial successes of the OPEC cartel at managing energy supplies, a concomitant increase in prices, and eventually in wage demands in the unionized monopoly sector – combined to help produce a decade-long spiral of increasing prices and rising unemployment now popularly termed "stagflation" (see Galbraith, 1981).

The stagflation crisis was compounded by the deficit financing used to fund the Vietnam war, which overheated an economy already operating at near capacity levels (Tobin, 1981:12). The overheated economy in turn reinforced the willingness of policy-makers to use recession-inducing monetary policies. These added a cyclical dimension to the rise in unemployment being caused by an ongoing process of plant closings, industrial restructuring to Third World production locations, and resultant "deindustrial-ization" (see Bluestone and Harrison, 1982).

A central feature of industrial restructuring was an attempt by multilocational corporate capital to control rising production costs by relocating plants to locations offering cheaper labor supply, easier labor control, and a more favorable political climate (see Bluestone and Harrison, 1982; Smith, Ready and Judd, 1985). The most obvious consequence of this strategy of capital restructuring was the exporting of primary manufacturing jobs to Third World countries and a concomitant increase in the US unemployment rate.

This in turn increased the demand for government transfer payments and social welfare spending at precisely the time that : inflation was increasing the cost of government services; capital restructuring was reducing government revenues derived from capital; and federal, state, and local taxation policies were shifting the burden of paying for welfare capitalism from businesses to households, and thus to labor. In this larger context, the "taxpayers' revolt" may be seen, in part, as a form of resistance by home-owning segments of labor to the rising costs of public and private goods, a stagnant economy, declining living standards, and a highly visible form of taxation, the local property tax.

At the national level, the public policies adopted to cope with the inflationary side of stagflation, particularly the tighter money supply, not only increased unemployment as an intentional recession inducing strategy; they also raised the cost of new business investment. This prolonged and deepened the recessionary tendency of the economy, even creating a selective depression in economic sectors like housing construction, which were highly dependent upon borrowed money. The high rate of unemployment created in the wake of these policies served to dampen wage demands and established the preconditions for Reagan's chief political success, the weakening of organized labor.

In light of these shifting political currents, it is important to examine closely the actual distributional effects of the post-World War II American welfare state. The claim has been made from many quarters that the expansion of the welfare state has dampened the capacity of "the economy" to produce profits, capital accumulation, and economic growth. It also is claimed that transfer payments from "productive" to "unproductive" population groups have been responsible for the fiscal crises of federal, state, and urban governments. How valid are such claims? Who has benefited from the expansion of US welfare capitalism and at whose expense? What have been its urban consequences?

THE SOCIAL DIVISION OF WELFARE

In each of the advanced capitalist welfare states two developments have complicated, in differing degrees, efforts to understand and measure the distributional impacts of welfare capitalism. The first has been the increasing reliance on "tax expenditures" as a policy tool (for an excellent definition of and explanation for the rise of "tax expenditures" see Surrey, 1973). They are a central component of what Sinfield means by "fiscal welfare" – the allocation of tax benefits to private individuals, groups, or organizations in order to get them to pursue a public purpose (e.g. investing money, conserving energy, enhancing skills). The second has been the dramatic rise of fringe benefits as a form of compensating employees in the monopoly sector of the economy. These benefits constitute indirect public subsidies to employers who can deduct them from tax liabilities as a cost of doing business. They also affect the availability of resources for financing directly provided public services because they are not treated as a form of taxable "income" to the people who receive them. In

Sinfield's (1978) terms, they constitute forms of "occupational welfare."

By the mid-1970s "tax expenditures" totaled over one-quarter of total budgeted expenditures of the federal government. Since then they have grown to nearly a third. Tax subsidized fringe benefits grew from 5.4 to 16.3 percent of total compensation between 1961 and 1981 (Stark, 1983:2). The largest tax expenditures were various growth-oriented tax credits, deductions, and shelters to corporations such as the investment tax credit, accelerated depreciation allowances, and industrial revenue bonds. Employees in the monopoly sector also were important beneficiaries of these pro-growth policies. Primary labor market workers enjoyed tax deferred "private" retirement plans, exclusion from income of medical benefits, and other forms of "occupational welfare."

Because of the growth of tax expenditures, tax shelters, and tax-avoiding corporate fringe benefits, the fiscal basis for financing the social services of US welfare capitalism has been significantly eroded. Ironically these sorts of fiscal benefits have been excluded from most studies of the impact of the welfare state on income, consumption, and investment (for exceptions see Mishra, 1977:111ff; Sinfield, 1978; Gough, 1979). This ignores the many forms of "income" that are provided either directly or indirectly through the tax code and which tend to offset the redistributional impact of formally progressive taxation schemes.

This is no small omission. Numerous subtle consequences, some deliberate, others unintended, follow from these *politically* produced, low visibility fiscal policies. For example, occupational welfare benefits tend to increase the legitimacy of corporations while reducing the legitimacy of government. Unlike social welfare services, occupational welfare is part of the incentive-reward system of the firm. By directly subsidizing individual workers in the primary, corporate-dominated sector of the economy by favorable tax treatment of fringe benefits, the state indirectly subsidizes corporate hegemony in the workplace. Without such policies the cost to corporations to insure a cooperative work force would doubtless be much higher.

Furthermore, as major unions successfully bargained to be included in these benefit systems, the interests of organized and unorganized workers diverged as much as those of the managerial and professional strata had previously diverged from their own. This transformation has been multi-faceted in its political implications. First, as Davis (1984) has pointed out, "as stronger unions bargained for 'welfare states in single industries' via contractual health and retirement supplementals, the general thrust for national, inclusive, welfare policies was diffused and weakened." Second, the segmentation of the categorical social policy entitlements which remained created new divisions between different groups and class segments based on eligibility criteria. This further undermined the legitimacy of welfare capitalism by producing new inequalities sensed as state sponsored "unfairness" by needy but technically excluded segments of the general populace.

The shrinking of the tax base by expanded fiscal and occupational welfare at the same time that a high rate of inflation was pushing middle income earners into paying higher marginal tax rates (i.e., "bracket creep") further undermined the legitimacy of the American welfare state and intensified the social division between the middle class and the low income recipients of the visible social programs of welfare capitalism. According to Treasury Department data, for instance, the median income family of four had their marginal tax rate increased from 17 percent in 1965 to 24 percent in 1980. This squeeze on real living standards was incorrectly perceived as being caused by too much "welfare" to the poor rather than too few corporate sector and professional ("yuppie") stratum taxpayers. Moreover, the material basis for financing the US social welfare state was adversely affected by the growth of "occupational welfare." As Stark (1983:2) has noted: "The growth of fringe benefits as a substitute for taxable wages extracts billions from the tax base and adds those billions to what is already a terrifying budget deficit."

Even less well understood than the significance of these forms of state provided "welfare" have been the urban impacts of these policies and their political basis. The complex interplay among the three different forms of welfare identified by Sinfield (1978) is perhaps best illustrated in terms of their consequences for US cities. For example, white flight, corporate disinvestment from central cities, and the urban concentration of low income population groups requiring social welfare services have all been viewed as separate "causes" of the fiscal crisis of central cities. Yet the interplay among these social phenomena has not been fully explored. That relationship is to be found in the socio-spatial consequences of the tax code in channeling business investment and taxpaying households out of central cities and increasing both unemployment and urban service needs among the less mobile segments of the class structure. The tax code, in turn, is an everchanging embodiment of the political basis of low visibility "fiscal welfare" policies.

Consider the following illustration. It has frequently been observed that home ownership tax deductions tend to redistribute resources upward in the class structure. Of the $22 billion lost to the Treasury by this form of "fiscal welfare" in 1980, for instance, one-quarter went to households earning over $50,000 annually (Goetz, 1981a). The emphasis of this sort of fact, found in most distributional studies, has been on "who" gets the tax subsidy and who is excluded. If the question is reframed to ask "where" the people getting the tax break enjoy the benefit, the connection between the policy and urban fiscal crisis becomes more apparent. In 1979, the Sunbelt states, with about one-quarter of the nation's population, nevertheless were the location of 63 percent of all new housing starts (Arroyo, 1981:27). The lion's share of new housing starts in the Frostbelt were concentrated in suburban areas. Both patterns contributed to urban fiscal crises in declining Frostbelt cities by subsidizing white flight.

The same has been true of the "fiscal welfare" granted to corporations to invest in new locations through the investment tax credit, accelerated depreciation allowances, exclusions of payments in aid of construction of new water and sewer facilities, the exclusion of interest on state and local industrial development bonds, and the sheltering of income that American-owned mutinational corporations earn from overseas operations until their profits are returned to the United States (see Marcuse, 1981; Nash and Fernandez-Kelly, 1983; Smith, Ready, and Judd, 1985). These tax expenditures have directly contributed to urban fiscal crises in declining central cities by subsidizing capital flight to new points of production.

Not surprisingly, blacks, female-headed households, and low income households concentrated in older central cities and their declining inner suburbs have been the most adversely affected by the job and revenue loss stemming from these "fiscal welfare" policies (see, for instance, Vidal, Phillips, and Brown, 1984). Thus, one key distributional consequence of the expansion of the low visibility fiscal welfare system for corporations and suburban and Sunbelt home owners has been an expansion in the number of urban households rendered eligible for public welfare assistance from the far more visible social welfare system.

This development in turn has fueled public resentment against the social welfare state. The victims of state subsidized economic restructuring and population deconcentration are blamed for the fiscal crisis of both the cities and the welfare state. The real causes are hidden in a host of "tax expenditures" which have no direct and visible impact on the public budgets they have thrown out of balance. When the fiscal crisis reaches the national level, low income public housing subsidies must compete with other priorities like defense spending, while tax deductions for home ownership remain intact and tax breaks to corporations to stimulate growth actually expand. Why has this situation come about? Who benefits from it and who pays? Where are the costs and benefits distributed?

WELFARE CAPITALISM: WHO BENEFITS?

Postwar welfare state capitalism in the United States was initially characterized by a sustained period of economic growth stimulated by Keynesian macroeconomic policies designed to stimulate aggregate consumer demand combined with an expansion of social policies intended to legitimize the negative human costs of rapid economic growth and change. This period is now threatened by resource scarcities, decreased rates of productivity and accumulation (Miller and Tomaskovic-Devey, 1983; O'Connor, 1984), and intensified international competition. The most prominent political response to this "accumulation crisis" (O'Connor, 1984) has been a political strategy ideologically justified as a return to "market capitalism" but supported by corporate financial and industrial elites in the monopoly sector. This strategy has been aptly termed "the recapitalization of capital" (Miller, 1978; Miller and Tomaskovic-Devey, 1983). It includes calls for: the contraction of social policies; cuts in corporate taxes and taxes on affluent households, supposedly to spur investment in basic industries; and an expansion of the domestic manufacturing sector by slackening the social regulation of pollution, investment tax credits, and various locational and technological modernization incentives that now fall under the rubric "reindustrialization." Reaganomics is the current, but by no means the only, political expression of this recapitalization strategy. (See Davis, 1986, for

an excellent discussion of the Democratic party's neo-liberal
variant of "reindustrialization.")

While the impact of Reaganomics on the "social wage"
component of US welfare capitalism has been significant (see
Piven and Cloward, 1982), that component itself has always been
a much smaller facet of the American welfare state than has been
true in Europe. For example, in 1978 direct social expenditures
for health, education and income maintenance have constituted
29.1 percent of Gross Domestic Product (GDP) in the Netherlands
and 21.9 percent in Sweden but only 15.7 percent in the United
States (Best and Connolly, 1982: 212). Despite markedly increased
levels of social spending in the USA between the early 1960s and
the mid 1970s, these social expenditures accounted for less than
16 percent of GDP in the United States prior to fiscal retrenchment,
as compared to an average of 21.8 percent in eleven major
European nations (Best and Connolly, 1982; Skocpol, 1987). As
Miller (1978:204) has noted, the American experience with
Keynesianism has demonstrated that "it is possible to have Keynes
without Beveridge, growth without a social minimum." Instead,
Keynesianism in the USA has relied heavily on three principal
instruments: high levels of military expenditures; stimulation of
individual consumer demand by periodic tax cuts which exceed
the share of the surplus allocated to collectively consumed social
services like public housing; and limited controls on private capital
investment. The movement toward a European model of a social
democratic welfare state was observable in rudimentary form in
the Great Society urban social policies of the 1960s. Even then,
the target of these policies was "the poor" rather than either the
working class or the whole citizenry as a matter of "right." In
any case, the trend was halted by the stagflation crisis of the late
1970s.

In the American welfare state, the most common varieties of
social welfare spending – Social Security, Medicare, disability
benefits – are financed largely through *horizontal* transfers. Rather
than transferring income from "haves" to "have nots" or from
capital to labor, horizontal transfers shift resources *within* the
working population from some categories of workers to others –
for example, young to old, healthy to disabled. Among horizontal
transfer programs, non-means-tested programs like social insurance
account for approximately 80 percent of income security payments.
Public assistance programs based on income account for less than
2 percent of GNP annually. The role of politics in these policies

has been to represent specific social interests; the role of the state has been to promote economic growth while mediating and rationalizing conflicting social forces within the working population rather than to act on behalf of the working population against those who own and manage capital resources.

Evidence abounds for the lack of public policies promoting significant income redistribution by social class in the USA (Reynolds and Smolensky, 1977). For instance, the ratio of public assistance to the earnings of common laborers has remained a relatively constant 25 to 30 percent since 1850 (Reynolds and Smolensky, 1978). Government benefits have generally been targeted to categories of the population which cut across class lines, e.g. farmers, veterans, college students, the elderly, the sick and disabled. Advocates of income redistribution have generally cloaked their appeals for greater equality of result in more indirect terms such as: " 'fairness' in taxation, relief for those 'unable' to work . . . and helping people get a minimum of essentials in order to assure 'equality of opportunity'" (Lapham, quoted in Reynolds and Smolensky, 1978:37).

In this overall cultural and ideological context, economic entitlements have been brought about by political organization. The major categorical entitlements of US welfare capitalism have been initiated by a combination of group capacity for political organization (e.g. farmers and veterans), shifting presidential electoral "mandates," (e.g. the Great Society), periodic popular mobilizations by social movements, and support from reformist professionals. The political conditions of the 1960s combining all of these factors (see Cloward and Piven, 1974) introduced new categories of beneficiaries and new programs into the American welfare state. These expanded in the following decade, as the ongoing economic crisis and restructuring of capital investment swelled the new categories with increasing numbers of eligible claimants, particularly in declining central cities. Program costs further increased as a result of earlier policy choices, made during less crisis-ridden periods, to index many middle-class transfer payment benefit levels to inflation. High rates of inflation throughout the 1970s, demographic changes resulting from increased life expectancies, rising unemployment, and increasing divorce rates, which increased the numbers of dependent children, all contributed to the relatively rapid growth in the cost of income support programs during the 1970s as compared to previous decades.

Having said this, it remains true that among advanced capitalist welfare states the United States remains a laggard, particularly in public spending for such key areas of social reproduction as employment training, subsidized low and moderate income housing, child care, family allowances, and related forms of social support (Wilensky, 1976; Heidenheimer, Heclo and Adams, 1975). In 1978, public spending for income support was $200 billion or 10 percent of GNP (Danziger, Haveman and Plotnick, 1980). The largest category by far was "social insurance," i.e., programs like Social Security, Medicare, unemployment compensation, and disability related programs, which accounted for three-quarters of this total ($132 billion) (Miller, 1978:204).

As T. H. Marshall (1972) pointed out long ago, "social insurance" is a basically capitalist institution to the extent that it calibrates benefits to the earnings a person has previously gained through wage labor. Moreover, the mode of social security funding, with a regressive cap on tax liability and matching contributions from employers and employees, is not redistributional. Social security tax burdens, with their regressive cap remaining intact, have grown from 9.8 percent of federal tax revenues in 1960 to 35.5 percent in 1983 (see table 2.4). The contributions of employers tend to be passed on to consumers as higher prices. The contributions of employees are tantamount to a form of forced savings. Hence a large share of the total costs is absorbed by workers themselves, with the most affluent employees paying at the lowest effective rates. In contrast, "income assistance" programs do redistribute resources progressively on the basis of need. In US welfare capitalism, the latter programs totalled $51.9 billion in 1978, or approximately one-quarter of total public spending for income support.

As a percentage of GNP, welfare state programs aimed at low income groups have shown very little growth since 1972. By official estimates, poverty in America was reduced by 25 percent between 1965 and 1972 but showed little reduction between 1972 and 1980 (Danziger, Haveman and Plotnick, 1980). Under the regime of Reaganomics it has increased (Davis, 1986). In contrast, by 1980 middle-class entitlements as a whole were four times larger than needs-based expenditures (Reich, 1984:17).

Furthermore, even this imbalance overstates the extent to which need is a policy criterion of the American welfare state. Only the food stamp program is designed to assist all people of low income. Most of the rest are categorical programs. Such programs treat people who have the same needs differently, depending on their particular characteristics. For example, single-parent poor families receive income assistance, two-parent poor families do not. Blind and disabled low-income people receive income support; "able bodied" poorly paid workers do not. Much of this categorization has been intentionally designed to create incentives for excluding categories of citizens who are expected to work (Danziger, Haveman and Plotnick, 1980).

When welfare state liberal political forces responded to black ghetto revolts by attempting to refocus needs-based targeting programs on the basis of *place* rather than people, as in the case of the 1966 Model Cities Program, pressures from Congress members whose districts were generally affluent and suburban, but who laid claim to including "pockets of poverty," were sufficiently resilient to force the transformation of the program into a general entitlement program. Over time, more and more places were deemed eligible for funding under Model Cities, yet the revenue base of the program was not greatly expanded. The result was an "urban poverty" program that neither served to demonstrate how resources could be concentrated to eradicate poverty nor to improve conditions materially in the places chosen for support. Resources were spread so thin that neither the tangible nor the symbolic impacts of the program were sufficient to enhance public confidence in the ability of the American welfare state to solve social problems. In this instance, the class bias in political participation, as reflected in congressional electoral politics, rather than any inherent tendency toward "governmental overload" was the root cause of the program's failure. The program failed because Congress members from wealthier congressional districts were able to redefine its purposes.

Likewise, in the mid-1970s under Republican administrations various "urban revitalization" programs were combined into the Community Development Block Grant Program (CDBG). As a result of the growing political representation of suburban interests in congressional politics, many large suburban counties that did not qualify for categorical funding of the specific "urban" programs they superceded, did receive funds under the consolidated block grant system. Given congressional realities (e.g. the 20 least urban states have 40 percent of the votes in the Senate), a major consequence of the shift from categorical grants to block grant revenue sharing was to tip the balance of resource allocation away from large central cities toward "a large number of small cities and large suburbs" (Gappert and Rose, 1975:43). In this way, available funds were once again spread over a broad range of eligible localities rather than concentrated in the central cities with the greatest social and economic needs (Barros, 1978:87). Although central city political elites lobbied intensely to prevent cuts in their allocations by altering the block grant formula, the newly eligible localities expanded program costs and thus placed political limits on future increases that might otherwise have gone to declining central cities.

These new forms of "place-based" inequality illustrate the importance of political avenues and structures in restructuring the American city. Uneven urban and regional development has been fostered by the historically specific political structures and processes of American federalism, by congressional politics, and by the state structures of public finance which account for the unique pattern of central-local intergovernmental revenue production in the United States. Another key dimension of US welfare capitalism distinguishes the USA from other advanced capitalist welfare states. The American welfare state has taken a more commodified form than the European state sector. Rather than directly expanding state-provided services, public spending has been dispensed to provide services indirectly by subsidizing private profit-making industries (e.g. health care and housing) or by subsidizing individual consumers of commodified services (e.g. college loan subsidies).

Likewise, a considerable portion of the subsistence payments going to low income families, as Gans (1972) has shown, merely get passed along to the owning classes as increased profits from rent, food, health care, and other commodified forms of consumption. Direct beneficiaries of "needs based" income support programs become conduits of benefits to indirect beneficiaries – hospitals, landlords, chain stores – who gain the most from the transfer payments the needy receive. As Taylor-Gooby and Dale (1981) have expressed the issue: "[S]hifting purchasing power around from one individual to another does not leave the private sector with fewer resources, it merely alters the structure of consumer demand according to whether individuals are net contributors or net receivers, or the relative profitability of different firms."

The American welfare state may be characterized as a resource transferring and "contracting out" state apparatus. One consequence of this particular form of welfare state – one which transfers significant parcels of state sovereignty from state and urban "managers" (see Pahl, 1975; Pickvance, 1984) to private individuals – has been the creation of an amorphous and invisible state sector. In this form of state structure "the state" is difficult for the average citizen to grasp as a "public" entity. Because state intervention takes place by indirect policies which induce parts of civil society to act, rather than by direct action by public administrators, it is very difficult for popular political forces to hold "the state" accountable for its extensive enmeshment in everyday economic and social life.

A related, but more subtle, consequence of this reliance upon private actors to achieve public purposes has been the cultural reinforcement of fragmented and "commodified" social relations. By expanding the model of individualized consumption from the marketplace to the political sphere and by stressing individual rather than social "rights," the "possessive individualism" of American culture is extended, reinforced and, ultimately, reproduced. Concomitantly, the cultural bases of social solidarity are narrowed, weakened, and undermined.

Having said this, it must be acknowledged that, for all of their deficiencies, since the inception of the Great Society, the American welfare state's complex entitlements did outperform the market's record of reducing poverty and social inequality in the United States. Between 1965 and 1980, the percentage of people officially living in poverty declined from around 20 to 14 million. When only income from private sources is considered, the "pretransfer" poor remained nearly constant over the same period (Danziger, Haveman and Plotnick, 1980). Thus, whatever progress was made during the 15 year period is entirely attributable to governmental cash and income transfers.

In the case of black Americans this accomplishment may be regarded as at best a "holding pattern." After two decades of on-again off-again federal anti-poverty efforts, urban revitalization policies, and affirmative action initiatives, black family income in 1981 stood at 56 percent of white family income, approximately the same as the income gap in 1960 (*New Orleans Times-*

Picayune/States-Item, June 5, 1983:16). This was true despite substantial black gains in educational achievement and electoral power.

In this context, the frequently observed stability of the pattern of income distribution throughout the postwar period, also may be viewed as a reflection of government transfer payments to the fixed income elderly and the poor having partially offset the regressive effects of a tax system that has grown less progressive and a public spending system geared increasingly toward middle class entitlements. A large part of the expansion in the 1970s of what James O'Connor (1973) has termed "social consumption" expenditures came in programs for middle-class beneficiaries such as veterans benefits, Social Security, and Medicare. Rather than promoting social redistribution, these polices engendered new forms of inequality. These three programs alone cost $200 billion to fund at the outset of the first Reagan term (in contrast to $50 billion for means-tested entitlements). They were among the sacrosanct "safety net" programs declared off-limits to Reagan budget cutters. The lion's share (fully 60 percent in the first round) of the cutbacks in "the welfare state" under Reagan were made in the $50 billion in programs targeted to benefit the officially poor (Wald, 1980; Pear, 1983).

The trend toward greater income polarization observable in the 1980s as a result of the changing occupational structure (see chapter 8 below) has been compounded by the fact that the public transfers, which at least achieved a holding pattern during the 1970s, have been significantly reduced by Reagan's budget cuts. As Mike Davis (1984:18) has succinctly put the issue: "[T]he 'victory' in the War on Poverty is largely an artifact of income transfers *within* the working class which leave structural unemployment situations intact. Begin to remove these federal income supports, as Reagan has recently started to do, and the original 1960 level of designated poverty reappears."

Not only has poverty reappeared, it has actually increased. This is because welfare benefits that are means-tested do not automatically rise with the cost of living, as do Social Security benefits. Their increase is dependent on the political choices of state and local government officials. Throughout the 1970s, a period of high inflation accompanied by various symptoms of state and local fiscal crisis, benefits to low income recipients failed to be extended, thus decreasing their relative value. Between 1969 and the beginning of the Reagan administration, for example, the overall purchasing power of such benefits decreased by nearly one-third (Wald, 1980:1; Pear, 1983:13). The political realities underlying the consolidation and indexing of middle-class benefits while eroding low income entitlements thus have been a major factor helping to explain the increased income polarization now plaguing many large American cities currently undergoing economic restructuring (see Fainstein et al., 1983).

The distributional inequalities characterizing federal housing policies have been even more pronounced than those attributable to the income transfer programs. Here too the parallels between more and less visible, more and less vulnerable, more and less urban, and more and less class-privileged policy structures are observable. In 1982, for example, the low visibility tax deductibility of owner-occupied (and, in large measure, suburban and Sunbelt) housing resulted in a loss of $25 billion in revenues to the federal government. In the same year, publicly subsidized rental housing for low and moderate income households (primarily urban) amounted to only $6.8 billion (Reich, 1984:177). Thus, nearly four times more subsidies were indirectly transferred to homeowners through the tax code than went to renters through direct government housing policies. Because there is an income "cap" placed on eligibility for rental subsidies, but no corresponding cap placed on the mortgage interest (and, until recently, the state and local property tax) deduction from federal tax liabilities, the overall effect of this dual policy structure has been to transfer wealth upward in the class structure. The policy structure also tilts toward preserving the suburban sprawl settlement pattern with all of its inequities at the expense of core cities.

The past inadequacies of the even more visible housing construction policies designed to provide housing for the bottom of the social structure are now so well known that a brief rehearsal should make clear why demands for entirely new policy structures have been forthcoming from both the left and the right, thus compounding the legitimation crisis of US welfare capitalism. These policy failures include:

1 the "ghettoization" of low income blacks in inadequately maintained large scale public housing projects and the resulting increased race and class segregation of American society (Hirsch, 1983);

2 the inability of local public housing authorities to persuade

impacted neighborhoods to accept small-scale "scattered-site" low income projects without fierce community resistance (Cuomo, 1974);

3 corrupt implementation, poor design, and excessive defaults in low income home-ownership programs (Herbers, 1972);

4 excessive subsidies to developers, landlords, and other suppliers of low income housing, with few strings attached (Gordon, 1977);

5 funding the highly visible low and moderate income programs at lower levels than need would require while imposing no limits whatever on tax subsidies for home ownership to the middle and upper classes, and, as a result;

6 driving a wedge of misplaced resentment between tax subsidized middle strata homeowners and rent subsidized lower strata tenants.

In assessing the impacts of public policies on housing distribution, the impact of urban development policies relying on low visibility tax expenditures also must be taken into account. Various urban policies subsumed under the rubric of "public–private partnerships" (see Smith, 1987) have sought to restore the property value of urban space by using tax incentives to stimulate private reinvestment in urban land. Where they have succeeded in this objective they have destroyed hundreds of thousands of available low rent housing units during the past three decades. Highway construction projects in urban areas have further reduced the available supply.

In the past decade, the movement of young urban professionals into previously low income neighborhoods in major cities which have expanded their professional service sector has further reduced the supply of housing units that can be "filtered down" to the poor (see Gilderbloom and Appelbaum, 1987). This process of "gentrification" is often perceived as purely "private," yet "gentrification" has been significantly abetted by the taxation policies of local governments which view it as a solution to rather than a symptom of the "urban crisis" (see Levin, 1985). Similarly, the recent spate of condominium conversions has been underwritten by favorable tax treatment of this form of "fiscal welfare." This has compounded the problem of housing distribution by reducing still further the overall supply of rental housing, not just for the poor but for middle income renters as well (Gilderbloom and Appelbaum, 1987). Who pays for these hidden forms of state intervention?

THE AMERICAN WELFARE STATE: WHO PAYS?

Reynolds and Smolensky (1978) have noted that before 1950 "government budgets seemed to reduce income inequality through a gradual creep upward in the relative size of government and ... through an apparently permanent displacement of the distribution of net income during the years of the New Deal," but that the overall distribution has shown little change since then. Despite the greatly expanded role of the state in the economy between 1950 and the 1970s, the forms of state involvement did not bring about a significant alteration in the degree of income inequality in the United States. This is true even though government spending had a positive redistributional effect between these years; this was largely offset by the increasingly negative (i.e., regressive) effects of *taxes*.

For example, considering tax changes between 1950 and 1970, roughly 50 percent of the redistributive effect of federal personal income taxes disappeared. Despite massive expansion of transfer payments since 1950, the wedge between before and after tax income redistribution has remained a relatively constant 15 percent. The decrease in progressivity of taxes virtually offset increased distributional progressivity of transfer payments. In addition to a long-term extension of income tax coverage down the income distribution scale, particular adjustments to the initial structure of the tax code have dramatically reduced income tax progressivity.

The extension of both fiscal and tax subsidized occupational welfare benefits within the working population has been quite unevenly distributed among different working strata. This is well illustrated in the cases of (a) the tax deductibility of educational expenses and (b) the exclusion of fringe benefits from tax liability. Consider first the difference between the tax treatment for retraining of displaced industrial workers and for acquiring improved professional skills by professional working strata.

Even those scholars who have minimized the long-term adverse effects of job dislocation produced by "deindustrialization" in the USA have identified major structural "imperfections" in the labor market such as worker immobility and underinvestment in worker training and retraining (Bendick, 1983:3). Because of the uneven regional impacts of deindustrialization, workers dislocated by capital flight find themselves looking for work in regions of limited opportunity. Because significant geographic and cultural distances separate regions, and because displaced workers have meaningful family, social and community ties, the "cost" of relocating outside their region is one that many workers are unwilling to make. For workers who own homes, the prospect of selling in a depressed market and having to buy in an inflated one in a growing region further reduces geographic mobility.

Since moving is problematic, many displaced workers must retrain if they are to find work in the places where they live. However, the American welfare state lags far behind other advanced capitalist political economies undergoing structural economic change in the extent to which the state subsidizes employment training and retraining (see, for instance, Body-Gendrot, 1987). The fiscal welfare system's treatment of people needing retraining is, in fact, a major barrier to effective "reskilling" of displaced workers. By not allowing the tax deduction of educational expenses for people acquiring new skills, while allowing it for those maintaining or improving their skills in existing occupations, the "fiscal welfare" system penalizes those who would self-organize to meet new employment conditions while rewarding stably employed professional strata.

A second example of the new forms of inequality generated by the fiscal and occupational welfare systems has been the dramatic growth of fringe benefits from only 1 percent of employee compensation in 1929 to over a third of total compensation for some privileged categories of workers by the 1970s (Reynolds and Smolensky, 1978:36). Overall, fringe benefits grew from 5.4 to 16.3 percent of total compensation between 1961 and 1981. The two largest of these forms of "occupational welfare," employee pension and health insurance plans, have also comprised a significant part of the expansion in "fiscal welfare" during the past decade. As table 2.1 demonstrates, these forms of "occupational welfare" have been skewed to favor professional and managerial strata and the monopoly sector blue collar labor aristocracy (which now faces the loss of this benefit structure because of capital flight to Third World production sites). Such benefits are generally not subject to taxation as income. Thus, employees at the upper end of the before-tax income scale also

Table 2.1 Employees with employer or union provided pension and group health plans, by occupation, 1982

Occupation	Total (in thousands)	With pensions		With health insurance	
		(n)	(%)	(n)	(%)
Managerial and professional	22,811	14,098	61.8	17,507	76.6
Precision products, craft and repair	12,443	6,437	51.7	9,312	74.8
Operatives, fabricators and laborers	19,223	8,449	44.0	12,906	67.1
Technical, sales, and administrative support	32,958	13,790	41.8	19,904	60.4
Service workers	16,507	3,722	22.4	5,658	34.1

Source: Statistical Abstracts of the United States: 1985 (US Bureau of the Census, Washington, DC, December, 1984): p. 421.

have been able to shield a progressively larger share of their real compensation from the nominally progressive income tax structure. Thus, the net impact of this change in the initial structure of the tax code has been a shift in "who pays" for state activities away from more privileged toward less privileged segments of the working population by a regressive redistribution of tax liabilities. Service workers in particular are deficient in "occupational welfare" benefits (see table 2.1). Those who must rely on the visible benefits of welfare capitalism are thus increasingly being supported by those middle to moderate income households who reside just above them in the income distribution scale. Viewed in this light, the new social antagonisms between fiscally excluded moderate income workers and public welfare recipients, while regrettable, is hardly surprising.

The loss to the treasury, and thus the net contribution to the current national "fiscal crisis" attributable to the dynamics of the occupational welfare system, is even more pronounced when we refocus our attention from employees to employers. Between 1974 and 1984, the two largest "occupational welfare" tax expenditures were the exclusion of employer contributions to pension plans and to medical insurance. These two losses to the Treasury rose dramatically, from $7.7 billion in 1974 to $68.1 billion in 1984 (or over one-third of the massive federal budget deficit in that year). The data presented in table 2.2 document the decade long spiraling rise of these leading occupational welfare tax expenditures. Table 2.2 makes clear that overlaid upon the inequalities in the distribution of specific tax benefits among different occupational strata has been an even more dramatic shift in taxation burdens from capital to households (and hence to labor, or at least to those segments of labor too politically weak to gain inclusion in the benefit structures of occupational and fiscal welfare).

In pursuit of new rounds of economic growth, the political managers of the American version of Keynesianism have relied on corporate tax cuts as the basic tool for ending recessionary economic downturns. These cuts have taken the form of both the addition of new deductions, credits, and allowances and the reduction of nominal tax rates to spur the growth machine. The former have been more significant than the latter in reducing corporate tax liabilities. As a result of the expansion of tax breaks to corporations throughout the postwar period, many large

Table 2.2 Occupational welfare, the two largest tax expenditures

($ in millions)

Type	1974	1975	1976	1977	1978	1979	1980	1981	1982	1983	1984
Net exclusion of pension and earnings contributions, employer plans	4,790	5,200	5,740	NA	9,940	11,335	19,785	23,605	NA	46,585	50,535
Exclusion of employer contributions to medical insurance	2,940	3,340	3,745	NA	7,105	11,080	12,075	14,165	NA	15,270	17,625
Totals	7,730	8,540	9,485	NA	17,045	22,415	31,860	37,790	NA	61,855	68,160

Sources: Estimates of Federal Tax Expenditures, Joint Committee on Internal Revenue Taxation, US Congress, Washington, DC: US Government Printing Office, 1975, pp. 8–9; *Statistical Abstracts of the United States: 1981*, US Bureau of the Census, Washington DC 1981, p. 254; *Statistical Abstracts of the United States: 1985*, US Bureau of the Census, December, 1984, p. 310.

Table 2.3 Effective tax rate, by type of industry, 1981

Sector	Percent of 1981 US income paid
Motor vehicles	48
Pharmaceuticals	36
Diversified services	30
Food processing	27
Retailing	23
Oil and refining	19
Diversified financial	17
Aerospace	7
Chemicals	5
Crude oil producers	3
Commercial banks	2

Sources: Joint Committee on Taxation, US Congress, USGPO, 1981; *New York Times* (March 20, 1983), Sec.3, p.1.

corporations paid little or no taxes. In 1981, for example, even before Reagan's regressive tax policies were enacted, although the nominal rate of corporate taxation was 48 percent, the effective tax rate varied greatly from industry to industry, ranging from a high of 48 percent for automobile manufacturers (which were disinvesting from domestic production and hence foregoing tax underwritten plant modernization at the time) to a negligible 2.3 percent for the larger commercial banks (table 2.3). Other segments of corporate capital which pay few taxes under present tax provisions include export companies, the insurance industry, the oil and gas industry, and the real estate and security industries. Not surprisingly, the major industries contributing to the campaigns of the members of tax writing congressional committees parallel the sectors that benefit most from differential taxation of corporations. The oil and gas industry, real estate, securities, the banking industry, public utilities, and trucking have been ranking contributors to the politicians who comprise the tax writing House Ways and Means Committee (*New York Times*, September 20, 1974:4).

The crux of the argument presented here is that the cumulative result of political processes of macroeconomic growth stimulation and congressional committee decision-making in the postwar

Table 2.4 The shrinking corporate tax burden: Major tax sources of federal revenues and their share of the total, by fiscal year (in %)

Tax source	1952	1960	1970	1980	1981	1982	1983
Corporation income	32.1	23.2	17.0	12.5	10.2	8.0	6.6
Social insurance*	9.8	15.9	23.0	30.5	30.5	32.6	35.5
Individual income	42.2	44.0	46.9	47.2	47.7	48.3	47.2

* Includes Social Security, Medicare, unemployment, railroad employment and federal employee retirement taxes.
Source: Office of Management and Budget, cited in *New York Times* (March 20, 1983), Sec. 3, p. 26.

period has been a redistribution of the burden of financing the American welfare state from profits to wages. As table 2.4 indicates, these processes have eroded the share of federal tax revenues derived from corporations from 32 percent in 1952 to only 6.6 percent in 1983. Reagan's initial round of accelerated depreciation allowances and other business tax breaks thus reflects a long-term trend rather than an abrupt departure from past practice. As Karen Anderson (1981) has noted, as early as 1954, "Congress allowed corporations to depreciate capital investments at rates faster than the actual deterioration of assets. In 1962, and again in 1971, these depreciation periods were shortened still further. Since 1962, corporations have also been allowed to take investment tax credits on the purchase of new equipment." As table 2.4 also makes clear, however, the accelerated write-offs and increased investment tax credits initiated by Reagan did intensify the rate of this long-term trend considerably. His policies reduced the corporate tax burden by over 90 percent, from 12.5 percent of revenues in 1980 to 6.6 percent prior to the passage of recent congressional "tax reform" legislation.

Ironically, in view of the commitment to growth that fostered many of these tax policies, the current structure of the tax system has begun to skew corporate investment in ways that are viewed as quite inefficient for the economy as a whole, producing sectorally uneven investment. As one commentator has expressed the issue: "The economy's best prospects for growth are . . . being lost as businessmen seek out 'loopholes' in the corporate tax code, much the same as individuals seek them in the personal tax code" (Wayne, 1983:1). As capital investment shifts to sectors with low effective tax rates, this causes overinvestment in some economic sectors (e.g. real estate), disinvestment in others, and ultimately, a sectorally unbalanced economy.

This sectoral unevenness is compounded by uneven rates of federal taxation between monopoly and competitive capital, a reflection of the relative political power of the two sectors. The effective rate of corporate taxation on Fortune 500 firms is 15 percent, compared with an average rate of 35 percent. The reason for this lies not in the economic inevitability of the corporate capitalist form of economic organization, but in the political power of monopoly capital to shape taxation policies. A lobbyist for a coalition of medium-sized competitive sector industries recently succinctly expressed the issue: "Taxes are not imposed by the market process, but by the legislative process and the Fortune 100 have had representatives in Washington to look after their interests while the mid-sized companies have not" (quoted in Wayne, 1983:26; see also Salamon and Siegfried, 1977).

THE SOCIAL BASE OF "FISCAL WELFARE"

Viewed in this light, the rhetoric of the Reaganite recapitalization strategy differs sharply from its reality. Although the rhetoric is anti-statist, the reality has been a reconstitution rather than a reduction of state activity. As I have expressed the issue elsewhere (Smith, 1984b:10-11):

The actions of 'human agents' on the political right have addressed the historically specific conditions of slow growth, inflationary pressures, and lowered productivity by promoting an agenda that has reduced the direct role of the state in planning and administration of everyday life, while increasing its indirect role in promoting capital investment and controlling inflation through a contradictory combination of expanded tax breaks to capital and monetary austerity.

The social base in the American electorate supporting this development has been largely drawn from middle-strata constituency groups who stand to benefit most from the policy shift. Davis (1984) has lucidly assessed the causes and consequences of the intensified political mobilization of middle-strata constituency groups allied with business Political Action Committees (PACs) in reshaping the political agenda of both major political parties in the United States during the late 1970s. This has been accompanied by political demobilization of blacks, Hispanics, and the unemployed. Overrepresentation of upper and middle-strata professional and technical personnel, middle managers, and "new entrepreneurs" at the electoral level has provided a social base of politically active voters supportive of the expansion of "fiscal welfare," the contraction of means-tested social welfare, and "deregulation" in order to "expand the frontiers of entrepreneurial and rentier activity" (Davis, 1984) through tax-writeoffs and deregulation of development, while expanding government contracting to the high-tech military-industrial sector.

The rise to power of the neo-liberal wing of the Democratic party, touting "new ideas" which are tantamount to more targeted versions of Reagan's supply-side nostrums, reflects the rise of new Sunbelt-based, defense and high-tech oriented, professional and technical middle strata as an important electoral power base within both major political parties. It also reflects the growing weakness of the Democratic party's traditional eastern and midwestern blue collar and minority constituencies in the face of slowed growth. This weakness results from the assumption of nearly all welfare state liberal policy proposals since 1946 that were redistributional in character that the policies would be financed by continuing economic growth. Traditional liberal social policy was premised on a redistribution of some share of the "growth surplus." In a slow growth or contracting economy such an approach simply did not work. The widespread awareness of this is reflected in traditional liberal Walter Mondale's defeat in the 1984 presidential election.

Vidich (1980) has identified a set of increasingly politicized capitalist class segments which also support the current reconstitution of welfare capitalism. This segment of capital comprises the mass communication, electronics, aircraft, oil, and machine tool industries. From their inception, these industries (which tend to be concentrated in the West and Southwest) have been "tied ... to politically determined market privileges – government contracts, franchises, subsidies, and tax writeoffs [which] have become a prerequisite for access to market opportunities." This set of capitalist interests has gained the support of their own managers, salaried employees, and even wage laborers who have come to identify their interests with the continued growth of their own economic sectors. As inflation, rising unemployment, and slowed economic growth threatened the alliance between these segments of capital and labor by undermining the living standards of workers in these "sectoral blocs," the "new" growth sector capital fractions developed a political strategy for reigniting the growth machine. They promoted policies which seemed to mark a return to "market processes" but which in fact produced even more politically determined market privileges in the form of accelerated depreciation schedules, "reindustrialization" policies geared to the "leading edge" growth sectors, and an accelerated defense buildup, which channeled more resources away from "old" civilian industries and toward themselves.

Finance capital joined in this strategy by promoting the notion that the mounting stagflation crisis was caused by a "capital shortage" which would impede future economic growth if social and tax policies were not changed to transfer resources to the capital investment sector (Miller and Tomaskovic-Devey, 1983:4). This "theory" of capital shortage gained wide currency as a result of the salesmanship of corporate business and financial elites, even though the level of private investment from 1965 to 1975, when corporate elites first began to demand huge tax incentives for investment, was actually quite high, exceeding the average investment ratio for the previous two postwar decades (Pechman, 1975).

By the late 1970s, this "capital shortage" perspective had attracted support within the Carter administration, whose urban policy analysts began a political redefinition of the "urban crisis" as a crisis of business disincentives for investment in older central cities rather than in terms of either inattention to the social needs of the people living in declining cities or the need to reform the past public policies contributing to urban decline and interregional job shifts – i.e., the past economic growth, defense, housing production, and business modernization policies of American Keynesianism (see Marcuse, 1981; Smith and Judd, 1983, 1984; Mollenkopf, 1983).

The Carter wing of the Democratic party was joined by leading neo-liberal Democratic politicians like Gary Hart of Colorado and Paul Tsongas of Massachusetts in promoting the idea that increasing incentives for private business investment was the best means to revitalize declining cities, reindustrialize America, and cope with the stagflation crisis. In this changing political climate, the supply-side tax and budget cutting policies of the Reagan-dominated Republican party may be regarded as simply an extension to its logical extreme of a long developing interest-based restructuring of perception, public policy premises, public discourse, and urban politics.

AMERICAN KEYNESIANISM AND THE TRANSFORMATION OF US CITIES

The impact of postwar Keynesian growth policies to stimulate business investment and aggregate consumer demand have had a profound impact on the form and function of American cities and regions (see Glickman, 1980). The partially unintended, partially purposive socio-spatial impact of the American version of welfare capitalism is perhaps the largest single "structural" element underlying the transformation of American cities into sprawling megalopolitan settlement spaces, the rise of the "Sunbelt" (Perry and Watkins, 1977), the restructuring of regional economic bases, and the conversion of some large formerly industrial cities in all regions into office parks for the multinational business service sector.

The policy mechanisms driving this new political economy, note Piven and Cloward, include:

> high levels of military and defense spending that stimulated the great boom in the Sun Belt; subsidies and tax credits for the construction and real estate industries that helped produce the great post-World War II suburban construction boom and the redevelopment of the older central cities to accommodate corporate administrative functions; infrastructure subsidies in the form of highway, water and sewer grants that spurred the suburbanization of housing and industry; farm subsidies that contributed to the continuing concentration of agriculture; somewhat later the use of investment tax credits as a strategy for economic stimulus (Piven and Cloward, 1982: 111; see also Smith, 1979:235–52).

We have already seen some of the ways that the three specific forms of "welfare" characterizing American welfare capitalism have worked as just described to redistribute burdens and opportunities on the basis of "place." We may now amplify upon these briefly.

Federal tax subsidies for housing have favored the types of housing that have encouraged the suburban sprawl pattern of residential development (Smith, 1979, ch. 6). New, single-family, owner-occupied housing has received favorable tax treatment at the expense of existing, multi-family, rental housing (Barros, 1978:113; Peterson, 1980:4, 13). The deductibility of property taxes from federal tax liabilities is a subsidy to homeowners, estimated at $15 billion for 1984 (Arenson, 1982:4E), which has gone disproportionately to suburban, non-metropolitan, and Sunbelt areas (Peterson, 1980; Arroyo, 1981). In 1981 alone, the deductibility of mortgage interest, which also has a decidedly suburban and Sunbelt distributional tilt, constituted a $19.8 billion loss to the US Treasury. The persistence of this tax incentive, even in the face of comprehensive tax reform, is an especially strong inducement for middle to upper income people to remain in suburbs and for continued uneven interregional development.

Federal Housing Administration (FHA) and Veteran's Administration (VA) loan guarantee policies have enabled many moderate-income working people to join the more affluent in the sprawling suburbs (Smith, 1979; Peterson, 1980:13). In addition to accounting for 25 percent of all new housing starts since World War II, FHA guarantees have been estimated to account for up to 40 percent of suburban sprawl (Markusen, 1979:5).

The business tax incentives for new investment enumerated earlier have encouraged investment shifts from central cities to metropolitan peripheries, older to newer communities, and the Frostbelt to the Sunbelt and overseas (Peterson, 1980:5; Marcuse, 1981). In 1981, the investment tax credit alone, which has been shown to be an "urban disinvestment" tax credit producing wasteful "surplus modernization," amounted to a $19.5 billion federal revenue loss (Marcuse, 1981; Arenson, 1982). The human cost of this incentive to disinvest from older but still useful capital stock has been a wasteful underutilization of "pools of unemployed labor in older cities, as well as abandoned productive facilities" (Peterson, 1980:6).

When these tax credits for new facilities are combined

with other key dimensions of public spending under American
Keynesianism including: federal research and development investments in space technology; expenditures for interstate highways;
water and sewer grants for new communities; direct defense
spending (following the political logic of the power of Southern
Congress members in locating defense installations); defense
procurement policies (providing a guaranteed market for western
and southwestern defense contractors); and energy and hydroelec-
tric development projects which have contributed significantly to
rural development in the South and West (Markusen, 1979;
Muller, 1981), it has been conservatively estimated that "from
the beginning of the New Deal through 1980 roughly $450 billion
was distributed from large northern industrial states to other
areas, mostly in the South and West" (Muller, 1981:39).

To these developmental policies must be added some dimensions
of the social policy agenda of welfare state liberalism, such as the
liberalized criminal procedures of the Warren Court and court-
ordered busing to achieve urban school desegregation, which have
been tied by conservative politicians to high crime rates in central
cities and threatened declines in "educational quality." Regardless
of the merits of these arguments, as James Coleman (1976) points
out, to the extent that they have found an acceptable niche in
public opinion, they have added a cultural dimension to the
demand for the more distant settlement spaces which the intended
and unintended economic development, defense, and energy
policies of American Keynesianism opened up. They also have
further weakened the social base of New Deal/Great Society
liberalism, thereby helping to open up the political space for the
emergence of the "reindustrialization" agendas of neo-liberalism
and Reaganomics.

Not surprisingly, the results of all these trends have been
accelerated under Reagan. To cite a central example of the uneven
regional impacts of Reagan's policies, the military budget increased
from $182.4 billion in FY 1981 to $264.l billion in 1984. In FY
1984 these massive defense spending increases of the Reagan
presidency went largely to the South and West. In 1984, 44
percent of direct military expenditures went to the South and 32
percent to the West, in comparison to 16 percent for the Northeast
and only 8 percent for the Midwest (Herbers, 1983:1, 14).
Between 1982 and 1984, nine of the ten biggest gainers, as table
2.5 indicates, were located in the West or South. Six of the ten

Table 2.5 The geographical distribution of direct federal military expenditures, 1982–84

States with largest percentage expenditure increase	%	States with smallest percentage expenditure increase	%
Wyoming	+75	Massachusetts	−6.4
New Mexico	+31	Maryland	−2.6
Arizona	+27	Virginia	−1.1
Montana	+22	Oregon	+0.7
Utah	+20	Delaware	+1.8
North Dakota	+19	Pennsylvania	+2.7
Texas	+17	New York	+3.5
Nevada	+16	West Virginia	+3.7
Georgia	+15	New Hampshire	+3.9

Source: Compiled from data in *New York Times* (December 20, 1983), pp. 1, 14.

states showing declines or quite low rates of growth were concentrated in the Northeast.

By 1985, however, because of the Star Wars initiative, Massachusetts and Connecticut, where major high-tech defense contractors and science-based university complexes are located, began to experience significant economic growth and concomitant "urban revitalization." This restructuring of federal spending priorities, combined with the expanded political-economic involvement of East and West coast cities in international trade and the export of business services to Asia, Latin America, and the Middle East is beginning to produce a new form of uneven regional development. This new pattern of interregional inequality is characterized by a continuing decline in the industrial heartland of the Midwest and growth in coastal cities and regions better situated to take advantage of the corporate-government alliance to reassert American global hegemony in the face of economic and political crises.

Subsequent chapters will fully address the complex question of the interplay between political-economic and state policy determinants in the transformation of US cities and regions in the postwar period. Before turning our attention to this central question, however, a few concluding reflections will help to set the stage for the subsequent argument.

CONCLUSIONS

American Keynesians have generally taken only limited interest in the normative dimension of government intervention. From their perspective, so long as the intervention stimulated greater aggregate demand and thus spurred new economic activity, both the form of the intervention (e.g. direct social expenditures or tax cuts) and the content of the intervention (e.g. guns or butter) were largely irrelevant. Yet it makes a great deal of difference to the character and quality of a society whether the state's major expenditures are missiles or social services; whether they compound or reduce social inequality; whether the social, spatial, and organizational "products" which the particular mix of social, fiscal, and occupational welfare benefits combine to foster are socially necessary, merely superfluous, or actually harmful; whether the social class structure and prevailing patterns of domination in the society are reinforced or altered by public investment. It also matters politically, as we shall see, whether state intervention takes the form of providing a highly visible public service or extending a relatively invisible fiscal welfare benefit.

The increased reliance on "tax expenditures" as a public policy tool in preference to direct public budget expenditures has been encouraged not only by the social base of support and the specific pattern of class alliances discussed in this chapter but also by the relatively less publicly visible character of this particular form of state intervention. An "expenditure" which has no immediately visible effect on the public budget is quite attractive to politically sensitive presidents and Congress persons at both ends of the mainstream American ideological spectrum. As Smith and Judd (1984:185) have noted: "Conservatives like to substitute subsidies buried in obscure tax codes for active policy because it gives them the ability to project the illusion of cutting government bureaucracy and spending. Liberals ... can claim to be pursuing social objectives, such as the creation of jobs [by fiscal welfare], without being accused of being 'big spenders' or 'budgetbusters.'" Despite the symbolic ability of many types of "fiscal welfare" to promise future growth, which creates the impression that people are getting something for nothing, such tax concessions withdraw substantial revenues from the public treasury. They thus entail very large "opportunity costs," i.e., lost opportunities for more publicly visible political processes to determine other public purposes for which the lost revenues might be spent if another method (e.g. a program, a direct subsidy) were chosen to provide them.

Moreover, as Friedland, Piven and Alford (1977:459–60) have shown, the form in which a policy is cast differentially affects its vulnerability to public pressures, including pressures for retrenchment when fiscal crisis conditions exist. Tax expenditures, like business tax breaks and homeowner tax subsidies, are insulated from public pressures for retrenchment by their low visibility. In contrast, rental housing supplements and direct welfare payments to low income citizens are vulnerable to such pressures because they show up as items paid for by general tax revenues.

More important, "fiscal welfare" policies also have been insulated from retrenchment pressures by the ideological legitimations surrounding their extension. As part of the overarching ideology of growth (see Smith and Judd, 1984; Wolfe, 1981), business tax breaks are sold as rewards for future contributions to expanding the productive forces of society, rather than as income transfers from labor to capital; uncapped homeowner tax deductions, justified in terms of growth expansion *and* social stability, are now popularly regarded more as a "natural right" than as a regressive transfer from renting to homeowning taxpayers. On the ideological and cultural level, the average American appears to be unaware that no other advanced capitalist country has seen fit to so lavishly subsidize suburban home ownership as a form of growth stimulation and a way of life (see Peterson, 1977, 1980; Heady, 1978).

The ideology of growth used to justify the particular forms of US welfare capitalism also has produced a spate of sectoral block alliances, which have served to reduce the play of class issues and class conflict in American politics. As Zukin (1980:593) has succinctly summarized the issue: "Not only does the state promote investment in growth to help finance its budgets, but it also promotes an alliance on the basis of growth between otherwise antithetical social groups that hope to profit from growth." In the area of urban redevelopment, for example, developers, bankers, municipal employees, and the building trade unions all gain from their participation in local growth coalitions. An important consequence is the dampening of consciousness of adversary interests between small and large investors in urban land (e.g. working class homeowners versus developers), labor and capital, management and employees. Each defends its own particular growth interest, segmentally protecting its own terrain. In this fashion, to extend the example, the short-term production of union jobs, landlord rents, tenant cost savings (e.g. by increasing the supply of office space), and developer profits cements an alliance in favor of rapid development even though the long-term interest of workers and tenants is not served by the lax enforcement of building codes sometimes triggered by the push for rapid growth.

The state cooperates in giving legitimacy and leadership to such alliances by both its actions and its inactions deemed necessary to promote rapid growth because of the support it gains from the sectoral block. The state then renews its short-term stock of legitimacy by avoiding latent social conflict through cementing such sectoral alliances. The cost to the public treasury to maintain alliances such as this has been a long-term drain on the state's material resources in exchange for political support. What Zukin (1980:593) sees as a central feature of US welfare capitalism generally seems especially applicable to the rise of the fiscal welfare state – namely that "once a particular terrain is awarded to a ... [sectoral bloc], the state guarantees the financing of further investment in this area for that group's benefit."

Against the views of both neo-Marxist and market liberal political economists, Keynesian political economists have expressed confidence that the periodic booms and busts of the business cycle could be effectively managed by economic stabilization policies, indeed, that well calibrated monetary and fiscal policies might even avoid these disruptive cycles. Keynesian macroeconomic policies were supposed to work flexibly, allowing technically informed economists and policy-makers to guide decreases in public spending during periods of growth to hold down inflationary pressures. Politically, that expectation proved unworkable. The logic of Keynesian market management rests upon market forces being sufficiently potent in a political economy for the market manipulatory tools of "fine tuning" and demand management to work.

If large sections of an economy are not subject to supply and demand curves – because of the social and political power of monopolies and oligopolies; the political production of market privileges by well organized "sectoral blocks" like the urban development and high-tech military sectors; the ability of the best organized segments of labor to join these growth-oriented "sectoral blocks;" and the desire of national politicians from both parties when in power to calibrate macroeconomic demand stimulating policies to the rhythms of election cycles rather than the needs of "the economy" – then Keynesian macroeconomic policy tools will be inadequate, and the results of manipulation often counterintuitive or even counterproductive (see Skidelsky, 1981).

For a short time, Great Society liberals tried to construct a social welfare block which even some radical analysts once mistakenly regarded as a potent "social industrial complex" (O'Connor, 1973), or at least a powerful, professionally led, "iron triangle" (Piven and Cloward, 1982). But as Minsky (1981–82:52) has said, once the political economy was set on a political course intended to simultaneously "improve the lot of the 'welfare poor' and increase the portion of output that goes to investment [via fiscal welfare] then the consumption standards of the working wage earning population must decrease." Of the latter, some have been protected by unions (at least until recently), others by professional skills. Those least likely to be protected by either – the unorganized, service workers, non-unionized industrial workers in right-to-work states, and the near poor – have ended up paying for the bulk of the upward and downward transfers of the American welfare state. This has further fragmented working-class consciousness by creating new social divisions within the working population and new antagonisms between the near poor and the welfare poor. These sources of delegitimation of Great Society liberalism, combined with the long-term inflationary bias of the Keynesian political predicament, and the stagflation crisis of the 1970s ended optimism among welfare state liberals and opened the door for criticisms of welfare capitalism from both the left and the right. It is to these criticisms and their implications for urban politics that we now turn.

3
Structural Marxist Urban Theory: Class Power, the State, and Urban Crisis

Conventional analysis of the politics and economics of urban problems is now in ferment. During the 1970s and early 1980s a new breed of urban scholars mounted a major assault upon the premises that had guided research on urban politics, community power studies, and urban policy analysis. These scholars rooted their work in a mode of analysis that combined many of the basic assumptions and objectives of structural Marxist social theory and applied them to the study of urban political economy. This chapter will address the major dimensions of the connections drawn by Marxist urban theorists between the general crisis of the advanced capitalist welfare state and general tendencies toward urban crisis. This will enable us to develop a more historically specific assessment of that relationship as found in the American political economy.

This chapter will first consider the central concern of structural Marxist urban theory – the specific relations through which structural economic conditions, class conflict, and the role of the state in advanced capitalist societies are viewed as determining *urban* political processes. The chapter then identifies some major gaps that have characterized Marxist urban political economy. Among the most important of these for our purposes are: (a) the gap between a general social theory which applies structural economic logic to explain the dynamics of urban development in all advanced capitalist societies and actual empirical research which reveals considerable differences among nation states in the ways in which economic and social crisis tendencies are politically mediated at the urban level; and (b) the relatively abstract, ahistorical, universalistic character of the discussion of the relationship among structural economic logic (economy), the social production of beliefs (culture), and political mobilization or quiescence (urban politics).

ADVANCED CAPITALISM, THE STATE, AND URBAN POLITICS

Structural Marxist urban theory has sought to develop a general theory of society that accounts for the relationships among the political, economic, cultural, and ideological dimensions of urban life. This concern has dictated a more systemic level of analysis than is common among students of urban politics. Classical community power studies, for example, have been concerned about the discrete actions of local actors in community politics, rather than with structured patterns of whole societies. The community power studies of the 1960s, as well as their criticisms (e.g. Bachrach and Baratz, 1962, 1963), were methodologically individualistic. That is, they tended to analyze the strategies of *actors*, whether individuals or social groups, seeking to maximize power over the agendas and decisions of local politics.

According to the early Marxian structuralist work of Manuel Castells (1975:10–11), such a limited focus is unable to account for the deeper-level "relations between political processes, urban contradictions, and general social interests, i.e., the economic, political, and ideological interests of the social classes which form the totality of society." Why is this the case? Most obviously, the study of the behavior of urban actors is by definition limited to the local community, while the urban problems that provoke local action are the result of society-wide, if not global, social forces and structural economic conditions. Examples in the USA include the mechanization of Southern agriculture in the 1940s and 1950s, the shift in industrial investment to the South, the Sunbelt, and the Third World in the 1970s, and the ongoing transformation of the American economic structure from an industrial to a service base. From these examples it should be clear, even to many nonstructuralists, that "community" power cannot be analyzed adequately apart from the wider context of economic and political conditions operating at the national and international levels.

Given this starting point, structural Marxist urban theorists assume that in capitalist societies the social structure is characterized by contradictory relationships between dominant and subordinate classes. The class relation regarded as central in orthodox Marxism is the contradictory relationship between capital and labor in the productive sphere. By the 1970s, studies of class relations in Marxist urban political economy were significantly influenced by the expansion of the welfare state within capitalism as an allocator of social resources. Following the early lead of Castells (1977, 1978), Marxist urban political economists began to focus on the sphere of "collective consumption," i.e., on the role of the national and local welfare state in producing and distributing collectively consumed urban social services such as mass transport, education, health care, and public housing. Struggles over the "collective consumption" of these public services became a means to identify the social stakes embedded in given modes of public service delivery that developed into distinctively "urban" political conflicts (see Preteceille, 1977; Dunleavy, 1980; and the critique of Saunders, 1981).

Moving beyond this concern with the politics of collective consumption, other critical urban theorists have sought to explain the changing social uses of urban space, and, in particular, to reveal the processes connecting the urban institutions, social movements, and political structures capable of maintaining or transforming the uses of urban space (see Smith, 1984a and b; Gottdiener, 1985). In this latter perspective, controversies over alternative uses of urban land are viewed as struggles between the mutually antagonistic social forces seeking to accumulate capital by transforming space and groups and class segments adversely affected by the transformation process. For David Harvey (1973, 1976, 1985) and other critical urban theorists (see Smith, 1979, 1982, 1984a and b; Gottdiener, 1985), including the later work of Castells (1984, 1985), the proper aim of social theory is to uncover the dynamic processes underlying the creation and transformation of urban space. Cities and regions become the focal point for the circulation of capital, the reproduction of (or change in) class relations, and the production of social conflict.

Both the "collective consumption" and the socio-spatial conflict perspectives represent major shifts in emphasis on the left from workplace relations to urban community struggles. Both structural Marxists and other critical urban theorists were forced to come to grips with the failure of the industrial working classes in advanced capitalist societies to convert concrete grievances found in the work place into a revolutionary politics. Surveying the landscape, they turned to the arena where social conflicts in the 1960s and 1970s were most evident, the arena of urban politics. Unlike earlier students of urban power structure, who analyzed such conflicts on a case by case basis, interpreting them as isolated instances of interest conflict (Dahl, 1961; Polsby, 1963) or elite manipulation (Hunter, 1953; Bachrach and Baratz, 1962; 1963), the newer breed of researchers sought to connect these local conflicts to an overall national political-economic context. They attempted to highlight recurrent, society-wide contradictions common to such local conflicts over collective consumption or socio-spatial change.

Casting their net beyond the boundaries of national political economies, some Marxist and critical urban analysts have chosen to analyze cities as parts of a much wider "world-system" of cities, depicting urban processes as dependent on the exigencies of the larger systemic features of world capitalism (see, for instance, Chase-Dunn, 1984; Hill, 1983, 1984; see also Smith and Feagin, 1987). From this perspective, local struggles over the built environment are interpreted as "expressions" of the accumulated contradictions of world capitalism. Community conflict thus becomes a mere "epiphenomenon" of the irreconcilable tension between capital and labor over the share of the social surplus to be devoted to further capital accumulation on a global scale versus the fulfillment of the human needs of living labor "in the community," e.g. housing, recreation, social and cultural uses of space.

Reflecting this concern for structural economic transformations of the "created environment" (Giddens, 1981), metropolitan regions have been depicted as a means for speeding the circulation of capital (Harvey, 1973, 1985; Castells, 1978). In this context, urban public policy problems like transportation and housing have been viewed as problematic arenas for social conflict precisely because they affect both the quality of life in residential neighborhoods and the interest that corporate and financial institutions have in the speedy circulation of capital. When the quest for neighborhood stability impedes speedy circulation, urban social conflict is the likely result. Because of the growing role of "the state" in both urban development and social policy (e.g. housing) the target of this conflict is likely to be the state.

THE ROLE OF THE STATE IN STRUCTURAL MARXIST URBAN THEORY

This brings us to a major area of disagreement within the neo-Marxist perspective – the role of welfare state capitalism and its relationship to urban social and political conflict. British structuralists like Pickvance (1976a, b) and Cowley (1977) emphasize those aspects of state provision of public services that they view as serving to *reproduce* capitalist social relations. Their reading of the welfare state, while focusing on activities of welfare state capitalism that are collectively consumed – e.g., health, education, and social welfare services – does not anticipate state policies as a major source of urban social conflict. In their view, the administrative agencies that manage the collective means of consumption (e.g. schools, welfare bureaucracies) are reproductive rather than redistributive institutions.

Viewed in this light, welfare state social service bureaucracies serve to reproduce capitalist social relations in two basic ways. First, their very existence serves to placate social discontent symbolically. Second, their basic economic function is to reproduce physically labor power in ways that insure that the working classes are adequately productive and effectively socialized instruments of production.

The welfare state's willingness and ability to provide high levels of collectively consumed services is explained by Pickvance (1976a:21) as a resultant of the need for a "collective capitalist" institution to resolve the contradiction under capitalism between short-term profitability and long-term productivity. For example:

> The fact that it is unprofitable, generally speaking to provide collective means of consumption and yet they are necessary to raise productivity is partly resolved by the State's undertaking the financing of such provision. Thus, the state steps in on behalf of capitalist agents, who, individually, find such provision unprofitable .... Thus, in addition to its functions of reproducing the political, legal, and ideological conditions of capitalist production, the state has a crucial economic role.

From this perspective, then, the capitalist state functions to directly *resolve* a basic contradiction of the ongoing economic order by its social welfare activities. At the same time, it indirectly serves to reproduce capitalist social relations by its dominant role in shaping political ideology. Ideologically, the state uses elements of welfare state liberal and even social democratic ideology to disguise the actual long-term beneficiaries of state activities and thus to depoliticize social service delivery. Additionally, state planners of public services, in Cowley's (1977:225) terms, superimpose an even more depoliticizing "ideology of problem solving and technical expertise on the political reality of class conflict." These excerpts capture the functionalist flavor that has characterized some of the structural Marxist writings in the British context.

Generally speaking, critical urban theorists writing in the American context have not viewed either urban development policy making or welfare state activities as inherently reproductive, cooptative, or depoliticizing (see, for instance, Mollenkopf, 1975, 1983; Piven and Cloward, 1982; Katznelson, 1976a; 1976b). These analysts have stressed instead the conflict generating and, indeed, politicizing dimensions of state activities. Thus, for instance, according to Mollenkopf (1975:294) the expanded state role in providing infrastructure services for economic development, inevitably politicizes many urban issues, such as neighborhood development and urban service delivery. In his words: "Of all the contextual factors which structure markets, the state is the most important. Land use patterns are inherently collective, public matters. They cannot be set up without government actions ranging from roads and sewers, to police and fire protection, to plans about how owners use their property. As a result, land use questions . . . inevitably become political."

The activities of American Keynesianism that have fostered the redevelopment and transformation of many central cities into command and control centers for both government and corporate power reveal, in Mollenkopf's view, the state's essentially contradictory role as guarantor of both accumulation (economic development) and social peace (neighborhood stability). In acting out this role he has envisaged the state developing a considerable degree of autonomy from "any given social stratum" including, presumably, the monopoly capitalist stratum (1975:253). In his most recent work, Mollenkopf (1983) has carried this argument even further, developing an argument about the decisive role of "political entrepreneurs" in urban development, which has prompted others to term him a "state determinist" (Gottdiener, 1985).

This conception of state power views the state within welfare capitalism as a sort of "mediator" between economic and social forces (see, more generally, Habermas, 1973; O'Connor, 1973, 1981, 1984). Thus the state has a considerable degree of "autonomy" from the forces of capitalist accumulation. This view of the state is at the heart of the expectation that the involvement of the state in urban development policy-making will inevitably politicize the policy-making process. If the state is more than a mere instrument of the dominant class – if indeed, its structural role is inherently contradictory – its actions, by definition are contradictory. Thus, the more that the state acts, the more likely are such contradictions to become expressed in visible public actions and policies. This in turn is expected to facilitate the mobilization of consciousness, sow the seeds of controversy, and hence foster politicization.

In this context, Katznelson, for instance, expresses no surprise that the community and not the workplace has become a main locus of political conflict. If, as Katznelson (1976a:22) has argued, the state has become visibly implicated in maintaining and reproducing contradictory class relations, and if the capitalist state's own growth is contingent upon the growth and reproduction of capital, then the state's intervention to "make the economy work," necessarily entails the state's direct distribution of the social class costs of growth.

Put more concretely, in a socially unequal society that is class stratified there are bound to be losers when the state acts to promote urban renewal, locate highway access ramps in residential neighborhoods, or otherwise restructure the uses of urban space. But the state's very involvement in the development process offers potential losers a clear and visible target against which to express discontent. Thus, while the struggle over urban space is class-based and economic, the main battlefield necessarily becomes the urban political arena. This in turn requires public officials to struggle skillfully against community-based social movements to channel mass discontent into manageable political rituals and routines (Katznelson, 1981; see also Smith, 1979; Smith and Borghorst, 1977, 1979, for discussions of the extent to which the local political managers of the urban redevelopment process have used both the ideology of economic growth and the material benefits of growth to buy off opposition and legitimate the dislocating side-effects of urban redevelopment).

The expectation that the involvement of the state in transforming urban space would produce highly conflictual local political activity in US cities was premised on the assumption that the state's role in the redevelopment process would be sufficiently visible to provoke focused resentment by potential losers. The model of political process underlying the theory of the state posited by Mollenkopf and Katznelson was drawn on the basis of the historical experience of the US urban struggles of the 1960s and early 1970s in American cities. At that time the role of welfare state liberal public policies in promoting urban renewal, locating low income scattered-site public housing projects in residential neighborhoods, and mobilizing and then absorbing the new social forces unleashed by the civil rights revolution into the new social policy structures of the Great Society was indeed highly visible. Much the same can be said for Castells' early versions of "collective consumption" theory, which were drawn on the basis of experience in a European context, where the role of the French state in urban development and urban social service provision were, and largely remain, highly visible targets for both provoking and channeling the discontents of everyday life into the "urban" sphere.

In the context of contemporary American urban politics, neither of these formulations is especially helpful. As we have seen in chapter 2, the growth of the low visibility benefit structures of "fiscal welfare" at the expense of more visible forms of state intervention has been especially pronounced in the past two decades in the United States. The highly visible social welfare policies of the Great Society have been replaced by low visibility fiscal welfare policies as the basic urban growth inducing and economic development tool of Keynesian welfare capitalism (see Smith and Judd, 1984). This shift in the mode of transferring resources and "contracting out" state sovereignty to "private" interests has secured politically determined market privileges for particular interests while obscuring "the state's" role in the ensuing transformation of opportunity structures, space, and society. Growing "privatization" thus has entailed growing depoliticization.

In this way, for instance, the visible and deeply resented

"bulldozer" symbolizing the displacement of urban renewal has been replaced by low visibility tax and loan subsidies promoting "gentrification" (see Palen and London, 1984; Smith and Williams, 1986). The last vestiges of publicly sponsored urban renewal have been rendered far less visible by being subsumed under the Community Development Block Grant scheme. Low visibility federal, state, and local tax incentives now help produce socially dislocating capital flight which is interpreted as a purely market process for which "the state" bears no "before the fact" responsibility. As we have seen, low visibility tax breaks for homeowners promoting continued metropolitan deconcentration have grown exponentially. Meanwhile, rent subsidized public housing projects, both large scale and scattered-site, have virtually ceased to be built. The urban social policy structures of the 1960s "War on Poverty" have been largely "defunded." The newer fiscal policy structures of the late 1970s and early 1980s have expanded steadily while obscuring both the role of the state in society and the social interests benefitting most from this use of state power. The emergent form of "hidden" welfare state apparatus is a blueprint for depoliticization rather than politicization, quiescence rather than conflict.

THE STATE AND URBAN FISCAL CRISIS

Focusing primarily on US welfare capitalism's extensive involvement in urban redevelopment policy-making, American urban researchers have paid scant attention to either the cooptative or the crisis-producing potential of the welfare state's "collective consumption" activities. Yet this has been a major theme among European Marxist urban analysts. This difference may well stem from the fact that the American welfare state has operated differently from its European counterparts. As we have seen in chapter 2, in our discussion of American "exceptionalism," a welfare state that offers more fiscal than social welfare, favors categorical rather than universal social services, provides most of the latter through transfer payments rather than directly, and finances the directly provided social services that it does provide (e.g. public housing, public transport, employment training) at relatively modest levels, does not fit well into theoretical formulations that envisage "the" state within capitalism as purchasing legitimation and securing the reproduction of labor power needed for capital accumulation by high levels of direct social expenditure (which in turn directly lead to both national and urban fiscal crises). It is apparent, then, that historically specific political differences among the advanced capitalist political economies in what the state does, how it does so, and how it pays for what it does, can help us to explain the differences that are to be found in various neo-Marxist theoretical accounts of the urban fiscal crisis.

Compare, for instance, the explanation for the fiscal crisis of cities offered by the early "collective consumption" theory developed in a European context by Manuel Castells and the explanation of urban fiscal crisis offered by the American neo-Marxist Richard Child Hill. When writing largely in a European context, Castells (1978) placed the crisis of the welfare state at the very heart of the urban fiscal crisis. He attributed the mounting expenditure – revenue gap to the withdrawal of a significant share of surplus product from the capital accumulation process to pay for the state's management of collective consumption activities such as health, housing, education and leisure.

Castells' analysis of the fiscal crisis of the city proceeds along the following lines. Initially, the collective consumption expenditures of the national state are functional for the capitalist order as a whole because they assure the necessary reproduction of labor, socialize the costs of benefits that otherwise might have to be paid for in wages, and thus shift economic demands away from capitalists toward the state (1978:12). Yet as they expand, collective consumption expenditures begin to impinge upon the process of accumulating capital for future investment on which the growth of both capitalism and the state ultimately depend. In response, finance capital, that fraction of capital most dependent upon speedy circulation, seeks austerity measures, including cutbacks in urban social services. State expenditures for collective consumption slow down, as the forces of accumulation recapture resources they viewed as lost to the accumulation process. At the "urban" level, where nationally designed and financed collective services are provided, service cutbacks, public service unemployment, and ineffective service delivery follow.

For Castells, it is *this* process of fiscal retrenchment of collectively consumed services, rather than the character of urban land use conflicts, or the drain on intergovernmental resources

posed by heavy infrastructure investment for economic development, which triggers the politicization of policy-making at the
level of local government. Castells (1975:10; 1976a) contends
that the contradictory nature of the expansion of the welfare state
under capitalism creates the potential for politicization as well as
cooptation. (On this argument more generally see Esping-Andersen,
1985.)

For Castells, advanced capitalist societies rest increasingly on
the consumption process (i.e., on the distribution of what Marxists
regard as "already realized surplus value"). Urban areas have
become concentrated seats of the management of collective
consumption. Given the growing link between collective consumption and the growth of advanced capitalist service economies,
new social contradictions emerge around issues of collective
consumption (e.g. effective mass transit, poor educational quality,
or inadequate supply of decent housing). Some of these contradictions find expression (as they have done in continental Europe) in
"urban" social movements. These movements protest the management of everyday life by the bureaucratic state. This is because the
major areas of administratively managed collective consumption –
health, housing, transport, and schools – are directly linked to
people's everyday lives and are uniquely suited to political mobilization. They regularly generate "political options linked to class
interests which form the social structure." (For his most recent
effort to theorize other social bases for the emergence of urban
social movements in addition to mobilization over issues of
collective consumption, see Castells, 1983.)

The welfare state initially blurs the class character of the
administration of collective services. It seeks to achieve social
stability by becoming "the manager of everyday life" as it
increasingly rations citizens' access to health care, housing, and
other social services. At the outset, the state's growing social
welfare activities successfully shift attention away from capital
and ease direct demands upon capitalists in the productive sphere
to provide higher wages and benefits. Major segments of capital
are thus enlisted as supporters of increased social welfare
expenditures. Yet, as the locus of attention shifts to the state,
contradictions emerge in the sphere of collective consumption.
Effective and equitable delivery of social services become political
questions. "Urban" political movements become part of the
emerging political structure. So also do state sector public employee

unions. The state–capital relationship which has obtained political quiescence begins to face the potential for political disruption.

To buy off such disruption, state expenditures rise. As they rise, more of the existing economic surplus is withdrawn from new production, circulation, and accumulation. Economic recessions follow, accompanied by state revenue shortfalls. Service cutbacks and public service unemployment, necessitated by the shortfalls, trigger the full politicization of the "urban" fiscal crisis as an expression of a fundamental structural crisis of the capitalist welfare state. Thus the national state's efforts to manage the urban system and engender political quiescence through the local administration of everyday life engender contradictory results. Conflict, not stability, is the end result of efforts by agents of the welfare state to reproduce the ongoing economic system, reproduce labor power, and compensate for the negative side effects of advanced capitalism. The structural contradictions of advanced capitalism cannot be eliminated. They are inherent in the structured inequalities upon which the system rests.

Richard Child Hill (1978), writing in an American context, presents a picture of the causes and consequences of urban fiscal crisis quite different from Castells' analysis. Hill (1978:214) defines capitalist urbanization in terms of the spatial order that results from economic activity. In the contemporary American political economy, Hill argues, capital accumulation no longer requires densely concentrated central cities. This has made possible extensive suburbanization, and the fiscal and socio-spatial inequalities that this has entailed. Moreover, the dynamics of capital investment and disinvestment have conferred vitality and prestige on some cities within national systems of cities (e.g. Los Angeles) and withdrawn it from others (e.g. Cleveland). (As we shall see below in chapter 4, suburbanization and uneven investment per se are not sufficient to explain urban fiscal crises, because interlocal differences in economic and social base do not automatically produce *urban* fiscal crisis in countries with political structures in which most locally delivered services are financed by centralized national political authorities.)

In Hill's analysis, even national systems of cities are only partial subsystems. The trend toward increased capital concentration in the hands of corporate institutions, combined with the rise of multinational corporations, has extended the reach of capitalism globally. Private economic organizations now span the globe, seeking to locate at the least expensive points of production, distribution, and exchange. One consequence of this development has been the financial decline of various central cities that have become victims of the global migration of capital, employment, and people to cities and regions now in the forefront of the world capitalist accumulation process.

What has been the response of "the state" to these conditions? According to Hill, older American central cities that have suffered from capital flight and population deconcentration have become the locus of large-scale "social control" expenditures by the state. This is because unemployment and underemployment are concentrated in older central cities, jobs have moved elsewhere, and the private sector that remains is small scale, highly competitive, and insufficient to provide employment for the existing population. Thus, many residents have become partially or fully dependent upon the state. Because state welfare services are indirectly custodial and regulatory, they perform a social control function. Furthermore, the poor and discontented among the population threaten crime and disorder which in turn engenders demands from other social strata for additional direct social control expenditures for law enforcement.

Because of the unique operation of American federalism and the widespread fragmentation of governmental authority in the American political structure, state and local governments must finance a sizeable portion of such "social expense" expenditures (O'Connor, 1973) as law enforcement and public welfare (Hill, 1984). The concentration of dependent populations in older central cities which lack an economic base to finance their share of such expenditures means that the urban fiscal crisis appears earliest and becomes most pronounced in such localities.

The accumulation process itself adds to this fiscal burden. It places demands upon state and local governments to subsidize directly capital accumulation by projects that increase labor productivity while subsidizing the reproductive costs of efficient labor power (e.g. schooling, health care). The upshot of all these expansions of state activity, particularly the state's social control functions, is the fiscal crisis of the *city*. For Hill, this crisis emerges first in cities hardest hit by a declining local tax base to meet various contradictory demands for public spending.

Eventually however, as a result of global capital mobility, the society as a whole experiences a structural gap between public expenditures and revenues. For Hill, the structural gap at the national level is viewed as an inevitable consequence of *any* political economy so organized that the state absorbs much of the cost of economic production while the surplus produced by economic activity remains privately appropriated. Private appropriation *per se* sets structural limits upon the revenue raising capacity of the state. Yet expenditure demands continue to mount. When the structural limit on state revenue raising is reached, the fiscal crisis of the *state* is at hand. (See also Palloix, 1977; and Esping-Andersen, 1985 on the political dimension of this crisis.) At the urban level in Hill's scenario this crisis has several political consequences. It forms the basis of increasingly class-based political conflicts. Middle-class taxpayers revolt against further revenue accumulation by the state. The users and providers of urban social services and social control activities struggle over who gets what, how, and at whose expense. Yet, unlike Castells and other European urbanists, Hill (1978:234) envisages urban political conflict as remaining largely contained *within* the working class, broadly defined. For instance: "The mutually antagonistic relations between city workers, community groups, and private sector workers [in their role as taxpayers] have confounded the mobilization of the central city labor force into a political coalition capable of transforming the character of city and society." Only occasionally do some issues, like utility rate increases or redlining by banks, redefine the axis of urban politics, engendering the class conflict that is appropriately targeted at the structural sources of the urban and national fiscal crises.

CONTRADICTIONS IN STRUCTURAL MARXIST URBAN THEORY

By now it should be clear that there are major problems reflected in the disagreements found within structural Marxist urban political economy. To summarize the disagreements, there is first the conflict between those who stress the welfare state's role as a mediator of class antagonisms and those who view its increasing role in the political economy as a harbinger of increased urban political and social unrest. Second, there are differences in the extent to which state structures and policies are viewed as capable of managing the political fallout of both the state's own contradictory functions and the process of global capital flight. Third, there are quite distinct and divergent emphases upon which type of state expenditure within welfare capitalism is at the heart of the urban fiscal crisis.

These differences reflect key deficiencies within Marxist urban theory which call for further theoretical refinement and empirical clarification. First, as noted earlier, there is a need to develop a social theory of urban political mobilization and quiescence which takes into account the different forms that "the welfare state" has taken in different advanced capitalist countries and the implications that different patterns of taxing and spending have for the question of political consciousness and action. In particular, the political consequences of the expansion of the low visibility but highly consequential "fiscal welfare" state as a new historical mode of state intervention need to be more fully explored. Although treated in this book as an expression of "American exceptionalism," because of "fiscal welfare's" most complete development in the American political economy, less direct and visible means of state intervention, including "fiscal welfare" are now being expanded in other advanced capitalist countries facing global economic crisis conditions (see Smith, 1984b; Szelenyi, 1984; Gorz, 1982). Moreover, advocates of fiscal welfare policies are now even being found in some state socialist political economies facing a mounting debt crisis (Wiatr, 1985). Accordingly, future research of a comparative-historical nature is needed to reveal: (a) which social forces in different national contexts benefit from this concealment of the state's role in society; (b) which social forces are disadvantaged by this development; (c) "who decides" this reconstitution of the social division of welfare; and (d) what implications the restructuring has for urban political mobilization or quiescence.

Second, in their effort to develop a general theory of the crises and contradictions of "advanced capitalism," many Marxist urban theorists have tended to blur the crucial distinction between the national and the local state. In so doing they have ignored important historical differences among advanced capitalist states along the following critical dimensions: (a) the relative political dependence or autonomy of local governments in different societies; (b) the national differences among the fiscal structures financing central and local government activities; (c) the different types of national, regional, and local political structures mediating global economic processes like capital flight; and (d) the different "urban" results produced. (For an exception see Hill, 1984; for further development of this argument see chapter 4, this volume.)

Third, the different historical experiences and empirical research settings of the various "fiscal crisis" theorists has produced a literature in which a host of factors compete with each other as leading contenders for the "culprit" behind the urban fiscal crisis. These include urban planning and land use policies, collective consumption expenditures, demands for social control spending, and expenses to finance the physical infrastructure and to reproduce the labor power needed for long-term capital accumulation. As already discussed above, none of the theorists has focused upon the contribution of mounting "fiscal welfare" losses in tax revenues to the fiscal crisis, preferring instead to argue about which politically or economically "necessary" expenditures slow down production, profits, and hence indirectly, state revenues.

Fourth, it is apparent that the difference in cultural settings among advanced capitalist countries also helps to explain why some theorists, like Castells, see the urban fiscal crisis as a collective consumption crisis inevitably leading to the development of urban social movements challenging state domination of everyday life, while others, like Hill, envisage class conflict over the effects of urban fiscal crisis having been contained largely within the working class, as various segments of the working population fight with each other to shift the relative burden of the crisis.

For example, Castells' early theoretical writings reflect his empirical interest in urban political issues that have reached the level of controversiality. Consider the following of his statements: "We cannot base urban research on the analysis of actors and of their strategies without first analyzing urban issues and the contradictions in the social structure which these issues express" (1975:11). This statement reveals both the strength and the weakness of Castells' initial variant of structuralism. In *The Urban Question* (1977) and other early writings, Castells was concerned with revealing the structural contradictions of advanced capitalism per se. From this perspective, such micro-level actors as historically specific individuals, groups, and institutions were seen as mere modes for expressing systemic contradictions both between and within socio-economic classes. In offering a number of concrete examples lending support to the notion that urban political conflicts are structurally rooted, Castells made an important contribution to urban political research, even before his more recent analysis of the culturally specific dimension of grassroots urban political movements (Castells, 1983). Yet in both instances, by tying his quest for more systematic empirical evidence to the observable practices of various social movements (see 1976b, 1978, 1983) whose level of political consciousness was already well developed and which provided nice illustrations of urban political conflict, Castells has engaged in a self-validating research strategy. Accordingly, he has not been able to shed light upon some of the more subtle processes (such as the gradual shift in the forms of state activity to "fiscal welfare") by which social and political conflicts often fail to materialize, even when structural preconditions are present (see chapter 2, this volume).

If he and other researchers of urban crisis and conflict (for instance, Research Planning Group, 1978) overlooked only issues which failed to become overt political conflicts because they were suppressed or manipulated from the agenda of urban politics by the deliberate actions of elites, this omission would be of limited consequence, since others have richly explored these phenomena (see, for instance, Bachrach and Baratz, 1970; Smith, 1979; Smith and Borghorst, 1979; Katznelson, 1981). But this literature has also tended to overlook what Steven Lukes (1974) has called the third face of power — the power that resides in the structure of any society's prevailing modes of acculturation, political communication, and consciousness. Historically specific cultural beliefs, reinforced by social processes of communication, become a powerful contextual constraint on collective action in all societies. They also become a basis for the legitimation of collective action and the forms that it takes when it does occur. In the advanced capitalist societies, in differing degrees and in different ways, culturally specific myths, symbols, and rituals often serve to reinforce mass beliefs in the appropriateness, or at very least, the givenness of the existing political and economic organization of society. Barring real and widespread crisis conditions, such myths, symbols, and rituals are likely to keep deep-seated social contradictions submerged from consciousness. Until quite recently, Castells (1983, 1984) and other urban researchers have been only minimally concerned about questions of specific national and community cultural values as a source of urban political dynamics. Thus, we must cast our net more widely to gain insight into the connections between socio-economic structure, cultural values, and political action operating in the contemporary American political economy.

But when we turn to Hill's work, we find that his precise understanding of the ways in which specific governmental forms in the American political system contribute to fiscal crisis is not paralled by an equally penetrating analysis of the mediating role of cultural values in urban political life. An analysis of this mediating role might have helped to provide answers to some of the questions Hill has left unanswered. Having suggested, for instance, that the substance of particular issues makes a difference in the degree and type of class conflict that declining central cities have experienced, Hill offers neither an analysis of *why* some issues in the American cultural context, like "redlining" by banks (see chapter 1) or excessive public utility rates are likely to redefine the axis of local politics, nor evidence of *how* such issues have redefined the terms of political discourse in particular places by raising class consciousness.

Numerous questions remain unanswered. Why have many signs of ferment and social conflict in American cities remained largely contained within segments of the working class? What cultural beliefs and ideological practices impede or facilitate the development of class-conscious opinion and social action? How do the mediating structures and processes through which cultural and political values are formed vary from country to country and even from place to place? Which dimensions of political and social structure unique to the United States defuse class-conscious opinion and action? In short, how is political life in urban America socially, politically, and culturally structured?

THE SOCIAL PRODUCTION OF POLITICAL QUIESCENCE

Numerous social theorists have called attention to the subtle ways that dominant beliefs, and the ritual acts that reinforce such beliefs, limit the range of political actions and public policies that various cultures come to define as legitimate. Gramsci (1971) insightfully addresses the extent and the ways that power can be exercised by means of cultural or ideological hegemony. In *The Poverty of Liberalism*, Wolff (1968) likewise argues that the central question of community power ought not to be who makes the decisions that are formulated as public issues, but rather, "how many matters of great social importance are not the objects of anyone's decision at all."

The power to shape the structure of preferences exists, although it often cannot be traced to particular acts. The answer to the question: "Who shapes the structure of preferences that shape and constrain the terms of political discourse?" often cannot be attributed to particular choices of individuals or even to specific acts of elite will. Rather, political conflict may fail to arise because: (a) the socially structured and culturally reinforced behavior of groups and classes within a society impose ideological constraints upon social action; (b) the prevailing practices of institutions and organizations are taken for granted by all politically active strata; or (c) the very wants that are translated into political grievances have been predetermined indirectly by assumptions emanating from mass media, dominant socialization practices, or structured inequalities in access to information about adverse social impacts (Lukes, 1974:21–2. On the operation of these cultural processes in the American context see Smith, 1979: ch 5).

In these ways, for instance, the American middle classes tend to believe that high levels of private consumption and high energy consuming suburban living standards equal the good life; that private automobile use is an irreversible social necessity; that cities are inherently harmful to human development; that America is the land of opportunity; that fiscal and occupational welfare benefits are "private" rewards flowing to productive segments of society rather than governmentally sponsored forms of upward redistribution to powerful segments of society; and accordingly, that poverty is the result of lack of individual initiative and moral worth, which should not be encouraged by overgenerous governmental social welfare transfers. Over time, such beliefs have taken on a life of their own, becoming powerful constraints upon political action and public policy (see, for example, Smith, 1979:chs. 5–6; James, 1972:40–44; Goodwin, 1972; Navarro, 1985:7–17; chapter 2, this volume).

Because this is so, future research in urban studies would benefit from a close examination of the cultural and ideological processes that determine how people in particular national and local cultural settings come to define their values and interests, prior to the point where "interests" are either mobilized into politics or deflected from consideration. In particular, urban researchers must adequately account for the current decline in social protest activities and class-based political mobilization at the very time that objective economic conditions and governmental fiscal austerity are worsening the plight of many working people and contributing to the increased polarization of incomes in many large American cities (see Sassen-Koob, 1984; Smith and Judd, 1984). What is needed, therefore, is a sound explanation of the episodic and transitory nature of class consciousness in American politics.

Clearly, the elaboration of cultural processes is a subject of investigation that must be undertaken in conjunction with, rather than as a substitute for, close scrutiny of the material economic and political roots of urban political life. Indeed, the study of culture cannot be separated from the study of structure. As I have tried to show elsewhere (Smith, 1979:ch. 5), the two are an inexorably linked duality. In any given social formation, the prevailing types of class divisions and alliances and their underlying residential, educational, work, and leisure patterns, organize the forms of communication structuring who talks to whom, and who does not. Stated more formally: the opportunity for communication is structurally predetermined, yet communication is the basic vehicle for acculturation as well as for intentional human action. Therefore structure and culture are complementary rather than alternative explanations of human action and inaction.

Although structurally shaped, communication does not take place globally. The rules, customs, and understandings that define a political culture vary from nation to nation, and even from place to place. The myths, rituals, and symbols that justify some modes of personal conduct and condemn others (e.g. what constitutes "political corruption") vary from class to class, region to region, and even among local subcultures within given nations. This is because acculturation is rooted in face to face interaction in settings where social learning takes place. "These settings – the family, the workplace, the neighborhood – are partially overlapping 'substructures of interaction' linked by one's position in the overall class structure of a society. . . .Through primary social interaction, discernable structures of thought and behavior are organized and communicated" (Smith, 1979:170).

Because structure and culture are interrelated, any study of cultural processes must be rooted in a clear understanding of such basically "structuralist" questions as: In any given social system, what are the structured rewards and punishments that shape the experiences that differently situated social strata have in school, at work, and in their communities? What are the structured channels of credit and access to public and private institutions that shape housing and neighborhood residential patterns? What degree and type of social interaction about common problems is possible for relatively disadvantaged social strata, given the prevailing physical structure of metropolitan areas? How are opportunities for primary social intercourse altered by material changes in land uses, and how are these, in turn, predicated upon the actions of those who control political power and manage capital investment flows?

In similar fashion, the investigation of structuralist questions such as these must be accompanied by close scrutiny of such basically "culturalist" questions as: To what extent does the ordinary language used by educational elites in schools, bureaucratic elites in workplaces, and political elites in general, distort, disguise, or otherwise legitimate the structured patterns of inequality that characterize particular societies? Are any distorted communications that one discovers an intentional consequence of elite manipulation? Or are elites, as well as other social strata, sometimes prisoners of the very structure of the language forms by which their culture has evolved and their political-economic practices have developed? In what ways do national, regional, and local cultural practices enable and constrain given forms of social action?

Frances Fox Piven (1976) provides a useful starting point for dealing with these issues, particularly as they relate to the question of why people act or do not act to shape their history. In Piven's view, political protest activities are socially structured, in so far as most of the time mass mobilization in liberal democracies is "structurally precluded." Why is this the case? First, all cultures encompass a "belief system and reinforcing ritual behaviors that define and justify certain modes of conduct as right or wrong, possible or impossible, and in light of these beliefs, what should be done in particular circumstances" (Piven, 1976:297). Thus, the beliefs that electoral forms are preferable to direct action and that the latter should be used only as a last resort often serve to preclude protest. The extensive ritual behaviors surrounding electoral politics reinforce these beliefs. Even when people become aware of their objectively unequal plight, this awareness may be offset by dominant myths and ritual acts that cause victims to blame themselves. These myths and rituals, developed in the context of unequal power, reinforce inequality. They serve to convince objectively deprived people to accept their plight, privatize their troubles, and loathe themselves.

Even if structurally deprived people begin to blame "the system" rather than themselves, their objectively unequal position in a society's opportunity structure (e.g. their unequal access to education and other means of survival) may impinge upon their sense of efficacy or convince them that individual conformity is less costly than collective defiance. Without such cultural constraints upon social action, class and other forms of conflict in distributively unequal societies would be more frequent and more consequential. But because structural and cultural constraints are especially compelling to those who are most deprived, "most of the time people conform to the institutional arrangements that enmesh them, which regulate the rewards and penalties of daily life, and which appear the only possible reality" (Piven, 1976:302).

Although Piven's research setting has been the American city, she offers a general rather than a culturally specific theory of political quiescence. Her stress upon the potency of electoral rituals for inducing conformity and quiescence can be applied to any society that has a democratic form. (See, for instance, Nelson, 1979, on the operation of these phenomena in the Third World context.) But collective defiance and class conflict are particularly difficult to trigger in the USA because the system is protected from disruption by a key dimension of American "exceptionalism" – the pervasiveness of pluralism as a cultural belief and of "pluralistic" governmental forms (see Smith, 1974).

Political forms often confound our understanding of political substance. For instance, the formal presence of numerous local political interests competing for advantage may mask certain basic similarities among the groups that are more significant than their differences. When structural analysis is superimposed upon local political controversies that reveal a multiplicity of local groups competing for power, the following sorts of questions may be framed: How are the actors in competition and conflict situated within the framework of the class structure of the city and society? Is there a common class position or common class interests that unify the contending parties? What is the social base of the range of groups that participates actively in national and local politics? Do the common interests of the politically active strata preclude any issues (e.g. redistributional issues) from reaching the political agenda? Does the existing pattern of political organization allow a politics of redistribution to materialize or do the competing groups confine themselves to distributional politics?

The point of these rhetorical questions is not minor. If the forms of political activity suggest that "partisan mutual adjustment" among the entire range of interests in a city or society is taking place when, in reality, "the private centers of power turn out to represent . . . a much smaller fragment of society" (Newton, 1976:43; see also Kay and Thompson, 1977; Smith, 1979), many who might otherwise become politically attentive and concerned are reassured. Some issues that might become politicized are depoliticized. Other potential grievances (e.g. biased access to political experience itself) are not even felt as troubles. Furthermore, the very idea of partisan mutual adjustment at the heart of American interest group pluralism makes little sense under conditions of substantive inequality. As I have said elsewhere:

Without a healthy measure of political, social, and economic equality, 'mutual adjustment' cannot be truly mutual. To the extent that adjustment lacks mutuality it is by definition asymmetrical, entailing relationships of domination and sub-ordination that are predicated upon existing social inequalit-ies. In this setting politics becomes a recorder of outcomes already inherent in the structured inequality of society, rather than a means for mutual adjustment. . . . (Smith, 1979:215).

Among the most fundamental of the inequalities in American society is the dominant position of corporate power in the realms of economics, politics, and culture. But the pervasiveness of pluralistic political forms can easily lead to a discounting of this inequality. Consider the example of a local political system characterized by the following conditions: (a) a large number of discernible local political actors, including city councilors, ward politicians, banking, utilities, and insurance company representa-tives, organized labor, and various local business, real estate, and neighborhood associations; (b) a political style characterized by both conflict and bargaining; (c) a major multinational corporation, fundamental to the city's economic base and its local tax revenues for financing the local government's sizeable share of public services, threatens to relocate; (d) the threatened relocation triggers a shared desire on the part of all of the above local interests to keep the corporation within the community; (e) this leads to a city policy of offering a variety of tax credits, subsidies, abatements, and other financial incentives such as industrial revenue bonds, to maintain the city's economic base and possibly to attract new industrial or commercial concerns to the community.

The end result of this situation is a sharp cutback in city employment and public services to the lower social strata because the local tax cut package presented to business and industry reduces city revenues. Yet conflict and bargaining still continue among the politically organized over the distribution of the remaining public services. The primarily middle-class actors inside the formally pluralistic local political system accept the basic economic and political organization of American society as a given. Accepting the "natural right" of private economic institutions to locate where they can make the most profit, and the "duty" of local governments to generate the lion's share of their revenues from local sources, they offer local "fiscal welfare" as a form of tribute to insure that their community will be viewed as profitable by extra-local economic organizations. These actions force fiscal retrenchment. Consulting the existing political structure of the city, public officials touch base with the politically organized interests. These interests manage to obtain minor gains or losses within the economic and political constraints that all have accepted as necessary, indeed desirable in the long run. The politically unorganized, service-dependent population suffers service cutbacks. Yet no one speaks up forcefully for them. Potentially sympathetic actors have been reassured by the continuation of pluralistic rituals and routines. Service cutbacks are made deep in the bosom of an anonymous welfare bureaucracy, with minimal resistance. (Lest the foregoing be viewed as a fictional account rather than an ideal-typical presentation, see Marcuse, 1981, on the management of the New York City fiscal crisis and the winners and losers in this process.)

CONCLUSIONS

The conclusion to be drawn from the foregoing is that "pluralistic" politics in American cities often amounts to little more than a tempest in a teapot. When all of the competing actors take the prevailing system of political and economic organization as givens, this limits what politics is about. Politics becomes a contest for marginal gains among the groups best organized to participate within that framework. Conflicts emerging in this context are circumscribed by the shared acceptance of the basic institutional constraints of the American political economy by all participating interests.

Substantive outcomes are often determined by the beliefs and practices that are taken for granted. The outcomes of urban politics are legitimized by the forms in which political life are cast. When formal elements mask substantive results, politics becomes apolitics, "mutual adjustment" an illusion. This is not the ideal setting for redistributional politics, the emergence of a "class for itself" or the conversion of fiscal crisis into social transformation.

4

The Social Construction of "Urban Crisis"

In an insightful essay on the relationship between national economic crisis and urban fiscal crisis Pickvance (1980:31–8) points out that there is no logically necessary relationship between the two. Their relationship depends on variations in particular political structures and culturally specific factors. Because of the mediating role of politics and culture, the empirical relationship between national economic decline and urban fiscal stress is not self-evident. Each occurs at different levels of the state and society. Neither is a mere reflection of the other.

Thus, for example, in the case of Great Britain, although there is overwhelming evidence of a longstanding national economic crisis, there was no appreciable urban fiscal crisis until very recently when the Thatcher regime *politically* cut central government grants to local governments to weaken the play of opposition parties at the level of the "local state" (see Parkinson, 1985). This is because the system of municipal finance used in the centralized British political system "acts as a buffer shielding the municipality's finances from its local economy" (Pickvance, 1980:31). In Britain, welfare payments are nationally provided: central grants to local governments account for nearly two-thirds of municipal expenditures; these grants contain a strong equalization element; and local governments with weak economies are not forced to rely on their remaining businesses for revenues to provide public services. Their ability to maintain necessary services even provides them with a resource to avoid the outmigration of their local labor force and to offer new businesses an incentive for locating there (Pickvance, 1980; on this aspect of the revival of Glasgow, see *New York Times*, January 29, 1986; on the weakening of these buffers against local fiscal crisis under Thatcher, see Parkinson, 1985).

The political structure of the US offers few of these buffers. In the United States, local government has been a major provider of direct government services including education, police, public health, and public welfare. In 1976 these four services alone constituted 62 percent of the operating expenditures of central cities of over a million people and nearly half of the local spending of all cities (Blair and Nachmias, 1979:15). Local property taxes, supplemented by state government fiscal assistance schemes, account for the lion's share of spending for elementary and secondary education. Federal subsidies account for less than 10 percent of these expenditures. Likewise, the unemployment and public welfare expenditures of American municipal governments are only partially financed by the national government. State and local governments facing economic decline must rely on their own diminishing tax resources to provide these services. Declining cities which have faced capital flight and population decline also have been required to finance a significant proportion of basic police, fire, sanitation, and street repair services out of declining local property taxes or increased debt. This places them in the unenviable position of adding deteriorating basic service quality or increased debt service to the list of ills adversely affecting population decline and the attraction of possible new business location.

Given the central role of governmental structure in channeling or withholding revenues from local political jurisdictions, the fiscal crisis conditions that many US cities have experienced in the past two decades cannot be regarded as mere reflections of the state of the national economy. Urban fiscal distress in older central cities was observable during the booming 1960s, a generally highly expansionary economic context (Hill, 1974; Pickvance, 1980). Furthermore, even as the general economy experienced stagflation in the 1970s, some economic sectors like energy and business and professional services experienced rapid growth. Accordingly, urban economies based on these sectors enjoyed the benefits of a growing local economy and tax base (e.g. Denver, Houston, San Francisco) and experienced few symptoms of urban fiscal stress. In contrast, metropolitan economies relying on declining industrial sectors like rubber and steel for employment and tax revenues (e.g. Cleveland, Buffalo) faced near bankruptcy. In the 1980s some of the same oil dependent Sunbelt cities that enjoyed fiscal solvency in the previous decade (e.g. Houston, most cities in Louisiana), but cut taxes when times were good and failed to diversify their economic base, have begun to experience fiscal crisis. This is attributable to a decline in the economic base needed to finance the increased service demands engendered by two previous decades of unplanned rapid economic growth.

It has frequently been observed that the formal powers of local governments in the United States to deal with local revenue needs vary considerably from place to place. Many growing Sunbelt cities, for instance, were able to finance growing service needs throughout the 1970s by annexing the taxing capacities of surrounding unincorporated suburbs. Frostbelt cities facing fiscal difficulties, but surrounded by fully incorporated suburban taxing jurisdictions, enjoyed no such powers. However, urban fiscal solvency depends not only on the character of the local economic base and the formal revenue producing structure of local governments; it also depends on the changing expectations that residents of cities have concerning the appropriate level and type of public services needed to improve the quality of their everyday lives. A growing body of research suggests that when everyday life is constantly buffeted by rapid growth and change, as has been the case in many Sunbelt localities, the demographic, economic, and social changes so produced also alter people's expectations concerning the need for government services even in traditionally low tax/low spending political jurisdictions (see, for instance, Abbott, 1981; Judd, 1983; Saxenian, 1984; Feagin, 1985).

In sum, the resources and constraints comprising the context with which the local political elites managing American cities must deal when addressing urban problems include both external and internal considerations. The "extralocal" factors are: (a) the political alliances local government officials are able to forge with political elites and policy-makers at higher levels of the state structure; (b) the state policies which provide material support for mediating local crises; (c) their city's locational advantages (e.g. its labor force characteristics, proximity to markets, and prevailing political "business climate") for attracting and retaining the private capital investment needed to sustain the local economy; and (d) the formal taxing and spending powers local governments have been assigned in the legal system. The resources and constraints of local political elites also include such "local" factors as: (a) the character of the internal political expectations and demands placed upon them by their citizens; (b) the extent to which their populations and their policy preferences are stable or changing; and (c) the extent to which localities have local institutional structures capable of responding to external demands. All of these external and internal considerations must be combined in any historically specific analysis of urban crisis, its causes, and how it is channeled or mediated through urban politics. This is the task to be addressed in this chapter.

NATIONAL POLICY AND URBAN CRISIS

Several interrelated dimensions of "urban crisis" in American cities were discussed in the urban affairs literature of the 1960s and 1970s. Although the "crisis" was defined in social, economic, and political terms as well as fiscally, most stress was placed on the fiscal crisis of declining Snowbelt cities. The "facts" that caused commentators to agree that an "urban crisis" existed are now widely agreed upon, although their meaning remains in dispute. The role that state policies have played in both producing and mediating urban problems also remains a hotly contested question. (Compare, for instance, the different interpretations of the role of the state and of national public policies in urban restructuring in the analyses of Fainstein, et al., 1983; Mollenkopf, 1983; and Gottdiener, 1985.) The following sections of chapter 4 attempt to give coherence to the complex social, economic, and political forces which combined to produce the particular forms of social and spatial inequality – blackening central cities, white flight, exclusionary suburbs, Snowbelt decline, Sunbelt boom, and mounting Snowbelt urban fiscal crises – which have been condensed under the rubric "urban crisis." Once this is accomplished, we will be in a position to distinguish these outcomes, in which the role of state policy looms large, from what appear at first glance to be the more "market" determined outcomes of the "new" urban crisis of the 1980s – capital flight, "deindustrialization," the social recomposition of selected large cities, and the restructuring of their economic functions. As we shall see, however, even those urban outcomes that appear to be the result of market processes operating in a separate container termed "the economy" have been shaped by the interplay of economic forces with the national, state, and local political processes. It is through this interplay that taxation, regulatory, economic development, and social policies vital to urban development are produced and political alliances are formed to sustain or challenge these policies.

Political Management of the Social Crisis of the Cities

The black urban rebellions of the 1960s were taken by national, state, and local political elites as a sign that an "urban crisis" existed and that it was a social crisis. The central dimensions of this "old" urban crisis are directly traceable to the impact of the policies of US welfare capitalism and the political strategies underlying them. To begin with, the high concentrations of low income blacks in large US central cities, has been traced to the massive urbanization of blacks following the mechanization of southern agriculture, a development stimulated and subsidized by federal agricultural and tax policies (Piven and Cloward, 1971). Prior to the Civil Rights movement of the 1960s and the desegregation policies that followed in its wake, the black migration to cities was especially pronounced in the central cities of the northeast and mid-west. This demographic shift was the result of the pull of industrial employment opportunities which encouraged black workers who had initially migrated from southern rural to urban areas to continue their quest for economic survival in the politically more favorable climate of northern industrial cities (Sackrey, 1973; Fligstein, 1981; Marks, 1985). In the 1970s, once segregationist legal barriers were removed, many large southern cities (e.g. Atlanta, New Orleans) began to experience increased black in-migration as a result both of continuing decline in demand for low skilled agricultural workers in the rural South and of return migration of blacks from economically declining Snowbelt localities (Smith and Keller, 1983).

Overlaid upon the black migration to central cities is the four-decade long movement of middle-class white taxpayers from central cities to suburbs. This demographic trend, sometimes attributed entirely to racism and attendant "white flight," was structured and underwritten by the Keynesian growth-oriented policies of the federal government in the areas of housing, highway development, water and sewer subsidies for new communities, and "fiscal welfare" for new investment. In similar fashion, the pattern of Sunbelt economic boom and attendant population flow from Snowbelt cities to the Sunbelt in the 1970s was significantly channeled by the tax, defense, and energy resource development policies of American Keynesianism (Perry and Watkins, 1977; Mollenkopf, 1983).

From the end of World War II until the mid-1970s, several major state policies contributed significantly to the socioeconomic and demographic changes underlying the urban problems of the 1960s and 1970s. Perhaps the most significant of these has been the sprawl-inducing interstate highway program. The massive deployment of funds from the Highway Trust Fund to build the vast network of interstate highways was tantamount to a population redistribution policy. Initially legitimated by the military-industrial complex as promoting "national defense" it was then sustained by the political strength of the auto-industrial complex (Whitt, 1982; Yago, 1983).

Other federal land use and housing policies that have importantly shaped the character of the US urban system have included: (a) Veteran's Administration and Federal Housing Administration mortgage guarantees which greatly enlarged the suburban middle class; (b) "fiscal welfare" policies excluding home mortgage interest and local property taxes from federal tax liabilities which greatly expanded suburban home ownership; (c) the toleration by the federal government of exclusionary suburban zoning; (d) the provision of a limited trickle of public housing, confined largely to central cities; (e) an urban renewal program, which, when it "succeeded" in altering urban land uses, did so by bulldozing low income rental housing and displacing low income urban blacks (Smith, 1979:ch. 6); and (f) a series of low income housing subsidy programs begun in 1968 as a Great Society response to the black urban rebellions and largely deemed failures by the Nixon administration and abandoned by the mid-1970s (for an interesting discussion of these policies and their urban impacts see Birkhead, 1975). Because the principal constituencies and groups comprising the Democratic party political coalition, particularly its local and state politicians facing urban fiscal stress, were interested in expanding the scope of federal patronage, even in the heyday of the Great Society, the social policies enacted to rectify the social crisis of the cities were diluted in impact by their widespread dispersal. The basic premise of the Great Society was to integrate black voters into the Democratic party coalition by the development of place-specific entitlements which could shore up as many Democratic urban regimes as possible. Thus, black urban poverty was treated largely as a problem of needy places rather than faulty labor market structures.

Beyond this fundamental political dimension of its policy design, the Great Society's efforts to reduce black urban poverty were further diluted by the institutional separation of the processes by which these policies were authorized and implemented and the process by which Congress appropriated expenditures to finance them. Thus, for example, place-specific entitlements, sold as a way to eliminate urban poverty, were spread even thinner to satisfy the imperatives of congressional patronage; effective targeting to needy people in central cities (and ultimately to the Democratic urban regimes which sought to integrate this constituency) was negated by the logic of the congressional appropriations process. As Herbers (1975:7) has pointed out, "small towns in Tennessee and Colorado, the home towns of influential Congressmen, got Model Cities funds intended for the ghettoes of big cities." Educational subsidies intended initially for poor school districts also were broadly dispersed because of this same political logic. Likewise, to gain political support for federal housing policies to aid minorities and the poor, lenders, builders, and realtors often benefited far more than the people they were ostensibly intended to help.

When the issue of expanding social welfare costs became politicized in the 1970s, neo-conservative and market liberal critics blamed rising federal budget deficits on neither these private interests nor on conventional pork-barrel politics, but on a presumptive "new class" of public employees bent on income redistribution. In the context of congressional distributive politics, the political weakness of Great Society liberalism was already apparent even before this conservative assault on the welfare state emerged. This is well illustrated by the case of the welfare state liberal effort in Congress, following the urban rebellions of the 1960s, to reduce the rental burden on low income public housing tenants. As poignantly expressed by Eugene Meehan (1980:286):

The crowning irony appeared in 1969 when the first Brooke Amendment limited tenant rent to 25% of gross income but provided no subsidy for housing authorities to make up for lost revenue. By the end of 1969, housing authorities in virtually all American cities were facing financial ruin. To take their condition as evidence that public housing has been tried and failed, as frequently happened in Congress and elsewhere, was a travesty.

These political realities of the struggle for federal dollars were already apparent in the waning days of the Great Society, as the increasing cost of financing the Vietnam war undermined public support for redistributional domestic policies. They accelerated in significance under the Republican administrations of Nixon and Ford. At first, the Nixon administration sought to weaken the political alliances forged between the national Democratic party and local urban ethnic and racial groups by attacking "national purpose" legislation such as the Great Society. Instead the administration called for a "New Federalism" which would use revenue sharing to provide state and local government officials with the resources to make "their own" decisions free from the heavy hand of "federal activism" (see Judd, 1984:334–42). Although opposed by Civil Rights groups, organized labor, and other social welfare liberals, the "New Federalism" initiative received the strong backing of associations of state and local elected officials, conservative critics of federal activism, and neo-conservative critics of Great Society urban policies.

With strong presidential support from Richard Nixon, the revenue sharing initiative was passed in the election year of 1972. In the wake of Nixon's landslide re-election victory, the growing political strength of neo-conservative ideological tracts, such as Edward Banfield's *Unheavenly City* (1970) and *Unheavenly City Revisited* (1974), and the growing popularization of market liberal critiques of the welfare state (see Friedman, 1973), a full-scale ideologically and politically solidified reaction formed toward Great Society social policies. Fostered by objective macroeconomic and fiscal conditions – recession, slowed growth, resource shortages (e.g. energy), balance of payments problems, and the absorption of the anticipated "peace dividend" by inflation as the Vietnam War ended – the Nixon–Ford social policy retrenchment strategy was reflected in the declaration that the "urban crisis" was over. This assessment was accompanied by cutbacks in appropriation requests for urban policies, impoundments of appropriated funds, the suspension of housing subsidy programs for low and moderate income urban residents, and an anti-urban restructuring of "New Federalism" revenue sharing formulas (Birkhead, 1975:60–1).

From Social to Fiscal Crisis

Like the place-based entitlements of the Great Society, the Nixon–Ford revenue sharing proposals were originally sold to the public as an aid to "needy places." In fact the policies used politically devised formulas that included local taxing effort (largely reflecting ability to tax) and insured that even wealthy suburbs would share in the aid. As Birkhead (1975:62) and Judd (1984:343–4) have shown, the impact of the Nixon–Ford initiated "New Federalism" has been conservative. Small scale and minor jurisdictions like townships and counties with very limited responsibilities received a disproportionate share of funds under general revenue sharing in relation to their objective needs. The tendency has been for general revenue sharing funds to be used by local jurisdictions to reduce debt, to cut taxes, or to operate and maintain public safety (police and fire protection) rather than to improve current operations of social services or to create new programs. During the 1970s approximately one-third of the revenue sharing funds going to state governments were used to cut taxes, a factor which contributed to their own revenue shortfalls in the recessionary early 1980s. The enactment and implementation of general revenue sharing was thus a key element in the political redefinition of the "urban crisis" from social to fiscal crisis. Not surprisingly, therefore, by the late 1970s general revenue sharing's distributional effect was a drop of "10 percentage points for the human resources portion of the federal assistance programs to states and localities" (Judd, 1984:345). Revenue sharing lacked the limited redistributional requirements imposed on local political elites by Great Society human resource programs targeted to benefit "the poor" as a categorical group. Therefore, national, state, and local public officials facing spiraling inflation in the general economy, were free to respond to the policy priorities of more fiscally conservative, general service oriented segments of society rather than to the anti-poverty agenda of the 1960s.

The "Great Inflation" (Harris, 1981) of the 1970s also contributed to the urban fiscal stress underlying the redefinition of "urban crisis" by driving up the costs of the basic goods and services provided by local governments. This made local officials increasingly cost conscious as municipal budgets were adversely affected by a variety of wider political-economic developments largely beyond the control of city governments. Inflation's impact on local budgets was many-faceted. Energy price shocks drove up urban transport costs, which already were far costlier than they needed to be in the 1970s because of a 50 year assault on efficient mass transit by the auto-industrial complex (see Yago, 1983). The rising demands of organized civil servants for higher wages reflected public employees' efforts to maintain living standards in the face of spiraling prices. Goods purchased by local governments such as trucks, buses, supplies, and equipment to maintain basic services all rose in cost. Inflation thus accounted for a substantial share of rising city spending throughout the 1970s. Campbell, Bahl and Greylack (1974) have estimated that for each dollar inflation adds to public expenses, it adds only 50 cents in additional revenue. Thus, by the mid-1970s high inflation in the national economy had become a central element of state and local fiscal distress.

Snowbelt cities were especially hard hit by these developments. Along with mounting inflation, declining industrial cities in the Snowbelt simultaneously faced declines in their revenue base and their ability to raise taxes by an increasing outflow of capital investment and taxpaying citizens. For example, in St. Louis between 1970–76 around 4,000 abandoned houses were torn down each year. In the greater Buffalo area between 1975 and 1979, 75 factories closed, thereby eliminating nearly 17,000 jobs (*New York Times*, January 5–6, 1981).

Faced with these critical conditions, many cities in the declining Snowbelt increasingly began to rely on borrowing to avoid either further tax increases or drastic expenditure cuts. Sometimes this was done without voter approval by the technique of "moral obligation" bonding first developed in New York State as early as 1960 to enable governments to raise revenues without raising taxes. When interest rates were low, the costs of servicing this debt were manageable. But by the mid-1970s the percentage increase in local government debt in relation to revenues began to rise dramatically (*New York Times*, November 2, 1975). In response, large banks began to scrutinize their local debt portfolios more closely. It was their refusal to purchase additional city debt which precipitated the fiscal crisis of New York City in 1975

(Block, 1981). When interest rates rose rapidly in the wake of New York's fiscal crisis, the fiscal condition of many northeastern and midwestern cities became critical. Such conditions began to close out financial markets and dramatically increased the costs of servicing state and local debt.

The tax burden for all US cities in 1978 averaged $201 per capita. Although measurable tax burdens tend to be much higher than this in large central cities, the range of variation among large cities is considerable. In 1978 New York City had the highest per capita tax rate of $842 per person. The comparable rate in Philadelphia, another large northeastern city, was $390 per capita. In that same year, Los Angeles, the largest Sunbelt city, ranked only slightly above the national average in per capita expenditures, at $239; while Houston fell well below the national average at $175 per person (*New York Times*, May 15, 1980:A23).

The urban fiscal crisis first came to prominence as a national political issue in the mid-1970s in the celebrated case of New York City. Between 1965 and 1975 New York's budgets had expanded at a rate of 15 percent annually, while it revenues, adversely affected by capital flight and the outmigration of industry, were increasing by only 5 percent annually (Weisman, 1975). If the federal government had been willing to assume New York's City's public welfare costs, about one-quarter of its total budget during the period of threatened default in 1975, New York's finances would have been solvent. But with a conservative Republican in the White House and a Congress unwilling to consider federalization of welfare costs during a period of mounting national economic crisis, no such policy was forthcoming. Instead, New York's elected political elites were forced into default when the city's large creditors refused to purchase additional city debt. As a result, the city's elected public officials lost power to a quasi-public board of fiscal overseers, the Municipal Assistance Corporation (MAC), comprised largely of representatives of finance capital. MAC chose sharp cuts in social programs, deferred maintenance, hospital closings, and cutbacks in education such as teacher attrition, larger classes, and a shorter school day as the route to renewed fiscal solvency (Alclay and Mermelstein, 1977; Marcuse, 1981; Tabb, 1982). The stage was thus set for a pattern of "resolving" fiscal crisis in other large central cities in the Snowbelt through a finance capital-led social construction of "fiscal crisis" as excessive social spending rather than declining banker confidence and artificially inflated credit terms for local government borrowing.

To obtain credit and avoid default many hard pressed central cities in the Snowbelt were forced to make concessions to bankers. This produced cuts in operating budgets and forced a deferral of needed maintenance. Following New York City's fiscal crisis, for instance, the fiscally distressed industrial city of Buffalo had to pay interest rates nearly double what they had been prior to New York's crisis only six months earlier. To obtain credit Buffalo was forced to agree to defer improvements in its water system, parks and playgrounds. This in turn continued the decline in the quality of everyday life, leading to further white flight, which compounded the revenue crisis even more (*New York Times*, November 2, 1975:6).

These virtually extortionary credit terms, in turn, forced some state and local public officials to turn to their own workers' pension funds as a major source of new credit (see, for instance, *New York Times*, October 7, 1975:18). This recapturing of past concessions made by the state and capital to labor contributed to the overall weakening of organized labor in the American political system as a whole, and helped pave the way for Reagan's successful anti-labor policies in the following decade.

Ironically, because of the relative autonomy of local and state political actions and government policies in the American federal system, the actions taken by state and local officials to cope with fiscal stress began to reverberate upward to the national level, reducing the ability of Keynesian federal policies to reflate the economy. By 1975 state and local government payrolls accounted for approximately 14 percent of the nation's total employment, having grown in the previous decade five times faster than federal employment and at a rate faster than total US employment. One consequence of this development was that by the mid-1970s state and local government taxing and spending policies began to offset the stimulative effect of macroeconomic growth-oriented federal tax cuts. Largely unable to run deficits, many state and local governments were faced with continuing service demands, well organized and increasingly unionized public employees, high inflation, numerous federal mandates to provide services unaccompanied by federal revenues, and tight credit markets following the New York City fiscal crisis. They were thus forced to finance growing operating costs by cutting services or raising taxes.

Nationally, the impact of this response to crisis conditions at the state and local levels was that although federal tax cuts sought to lift the economy out of periodic and deepening recessions, as in 1974–5, states and localities moved in the opposite direction, "taking stimulus out of the system in an effort to achieve fiscal respectability" (*New York Times*, December 2, 1975:64). The different political interests operating at the different levels of government produced contradictory actions and incompatible results.

ECONOMIC CRISIS AND THE TRANSFORMATION OF NATIONAL URBAN POLICY

In this context of stagflation, growing national economic crisis, and state and local fiscal distress, Democratic presidential candidate Jimmy Carter narrowly defeated Republican Gerald Ford for the American presidency in 1976. As a Democratic president, who had been elected by holding together the New Deal alliance of the South and the industrial heartland, Jimmy Carter initially responded favorably to the interests representing the declining industrial cities that formed a key element of his electoral base. The Carter administration at first attempted to develop urban policies that would appeal to capital, labor, minority groups, and local political elites in the declining regions of traditional Democratic strength. Revenue sharing funds were redeployed to the benefit of economically distressed cities by adding an excess unemployment factor to the distribution formula (Markusen and Wilmoth, 1982). The Comprehensive Employment and Training (CETA) program and Community Development Block Grant (CDBG) program were significantly expanded. In 1977 extensions and expansions of anti-recessionary fiscal assistance programs lent support to fiscally distressed large central cities by using distributional formulas heavily weighted in favor of declining Snowbelt urban centers (Smith and Judd, 1984). In that same year Carter's Urban Development Action Grant (UDAG) program was pushed through Congress to provide federal dollars to help stimulate private investment in selected cities. The intended beneficiaries were communities facing population decline, a declining tax base, and significant neighborhood deterioration or abandonment. Yet, as so often in the past, to gain passage of this "urban" revitalization policy, Carter was forced to set aside one-quarter of the project funds for cities of less than 50,000 people that were located outside of standard metropolitan statistical areas (SMSAs) (Gist, 1980:238).

By 1978, however, several considerations in the wider political-economic environment prompted the Carter administration to reassess its commitment to the economically declining and fiscally distressed central cities of the Snowbelt. These have been summarized by Smith and Judd (1984:181):

> The mounting global and national economic crisis of prolonged stagflation prompted a general reconsideration of demand and inflation stimulating social policies. Pressures at the elite and mass level began to be felt to keep federal spending down. The passage of Proposition 13 in California symbolized the gathering strength of the "tax revolt" nationwide and prompted similar campaigns by fiscal conservatives in several states. These developments, in turn, aided fiscal conservatives in Congress and encouraged a go slow approach in the White House (Markusen and Wilmoth, 1982). The approach was both reflected in and reinforced by the failure of Carter's Urban Development Bank proposal. Once intended as the cornerstone of an *urban* reinvestment strategy (see Smith, 1979:ch. 6), the policy evolved into a general policy of trickle-down growth stimulation by allocating loans and grants to depressed urban *and* rural areas. Even when so diluted in focus and reduced in intended size, the proposal failed to make it out of a congressional conference committee. By this stage of the Carter presidency . . . the sole legitimation of urban policy had become the stimulation of new capital accumulation. . . .

Thus, by the time Carter proposed a "New Partnership" to conserve American communities in March, 1978, the logic of the policy constituted a redefinition of urban crisis as a mere reflection of the general national economic crisis. "Urban areas" were expected to cooperate with federal "fiscal welfare" and subsidy policies to aid business. The justifying rhetoric of the New Partnership shifted focus from distressed cities to distressed "communities" and "urban areas," including suburbs and "pockets of distress" in the Sunbelt. It called for a restoration of "business confidence" to protect current capital investment, and for the use of federal "leverage" to stimulate private economic development as a means of creating jobs. This approach served to redirect federal "urban policy" toward revitalizing not distressed cities but the increasingly footloose private sector (*New York Times*, February 1, 1978:1, 38; April 2, 1978, Sec. 4:1; Smith and Judd, 1984).

Once he departed from his early efforts to reward the black urban constituencies that had been so crucial to his election, Carter's "national urban policy" proposals accelerated the already perceptible shift from social welfare Keynesianism to fiscal welfare Keynesianism discussed earlier. The refocused policy called for three basic forms of "fiscal welfare": (a) capital subsidies and tax incentives for businesses either investing in "pockets of distress" wherever they occurred, or for hiring marginally employable workers in such places; (b) tax incentives to capital investors for "targeted" investment and job creation; and (c) the creation of a National Development Bank to offer grants, loans, loan guarantees and tax subsidized Industrial Revenue Bonds (IRBs) for private sector companies willing to locate in "targeted" areas.

The extensive reliance upon the symbolism of "fiscal welfare" as the lure to bring about "urban revitalization" masks several undesirable consequences of this approach to state policy. First, locating firms in distressed areas is not the same as creating jobs for workers living in those areas. For instance, when the Digital Corporation, a leading producer of electronic computers, relocated from the Route 128 high tech belt surrounding Boston to the inner city South End neighborhood, it employed few local workers. It also increased pressures for gentrification and worsened traffic congestion and pollution in the South End (National Urban Policy Collective, 1978). Similar distributional effects were observable when Hewlett Packard and several other Silicon Valley computer and microelectronic firms relocated to the city of Roseville, California (Tarallo, 1987).

Second, business subsidies through the tax code to indirectly create employment result in lost opportunity costs to use these tax revenues to more directly assist displaced or marginal workers or to more creatively produce new employment – e.g. employment retraining, neighborhood-based producer cooperatives, technical assistance to self-organized groups of currently unemployed workers with particular capacities and work histories.

Third, the shift from reliance on direct social policy to fiscal policies to induce private businesses to achieve public policy goals, embodied in Carter's approach to urban policy and accelerated greatly under Reagan, represents a shift of the public tax burden from corporations to individual workers. As we have seen, the effect of this shift has been a restructuring of class relations by creating new social divisions among the working class and exacerbating antagonisms between those receiving and those paying for welfare state entitlements. This largely public policy induced transformation of the social structure in turn has served to weaken the legitimacy of "social welfare" as a policy approach (see Smith and Judd, 1984). Thus, potential demands for more extensive and effective "collective consumption" are derailed while simultaneously reducing the material revenue base of the national and local governments through tax cuts. In this political context of "American exceptionalism," characterized by corporate hegemony, left-liberal political weakness, and the rise of the "fiscal welfare" state, the arguments drawn from European experience that the urban fiscal crisis has been produced by the struggles of "collective consumption" movements for more and better social services does not fit the facts of the American experience.

THE MYTH OF SUNBELT BOOM AND THE SPREAD OF
FISCAL CRISES TO THE SUNBELT

In the late Carter and early Reagan years, the urban expenditure–revenue gap spread to encompass cities and regions once thought to be immune from urban fiscal crisis. In 1978, for example, in the nation's central cities of 250,000 people or larger, public expenditures rose at an average rate of 8 percent while available revenues increased by only 4.8 percent (Herbers, 1980:26). The spread of symptoms of fiscal crisis to large central cities in all geographic regions calls into question both the conservative argument that urban fiscal crisis is a unique byproduct of excessive social spending by northern liberal Democratic mayors and the argument advanced by many liberals in the Northeast and Midwest that interregional capital flight was the sole culprit accounting for urban fiscal crisis.

Growing Sunbelt cities have been treated in the literature as likely to remain more fiscally solvent than declining Snowbelt cities (see, for instance, Lupsha and Siembieda, 1977; Mollenkopf, 1983; but see the perceptive predictions in Firestine, 1977; see also Abbott, 1981 and chapter 9 below for counter-evidence). The argument has been advanced that because of their traditional low tax, low service political culture, lack of a trade union tradition, rapid rates of growth, and legal ability to annex their developing suburbs, Sunbelt cities are unlikely to experience fiscal crises. The Fainsteins, for example, cite empirical data from Muller (1981) to support their conclusion that the new post-industrial cities of the Sunbelt are fiscally solvent, and that their relative solvency stems from "low taxation, low expenditure regimes, and produces greater levels of social inequality than would be tolerated in the old cities of the North" (Fainstein and Fainstein, 1981:5).

Several realities complicate this image of fiscal solvency in post-industrial cities of the Sunbelt. First, the political development of low taxation/low expenditure political regimes has been more characteristic of southern and Rocky Mountain cities than of the western Sunbelt cities along the Pacific Rim. The latter, particularly in northern California, have always had strong trade union traditions. They have also offered a wide variety of local public services and have accepted the leading role of the state in their economic development (see Shapira and Leigh-Preston, 1984:37–44).

Second, the image of "Sunbelt" political and economic development driven largely by regional relocation of capital investment in search of cheap and politically docile labor pools has been overdrawn as an explanation of the Sunbelt's growth and its presumed fiscal solvency (see Smith, Ready, and Judd, 1985). This explanation does not fit well as a characterization of the political and economic development of western Sunbelt cities, which have been more dependent for their economic growth on importing skilled labor than on their available supplies of less-skilled labor (see Shapira and Leigh-Preston, 1984:37–44). This explanation works best in accounting for industrial development in both urban and rural areas of the South where "branch plants (as in textiles, electronics, and light manufacturing) have been established to exploit available supplies of less-skilled labor" (Shapira and Leigh-Preston, 1984). It also helps account for the spread of "new sweatshops" (see chapter 9 below) in both urban and non-metropolitan localities in those regions which have attracted large pools of illegal immigrant labor (e.g. New York, Chicago, Los Angeles, Silicon Valley).

Third, as Seyler (1979) has demonstrated, most of the available research on non-metropolitan industrialization in all regions of the country has shown that such peripheral areas rather than central cities "are hosting more mature, often slowly growing or nationally declining industries." Since much of Sunbelt (particularly southern) industrialization has been of this type, this helps to explain the apparent anomaly of widespread plant closings and "deindustrialization" of previously high growth non-metropolitan communities which have only been industrialized for two or three decades. Intensified international competition has ushered in a period since the early 1980s of increasing plant closures and relocations: for example, the migration of footloose microcomputer assembly plants from California's Silicon Valley to Pacific basin countries; the relocation of light manufacturing assembly facilities from South Carolina to Central America (see *New York Times*, October 27, 1982:1; March 19, 1983:1). In highly competitive sectors operating in the international economy, the Sunbelt's previous locational advantages (e.g. lower taxes, more favorable "business climates," less expensive and/or more cooperative or "flexible" labor pools) are no longer sufficient to insure either the economic base or the non-antagonistic labor-management relationships and pro-business ideology assumed to underlie its imputed fiscal solvency.

Fourth, in addition to failing to anticipate the actual community and fiscal impacts of Sunbelt "deindustrialization," the image of Sunbelt growth as depending largely on interregional industrial relocation also has failed to take into account several key features driving Sunbelt development. These include: (a) the central role of the federal government in shaping and subsidizing the (uneven) development of the West; (b) the importance of the expansion of indigenous service-performing jobs, including government, business, tourist, and recreation services in Sunbelt regional economic growth (Shapira and Leigh-Preston, 1984); (c) the concentration of the lion's share of Sunbelt growth in just three states – California, Texas, and Florida; and most importantly, (d) the social and political changes produced by the economic and demographic changes accompanying Sunbelt growth (Abbott, 1981; Judd, 1983; Saxenian, 1983; Plotkin, 1983; Johnson,

Booth, and Harris, 1983; see also chapters 8 and 9 below). Particularly in the most rapidly growing cities (e.g. San Jose, Denver, San Antonio) local political systems have experienced significant increases in the level of political demand for improved community services, effective growth management and control policies, and a better quality of neighborhood and community life as a result of the mounting social costs of unregulated rapid growth (see especially Plotkin, 1983). This has begun to alter the structure of demand on the expenditure side of the expenditure/revenue balance sheet.

Fifth, the vaunted power of Sunbelt cities to "annex" their growing suburban tax bases has been characteristic of a few large southern cities rather than of the political structure of the Sunbelt region as a whole. Thus, for example, the city of New Orleans lacks annexation powers; yet its local political elites face high rates of voter turnout and the contradictory pressures of a popular low tax ideology *and* continuing service demands from neighborhood groups at all levels of its local class structure. Thus, the city has faced chronic fiscal crisis conditions for the past two decades (Smith and Keller, 1983).

Finally, annexation itself entails costs as well as benefits. Consider the case of Houston, now the nation's fifth largest city. Houston is often singled out as a major example of the absence of fiscal crisis tendencies in the Sunbelt, because it has the lowest level of per capita public expenditures of the largest American cities and has annexed the lion's share of its sprawling suburbs. In the mid-1970s for instance, New York City spent $1,200 per capita on public services compared to Houston's $160 per capita (*New York Times*, December 4, 1975:35). Houston has no welfare program and the program provided by the State of Texas is limited and punitive (Sterba, 1976:1, 24).

Yet even here, where low per capita taxation rates prevail, the citizens of Houston have had to pay a wide variety of hidden "taxes" in other guises. First, although Houston has directly provided fewer basic services than other large American cities, basic services have been required to finance the metropolitan infrastructure for its extended growth. To pay for such expenditures, 200 special taxing districts have been created in metropolitan Houston. This fragmentation of taxing districts has disguised the actual fiscal picture of Houston. As one commentator (Sterba,

1975:35) writing at the peak of Houston's economic boom years of the 1970s, has pointed out, under what then looked like a healthy fiscal climate:

> [S]ome of the districts are mounting billions of dollars in future indebtedness. [The districts] are formed to aid real estate developers by issuing government bonds to build streets, sewers, drainage and other land improvements. Instead of paying for these improvements in the price of their houses, home buyers find themselves paying high property taxes. When the city annexes the next development, it assumes the bond burden. In effect city taxpayers end up paying for suburban sprawl.

Second, in traditionally low service cities like Houston there is a complementary hidden "tax" in the form of the need for citizens to compensate for inadequate public services by private expenditures of various kinds, e.g. neighborhoods which hire off-duty policemen to privately patrol their areas; individuals who spend more than they otherwise would for car repairs because of inadequately maintained streets and roads. Third, despite the limited character of direct taxation, now that the international oil economy pricing structure has collapsed, and the Houston economic boom has abruptly ended, the previously much-heralded "Oil City" can no longer find sufficient tax revenues to meet current operating expenses for the services it does provide (Hill and Feagin, 1987). This has provoked a severe fiscal crisis in a city which only three years ago was still thought of as a "boomtown" worthy of emulation by less successful rivals in the global competition for economic growth (Smith and Keller, 1983).

POLITICAL CONTRADICTIONS OF SUNBELT DEVELOPMENT: THE MYTH OF POLITICAL QUIESCENCE IN THE SUNBELT

By the 1980s, Houston, along with a number of other large Sunbelt cities, had developed extremely rapidly (e.g. Denver, Phoenix, San Jose, San Antonio, Dallas), often unchecked by the constraints of coherent public land use planning and regulation. Research into the major results of this mode of development has revealed a host of community problems including: overdevelopment in inappropriate areas accompanied by poorly drained land leading to frequent flooding; subsidence of soil; overcrowded freeways; polluted air; overused and potholed streets; inadequate garbage collection; and inadequate water distribution systems (Bernard and Rice, 1983; Smith and Keller, 1983; Feagin, 1984; Saxenian, 1984; Sawers and Tabb, 1984).

At the level of urban politics the local responses to these problems reveal the contradictory role of the local and national governments in the American federal system. In a number of rapidly growing Sunbelt cities the decline in the quality of everyday life caused by uncontrolled rapid growth has contributed to the development of new neighborhood-based local political coalitions demanding growth controls, improved delivery of local public services, and liveable neighborhoods (see Abbott, 1981; Saxenian, 1984; chapter 9 below). This has been true even in places like Houston, once thought to be bastions of free-wheeling capitalism and unregulated growth (see Hill and Fergin, 1987).

Ironically, the rise of these new local political currents in rapidly growing Sunbelt communities began at precisely the time that national economic and political developments were prompting the late Carter and early Reagan presidencies to usher in an extended period of sharp cuts in federal financial support for state and local governments. This has brought a number of interrelated contradictions to the surface. Because of developments discussed earlier, between 1977 and 1981 the rates of interest that state and local governments had to pay to borrow money almost doubled (*Business Week*, 1981). This was combined with federal cuts in fiscal assistance to state and local governments, whose fourfold increase during the 1970s had enabled many states and localities to avoid fiscal difficulties. Furthermore, as a direct result of Ronald Reagan's growth-oriented federal tax cuts, the 30 state governments which had previously tied their tax structures to the level of federal taxes paid by their citizens, began to experience pronounced revenue shortfalls in the early 1980s.

In this context, several contradictions became apparent at both the national and the state and local governmental levels. First, the decrease in state and local expansion attributable to declining federal financial support in the late Carter and early Reagan years contributed to prolonging the national recession of 1980–83 by taking part of the stimulus out of the economy provided by Reagan's massive tax cuts. Second, growing Sunbelt cities faced a mounting imbalance between the basic public service and local infrastructure requirements generated by their economic and population growth and declining federal capital investment subsidies and increased local borrowing costs. At the same time, declining federal revenues and reduced grants-in-aid increasingly forced Sunbelt cities and states back upon their own fiscal resources to meet growing popular demands for "managed growth," improved services, and a better "quality of life."

This contradictory situation helps to explain the resistance that developed to Reagan's second and subsequent rounds of budget cuts from state and local government officials, including many key Republican mayors and governors from the Sunbelt. To illustrate this tension concretely, one of the exceptions to its generally pro-Sunbelt tilt has been the Reagan administration's effort to cope with high budget deficits by slowing down the use of federal revenues for capital spending projects, including projects in new growth areas. Thus, for example, in refusing to fund water treatment facilities in suburban areas of Orlando, Florida, the Reagan administration argued that: "if people wanted new communities they could finance them themselves" (quoted in Herbers, 1982). The irony underlying this position is that the continuing rapid growth of Sunbelt communities, encouraged by the overall thrust of Reagan policies, has left many newer localities with inadequate infrastructure facilities. Reagan's general cutbacks in support for local governments and his specific capital spending policies are bound to compound these existing inadequacies. This could put a brake on continued Sunbelt economic growth, unless local taxes, local user fees, and local public works spending are increased substantially in these jurisdictions.

This policy predicament in Sunbelt communities has been compounded by the fact that the national fiscal crisis produced by Reagan's taxing and defense spending policies has increased the federal government's use of borrowing to offset its own expenditure/revenue gap. State and local governments seeking credit to finance public works projects have increasingly been "crowded out" of credit markets by the nation's two most powerful borrowers, the federal government, borrowing to reduce its deficits, and large corporations, pursuing a new round of consolidations and mergers in the early 1980s (Miller and Tomaskovic-Devey, 1983). Moreover, the entry of new competitors for subsidized credit, namely the "public–private" local growth coalitions seeking to stimulate profitable development patterns through issuing Industrial Revenue Bonds and Industrial Development Bonds (Smith, Ready, and Judd, 1985; *Business Week*, October 26, 1981:135–81) has exacerbated the plight of general purpose local government jurisdictions even further in their quest for an effectively developed basic infrastructure.

This neglect of the basic infrastructure of US cities – their streets, bridges, sewers, water supplies, and utility systems – addresses a basic question in social theory introduced in our earlier discussion of structural Marxist urban theory. It is to this question of the state as "collective capitalist" that we now turn.

THE URBAN INFRASTRUCTURE CRISIS: THE MYTH OF THE STATE AS COLLECTIVE CAPITALIST

It was argued above that the "collective consumption" thesis developed in a European context by Marxist urban political economists was not especially helpful in explaining the fiscal crisis of US cities. What can be said of the related argument that the socialization of the costs of urban infrastructure to foster efficient capital accumulation is the culprit producing urban fiscal crisis? (For discussions of this view see chapter 3, this volume; Kennedy, 1983.) In the American context, the weight of the historically specific evidence contradicts the thesis advanced by some Marxist urban theorists that the urban fiscal crisis stems from excessive public spending on social capital expenditures. More commonly, major US central cities have experienced local fiscal stress stemming from the socio-spatial biases of American Keynesianism at the national policy level – i.e. from the tendency for public expenditures and taxation policies to stimulate new growth in suburbs, the Sunbelt, and the metropolitan areas where high tech military spending is concentrated. Local political elites are then forced by the political structure of American federalism (now reinforced by reduced intergovernmental transfers under Reagan) to cope with revenue shortfalls on their own. Thus, they have deferred the maintenance of their water, sewer, utilities, and bridge systems as an *effect* of their revenue predicament rather than allocating resources to such expenditures as a cause of fiscal crisis. As well documented by Choate and Walter (1981a and b), local government capital spending declined from 4.1 percent of GNP in the mid-1960s to 2.3 percent in 1977. By 1980 it had dwindled to 1.7 percent of GNP.

Despite a pressing need for funds to repair crumbling streets, sewers, bridges, public buildings, and municipal water systems, local fiscal crisis conditions, combined with declining federal revenue sharing, increased interest rates for municipal bond issues, and declining local revenues from sales taxes during the 1980–82 recession, caused many municipalities in all regions to postpone such necessary capital projects. According to a survey of 301 cities undertaken by the Joint Economic Committee of Congress in 1981, the cities surveyed were able to carry out only 60 percent of the capital projects they had planned (Herbers, 1982:12).

By 1981 a special section of *Business Week* (October 26, 1981:l35-81) entitled "State and Local Government in Trouble," documented the consequences of this failure to invest in the maintenance of the existing infrastructure: obsolete and decaying bridges; leaking water and sewer mains; deteriorating buildings; insufficient capacity of wastewater treatment systems at the local level, and crumbling highways and deteriorating rail beds at higher governmental levels (see also, Pierce, 1980:11; *New York Times*, November 12, 1981:12; Choate and Walter, 1981a and b; Herbers, 1982).

Several complexly interrelated factors account for the sharp absolute decline in national physical capital investment from $33.7 billion in 1965 to $24 billion in 1980. Beginning in the mid-1950s, with the expansion of federal spending under the National Defense Highway Act, the federal government began to absorb a larger share of public works expenditures. In 1957, 10 percent of the expenditures for infrastructure were derived from federal dollars; by 1980 the federal share of public works had grown to 40 percent.

Federal growth-oriented Keynesian policies favored new construction over repair of existing facilities. State and local politicians in the new growth areas initially benefitted from the public visibility of the new highway, water development, sewage treatment, and drainage projects in their areas, for which they could take credit. The urban deconcentration, sprawl, and uneven regional development pattern produced by the growth-oriented and military Keynesian federal taxing, spending, and procurement policies, required enormous capital investment to sustain it.

These new growth priorities drained resources from older central cities, which could no longer maintain their underutilized physical facilities. Ironically, such places also faced reduced expenditures for highway and urban redevelopment infrastructure projects because successful neighborhood protest against the adverse residential impacts of the highly visible "federal bulldozer" had produced a federal moratorium on completion of many central city highway access ramps. In addition, the enthusiasm of national Democratic politicians was dampened for redevelopment projects which revealed deep cracks in their urban coalition (see Lupo, Colcord and Fowler, 1971; Smith and Keller, 1983; Mollenkopf, 1983).

When such cities responded to urban decline, disinvestment, and population loss by making *local* improvements in their infrastructure to promote private investment, these supposedly "productive" social capital expenditures often failed to lure capital back to declining cities. As Michael Kennedy's (1984) quantitative analysis of factors contributing to fiscal stress in the 130 largest US cities shows, the central cities' efforts to attract private capital investment as a solution to their fiscal problems by making improvements in the urban infrastructure may actually worsen their fiscal condition. This is because the fragmentation of governmental jurisdictions in the American political system has made it possible for surrounding governmental jurisdictions to capture the new investment benefits generated by such social capital investment as road and mass transport improvements which improve access of suburbanites to the amenities of the urban core. In the central cities themselves new investment may be insufficient to offset the initial costs of infrastructure improvements, thus compounding fiscal stress.

Meanwhile, at the national level, from the late 1960s onward, the overall pie of federal public works began to shrink. Initially, delays in physical capital maintenance projects were prompted by the costs of financing the Vietnam war. Then, the rising costs of federal cost of living adjustments (COLAs) in middle-class entitlement programs, the increasing share of federal resources devoted to Sunbelt expansion (Mollenkopf, 1983), the resistance of Snowbelt congressional politicians to new Sunbelt water development projects (*New York Times*, March 24, 1986), and the sheer weight of inflation, combined to reduce the federal share of GNP devoted to public works.

Two key aspects of the "exceptionalism" of the US state structure – American federalism and the pork barrel politics of federal public works spending – further undermine the image of the US state as a kind of "collective capitalist" insuring the rational allocation of resources to the urban and national infrastructure to insure efficient capital accumulation in the long run. Instead, at the congressional committee level, pork-barrel politics has given a symbolic green light to the kind of political relations at lower governmental levels that have led to mounting waste, fraud, rising costs, and reduced effectiveness of public infrastructure spending. Governmental fragmentation of responsibility for maintenance of infrastructure among over 3,000 counties, 35,000 local governments, 26,000 special districts, 2,000 area-wide units, 15,000 school districts, and 200 interstate compacts has facilitated the insulation of local public works jurisdictions and reduced the public visibility and accountability of local public works politics. Moreover, it has expanded the influence of yet another sectoral block. This block includes the construction industry (constituting a major competitive economic sector of 478,000 firms), contractors, and unionized construction workers. Choate and Walter (1981a) have documented the widespread incidence of waste and corruption involved in the allocation of public works pork-barrel contracts within this internally competitive sectoral block.

Political alliances at the local level, which Molotch has termed local "growth machines" (see Molotch, 1976; Molotch and Logan, 1980) have frequently played a leading role in organizing the interests of particular firms operating within this sectoral block around land-based locational questions to tilt federal infrastructure development programs to their own particularistic purposes. For example, waste treatment subsidies provided by the Federal Water Pollution Act have been used to promote particular patterns of urban expansion or to cement particular alliances in the politics of local public works contracting (*New York Times*, November 12, 1981:12).

An understanding of the operation of the historically specific political processes characteristic of this "contracting out" dimension of the amorphous US state apparatus, helps us to move beyond the functionalism of those versions of structural Marxist urban political economy which envisage the capitalist state per se as necessarily engaged in the long-range planning which individual capitals are incapable of pursuing on their own. Rather than smoothing out the competitive and antagonistic relationships of the economic marketplace by planning for long-term accumulation, the social relations of the fragmented and pluralistic American political structure seem to have produced a collusive but no less antagonistic struggle for political access, contracts, preferments, and market advantage among alternative land-based growth coalitions.

Antagonistic competition has characterized the relationship among alternative growth coalitions at the local level seeking to channel diminishing federal spending. This interlocal competition has been exacerbated by the contradiction between the pervasiveness of the ideology of growth on the one hand and the objective resource constraints which have diminished the size of the federal resource transfers upon which future real growth often depends. The same intense competitiveness has been true of the relationship among different cities seeking to capture their "fair share" of new economic growth in an increasingly global political economy (see Goodman, 1979). It has been further intensified by structural changes in the national and world economy – which have freed corporate capital investment from previous dependencies on local agglomeration economics, enabling a reorganization of production, management, assembly, producer service, and distribution activities into multiple operational units scattered across the globe (Storper, 1981; Scott and Storper, 1986; Peet, 1987; Smith and Feagin, 1987). The case of civic boosterism by the dominant local growth coalition in the Sunbelt city of Atlanta well illustrates the character and intensity of this interlocal competition for new private investment on a global scale that now characterizes urban politics in the United States.

SUNBELT BOOSTERISM IN GLOBAL PERSPECTIVE

In addition to their mounting service needs and demands, tighter credit terms, and reduced direct federal support, some large Sunbelt cities also experienced white flight during the 1970s and early 1980s. Following a surge of population growth in the 1960s, Atlanta lost 14 percent of its overall population and a full 43 percent of its white population in the 1970s. This population movement was paralleled by a shift of job growth from the core to the perimeter of the metropolitan area (*New·York Times*, March 20, 1983:E3). To cope with employment restructuring, population decline, and fiscal stress Mayor Andrew Young persuaded his predominantly black political base to accept a regressive local sales tax increase while offering homeowners and corporations property tax relief as an incentive to stay put. Economic restructuring and population decline have also prompted Young to join the intensive competition among local governments to attract new national and international business investment to the Atlanta metropolitan area. This interlocal competitiveness was initially manifested in the efforts of Snowbelt state and local politicians to tilt their taxing and spending policies in a pro-business direction to attract new investment. It has now been extended to state and local officials in many Sunbelt cities facing similar problems of industrial restructuring, white flight, and structurally induced employment and revenue losses (see Rawls, 1983:12).

In the case of Atlanta, a new kind of metropolitan-wide growth coalition has been formed in response to the crisis conditions precipitated by the metropolitan region's dependent position in the international economy. Using a network of international business contacts made as a result of his United Nations ambassadorship, Mayor Young has initiated an aggressive campaign to attract international business to the Atlanta metropolitan area. Atlanta and its six surrounding counties have launched a $3 million effort to market the entire metropolitan area as an attractive location for services, sales, distribution, and high technology industries. The local political elites in these jurisdictions have been joined by state government officials, local businesses, and the Atlanta Chamber of Commerce in a "public–private partnership" called "Advantage Atlanta" to stimulate renewed economic growth. The sales effort of this metropolitan growth coalition has stressed the work ethic of the regional labor force, the region's favorable transportation advantages, and its allegedly superior "quality of life." The governor of Georgia, George Busbee, has explicitly used as a selling point the fact that the metropolitan labor force "with its lack of enthusiasm for labor unions...[kept] the unemployment rate in the Atlanta area among the lowest in the nation" during the last major recession (Rawls, 1983:12).

Atlanta's pro-growth coalition's effort to forge metropolitan-wide political unity in the face of intensified interlocal competition for international capital investment illustrates a major political consequence of the most common current definition of "urban crisis" – the shift from social and political to economic perceptions of "crisis." There is a contradictory awareness on the part of state and local political elites that both too rapid growth and too little growth in the economic base of local community life are likely to expand the role of the local state in civil society both as a facilitator and regulator of economic growth processes and as a mediator of threatened or actual economic decline. Despite the still loud proclamations that "market forces" are the harbingers of new rounds of growth, state and local government officials have not been able or willing to forgo the role of "public entrepreneur" in community economic development. This role has been thrust upon them by both their structural position as "middlemen" between capital and local communities and their instrumental need to generate sufficient tax revenues to provide them with the resources to carry out their mediating role.

This role is significantly constrained, however, by the nearly universal availability of tax incentives designed to retain existing businesses and induce new business investment. The result is often a subsidy to multilocational capital for locating where it wishes, at the cost of sizeable loss of tax revenues to state and local governments. As Smith, Ready and Judd (1985:195) have pointed out, the emergent economic and political context enmeshing public economic development entrepreneurs is a classic instance of the tragedy of the commons. Local political elites "are loathe to criticize the argument that tax incentives are beneficial, or to question the effectiveness of the other instruments which attempt to promote economic development, for fear that the first to say 'no' will be excluded from whatever growth does take place in the national economy."

The formidability of the task of the new "public entrepreneurs" is made even greater by new global conditions affecting the real possibilities for community economic development. These conditions include: the increased concentration and fluidity of investment capital; peripheral industrialization; intensified international competition between core and peripheral producers of goods and services; Third World political instability; intensified labor migration flows; and capital restructuring by core country multinational corporations to reestablish favorable conditions for profitability in an increasingly uncertain environment.

Our understanding of the dynamics of the new international

system is still incomplete (compare, for instance, Portes and Walton, 1981 with Frobel, Heinrichs and Kreye, 1980). Nevertheless, it has become clear that global capital restructuring by multinational enterprises has produced a new global–local interplay. Local communities, including local political and social structures and prevailing political alliances in core and peripheral countries are increasingly affected by changes in the patterns of international trade and investment, trends in the organization and control of production under conditions of increased uncertainty, and trends in labor migration. What implications does this process of global economic restructuring have for the future economic and political development of US cities?

CONCLUSIONS

In the larger political economic order of the United States, where the strict division of labor between market and state requires local officials to mediate between corporate control of economic functions and electoral control invested in local communities, the social construction of the local "business climate" has become the central task of the political elites of the local state. As was suggested in chapter 3, the material and ideological constraints under which this social construction of reality has been politically managed define the outer limits of "hegemony." In US cities, the current political management of economic restructuring by state and capital has weakened direct political challenges to capitalist hegemony. The "good city" is now commonly defined as one in which corporate domination of productive relations is uncontested, the community adapts to economic change without resistance, and corporate influence over the local state is accepted as a benign expression of "partnership." Fortunately, as we shall see, not all of the popular forces involved in the economic and political changes currently shaping the US urban system are as captive of this social construction of reality as are the local growth coalitions and the supportive local officials who have been shaped by the new global constraints on the forms of state intervention in civil society.

Before continuing our analysis of the relationship between global economic restructuring and urban politics in part IV, we turn next in part III to the sustained effort by New Right social forces to consolidate this emergent ideological hegemony by calling for a full-scale return to "the market" as the best way to revitalize American cities. The theoretical postulates constituting the market capitalist ideological distortion of political and economic power relations are subjected to critical scrutiny in chapter 5 (part III). Chapter 6 next considers the ways in which the ideology of unleashed market forces has been deployed in debates over urban policy. Chapter 7 then analyzes the political power shift reflected in the urban and regional impacts of the state policies of Reaganomics. Once this is accomplished we will be in a better position to understand the nature of the current national political and ideological context affecting local responses to global economic restructuring.

Part III

Market Capitalism and Urban Development

5
Market Capitalist Political Economy: The Depoliticization of Policy Making

Popular American use has equated "liberalism" with the welfare state capitalism that has characterized the basic direction of federal urban policies since the New Deal. Market capitalist social theorists object to this usage. They insist on maintaining the classical use of "liberalism" in European social thought to designate a social theory dedicated to reducing the role of the state in economic life in the belief that thereby the individual's freedom will be enhanced. In the United States, market liberals often are termed "conservatives." This designation tends to confuse devotees of the free market with traditional conservatives who favor substantially greater social control of individual behavior than market liberals find tolerable.

In this chapter the terms "market liberalism" and "market capitalism" will be used interchangeably. Market capitalist political economy will be explained and subjected to critical scrutiny. Milton Friedman's theoretical defense of market capitalism will be treated as the paradigm case of market capitalist social theory. In the next chapter the implications of this approach for urban public policy will be considered. Although not an urban political economist per se, most of Friedman's central policy concerns – public education, housing, crime, urban redevelopment, minimum wage legislation, labor law and tax policy – all have profoundly urban impacts. Where appropriate in the next two chapters, the views of other policy practitioners who have applied market capitalist tenets to actual urban policies will also be considered (see, for instance, Savas, 1974, 1981, 1983).

MARKET CAPITALISM AS SOCIAL THEORY

Market capitalism is a social theory that seeks to limit the role that state policies might play in distributing life chances. Possible benefits of redistributive allocations by the state are invariably weighed against the possible harm they might do to the market as a central means of social organization and economic integration. For instance, market capitalists perceive urban policies which seek to redistribute resources by region or class as potential threats to work incentives and to the increased economic productivity and social prosperity that is assumed to follow from market processes. This does not mean that market capitalists are entirely laissez faire. They favor those state actions which can be shown to reinforce the operation of market mechanisms (Room, 1979:49).

Market capitalists differ from Keynesians in their belief that unstimulated and unregulated market forces are more likely to produce prosperity than is the "mixed economy" in which the capitalist state is managed by economic technocrats who rely heavily on the stimulation of aggregate demand and the "smoothing out" of business cycles as central engines of economic growth. For market liberals the free market, despite periodic fluctuations, is the best long-run route to increased economic growth. Because of this belief, market liberals oppose all public policies which separate access to life chances from labor market rewards (Room, 1979:50).

Fearful that state-financed social services will inevitably become bureaucratized, combative against the tendency toward empire-building by the heads of public agencies (Niskanen, 1971), and concerned that this tendency will inevitably withdraw resources from productive uses, market liberals wish to radically reduce the scale of government in providing or financing public services.

Somewhat less hostile to selective, minimally set transfer payments, because these protect the market against charges that it produces destitution along with prosperity, while, in their view, enhancing the power of "consumer demand," market liberals have been more willing to support some forms of minimum floor under the market allocation of incomes. This, however, is only accepted if government support for the "truly needy" takes the form of cash transfers (e.g., a "negative income tax") or vouchers, rather than services.

All directly provided urban social services are dismissed, often without empirical examination, as inherently wasteful and paternalistic. Vouchers are touted as introducing sound market principles into government policy. Even though some market capitalists accept the provision of educational or health subsidies to those most in need, in the form of vouchers to service users, they uniformly oppose direct subsidies to providers of these services. In their view, such currently collectively provided and consumed services should be privatized (see Savas, 1982). They should be privately purchased in the marketplace as commodities, in much the same way one would purchase soap or appliances. As Savas (1983:452) has put the issue: "By privatizing, contracting out, franchising, issuing vouchers and relying on voluntary institutions, municipal monopolies can be broken up and forced by competition to deliver services more efficiently."

Another market capitalist complaint about collectively consumed public services is that their existence stimulates excess political demand for their expansion. Demands begin to outstrip the capacity of government to respond, thereby both draining tax revenues and fostering social instability. Since, in their view, both limited taxation and social stability are necessary to enable market processes to function predictably and efficiently, market liberals eschew nearly all collective consumption policies of the national and local welfare state. Their argument seems to be that if the door is opened a crack, insatiable demands for universal provision will ensue, bankrupting both state and society in the long run (George and Wilding, 1976).

Having now settled on the general premises of market capitalism which bear upon questions of urban public policy, we may consider in greater detail the basic principles and postulates of market capitalist political economy. Once this is accomplished, we will be in a position to consider the implications of this approach for urban policy and to subject its policy implications to critical scrutiny in the next chapter.

MARKET CAPITALIST UTOPIA: THE DEPOLITICIZED ECONOMY

Market capitalists operate on the basis of several underlying assumptions about the dynamic and integrative social consequences of unfettered free markets. The constant hope of market liberal political economists is for a "liberated" economy – an economy guided by the dynamic of individual self-interest unchecked by the "dead hand" of state planning (see Butler, 1981) or the "perverse" influence of politics. The leading market capitalist Milton Friedman holds that if the state's role in economic affairs were severely limited and economics were freed from the pernicious and collusive effect of politics, free markets could be expected to: liberate individual creative talent; promote voluntary cooperation; avoid the concentration of political and economic resources required for centralized economic planning; expand political freedom by radically separating political and economic power; and, somewhat paradoxically in light of this, depoliticize both civil society and the policy-making process.

According to Friedman, reducing the role of the state in economic affairs will, ipso facto, enlarge the role of the individual entrepreneur. The individual thus becomes the basic unit of analysis in market liberal political economy, and creative entrepreneurship the basic goal of its devotees.

Friedman posits a "constructive" justification for diminishing the role of politics and the state in civil society. In his view, individual genius rather than governmental initiative has been responsible for the most creative advances in the arts, sciences, and economic development. The cultivation of such genius requires a climate in civil society conducive to variety, diversity, and experimentation, values often given short shrift by centralized bureaucratic states. Accordingly, market capitalism, which from Friedman's perspective gives free reign to a wide variety of individuals (and their surrogates, economic organizations), is pictured as the best way to promote individual creativity, experimentation, and, through these, social progress. Thus, for Friedman, the state ought to play only the quite limited role in economy and society of protecting markets and "voluntary" contracts and insuring the common defense.

For market liberals like Friedman, the meaning and value of human freedom is bound up in free and voluntary interrelationships among people. Social freedom entails the maximization of individual power, mobility, and choice. The fundamental task of social organization thus becomes the coordination of the diverse economic activities of large numbers of self-interested, interacting individuals, without unduly inhibiting individual mobility and choice.

In developed societies, individual freedom must be reconciled with growing economic and technological interdependence. Two of the basic modes for coordinating activities of a complex economy characterized by a specialized division of labor are planning and the market. Friedman chooses to equate "planning" with one type of planning – coercive, central direction. (On decentralized, democratic planning models see Smith, 1979: ch. 6; Alperovitz and Faux, 1984: ch. 15). This provides a stark contrast with his preferred definition of a market – "the voluntary cooperation of individuals." He sets out to find a way in which this can be accomplished without expanding the coercive power of the state.

In Friedman's view, private "voluntary" arrangements are preferable to state action to achieve objectives deemed desirable by "citizen-consumers." From this perspective, it is preferable that collectively consumed urban services like housing, health care, and education be provided to individual "consumers" at a price by competing private providers, based on *ability to pay*, rather than either distributed universally to "citizens" by the state as a matter of *right*, or redistributed to needy people, or declining cities, on the basis of *need*.

In Friedman's political economy, market allocation is clearly preferable to state planning arrangements. This is because he believes that economic transactions in a market capitalist economy are characterized by the following attributes (1962: ch. 1):

1 mutual voluntariness between producers and consumers;
2 information about products and services that is both pertinent and sufficient to enable producers and consumers to engage in rationally self-interested mutual exchanges;
3 production and consumption units that are each small enough to bring a substantial degree of equality to the bargaining process characterizing market exchange;
4 institutional arrangements by the minimal state that are conducive to the maintenance of free and voluntary exchanges among producers and consumers; these include: (a) laws against monopoly; (b) laws that prevent physical coercion and enforce contracts; and (c) provisions to compensate third parties to market exchanges from adverse externalities or "neighborhood effects."

Apart from outlawing monopoly, how does Friedman view the problem of maintaining small units of production in the age of large corporations? In its simplest form, the free market model of economic organization posits a great multiplicity of competing buyers and sellers as a basic prerequisite of voluntary exchange. In such a context, according to Friedman: "The consumer is protected from the coercion of the seller because of the presence of other sellers with whom he can deal. The seller is protected from coercion by the consumer because of the other consumers to whom he can sell" (1962:14). It is this logic which prompts Friedman to oppose the role of the welfare state in the advanced capitalist societies as both a concentrated provider of services like schooling and a concentrated consumer of goods and services of the "private" economy through government procurement and contracting.

Despite his awareness of the growing governmental scope in economic affairs, Friedman paints a glowing picture of lilliputian units of private economic organization. He contends that private enterprise in American society is characterized by sufficiently small units to maintain an open and competitive marketplace that fosters well-informed and voluntary exchange. He thus glosses over the implications of corporate concentration of economic *and* political resources for both his theory and for contemporary urban life. By defining the "enterprise" as a valid surrogate and essential intermediary "between individuals in their capacities as suppliers of services and as purchasers of goods" (1962:13, 14), Friedman avoids having to deal with the historical changes that have supplanted competitive capitalism with a three sector economy, including a competitive sector, a monopoly sector, and a state sector. These sectors create jobs, affect prices, and shape investment (see Galbraith, 1969, 1973; O'Connor, 1973). Especially overlooked is the growing role of national and multinational corporations in setting prices, shaping investment, restructuring urban economies, and influencing the public policies of local, state, and national governments.

It is government, not corporate power, that is the chief antagonist in Friedman's social philosophy. His fear of concentrated governmental power in the service of explicitly political ends prompts Friedman to develop the paradoxical argument that free and voluntary markets are the sine qua non of both political freedom and the *de*politicization of social life. A skeptic might ask: What good is political freedom in a context in which most important issues of social life are decided by markets rather than politics or planning? But such obvious contradictions do not seem to bother Friedman. His single-minded concern about the threat to individual liberty posed by concentrated state power prompts him instead to argue that while political and economic freedom are indivisible, political and economic power must be kept separate.

Friedman regards the very concept of democratic socialism as contradictory. In his view, any political arrangements designed to insure the individual freedom of the democratic citizen are bound to be frustrated when combined with highly centralized economic planning arrangements, even if these are periodically subject to modification in response to electoral mandates. This is because in his view "economic freedom" – narrowly defined as the unfettered pursuit of *individual* material well being – is both an inseparable dimension of "freedom broadly understood" and a necessary means to achieve meaningful political freedom.

For Friedman, competitive capitalist economic arrangements promote this sort of political freedom by directly insuring economic freedom. These arrangements radically separate politics from economics, a goal that socialist political economists and even most welfare state liberals reject as unrealistic. When political power and economic power are kept in separate hands, and the former is limited in function, Friedman believes that social power is by definition more broadly dispersed. In this model, power in each sphere "offsets" (i.e. checks and balances) the other (1962:9). By this logic, competitive capitalism becomes a necessary, if insufficient, condition for political freedom.

Despite his apparent fondness for political freedom, Friedman is radically unwilling to expand the range of issues through which the individual's political freedom might be expressed. In his view, just as market choices are preferable to planning, so too are they preferable to political decisions in the arena of public policy-making. Friedman expects that properly functioning markets will enhance the degree of cooperation and social integration in society. Accordingly, he believes that market capitalism will depoliticize the making of public policy. By fostering voluntary actions, markets are expected to "reduce greatly the range of issues that must be decided through political means, and thereby to minimize the extent to which government need participate directly in the game" (1962:15). Politics is castigated for suppressing minority opinion, enforcing social conformity, responding too frequently to the tyranny of the majority, and thereby ignoring a wide variety of individual preferences.

In his recent major book, *Free to Choose* (1979), Friedman (with Rose Friedman) expands upon his desire to extend market forces from the realm of economics to politics and public policy implementation. Following the lead of political analysts in the area of "public choice" theory (see Tiebout, 1956; Buchanan and Tullock, 1962), Friedman here treats both economy and polity as "markets in which the outcome is determined by the interaction among persons pursuing their own self-interests (broadly interpreted) rather than by the social goals the participants find it advantageous to enunciate" (1979:x). The villain of *Free to Choose* is a supposedly "new class" of civil servants that spend peoples' income paternalistically rather than allowing people to spend it themselves. This culprit is allied with "special interests" who have captured government resources for their own purposes (p. 7), thus expanding the role of government in everyday life and draining resources from the pockets of individual consumers (1979:6–7; see also Shackleton, 1980).

Over against this image of politics and public policy, Friedman counterposes the free market, as a last bastion of individualism, minority opinion, diversity and choice. He believes that market decisions are more adaptable than are political decisions to the variety of points of view (preferences) that people may have for collectively as well as for individually consumed goods and services. As he puts it, in the political allocation of goods and services, "the number of separate groups that can in fact be represented is narrowly limited, enormously so by comparison with the proportional representation of the market" (1962:239). In short, once viewpoints are expressed on public issues, majority preferences on the type and level of public goods and services that are collectively consumed must be accepted by those whose preferences differ from the majority. While the politically alienated can move to another political jurisdiction ("vote with their feet"), the costs of doing so are greater than in the case of expressing dissatisfaction in the private marketplace by giving one's business to another firm. This is especially true in the case of federal policy decisions which offer *indivisible* public goods like national defense.

It also applies to any public policy that sets particular types and levels of collection consumption, e.g. for schools, housing, and health care services in response to political preferences. Once the bundle of goods and services to be collectively consumed is politically determined, and the level of public support for the bundle is set, those who prefer more or less taxing and spending or the consumption of items (e.g. the arts) left out of the package, are "coerced" to conform to majority will. The upshot is that because collectively consumed urban social services are difficult, if not impossible, to disaggregate in the political marketplace, Friedman prefers that their provision be left as much as possible in the hands of the economic marketplace.

This chain of reasoning forms the basis of Friedman's much heralded scheme to replace urban public education with a system of educational vouchers given to each student to allow "shopping around" for suitable schooling. His voucher proposal, as well as related efforts by devotees of market solutions to public policy problems in health care, housing and ghetto employment, will be critically examined in the next chapter. For now it is sufficient to note that the major consequence of the adoption of such an approach would be to reduce the role of politics, planning, and the state in urban policy. Not only would market capitalist political economists limit the role of the state in promoting or regulating the private economy; they would also expand the role that the market now plays to encompass many areas that have come to be regarded as legitimate domains of public decision-making, such as urban public education, social service provision in health care, and garbage and trash removal.

The ultimate goal of market liberal political economy is to reduce as much as possible the number of public issues resolved by national and urban politics. In part this is because of their limited definition of politics. For the market liberal, politics should be concerned with little more than the allocation of various bundles of collective consumption that cannot be easily disaggregated, like national defense. But in part it is also because of their belief that voluntary market arrangements are more conducive to stability and social integration than are the collective mechanisms for resolving political conflict. In the context of majoritarian political arrangements for resolving conflict among diverse minority points of view, "politics" so defined, inherently entails coercion, conformity and, indeed, even suppression of the preferences of political losers. This, in Friedman's view, "tends to strain the social cohesion essential for a stable society" (1962:23).

Here Friedman conveniently ignores the very real stresses upon social cohesion and stability historically posed by competitive market arrangements which also have had losers and winners. This is in fact one of the very justifications of the market – its highly touted capacity to reward the efficient, weed out the "lemons," and provide "work incentives" for those at the bottom of the social structure. Not only does Friedman ignore historical evidence of the dislocating effects of competitive capitalism, he actually holds that an unbridled market would *reduce* social strain by "rendering conformity unnecessary with respect to any activities it encompasses" (1962:24). Such formulations, which mask the coercive aspects of economic exchange relationships in actual class stratified societies, contribute to the ideological "hegemony" (Gramsci, 1971) by which dominant social interests are enabled to maintain and reproduce their power and privilege.

Since the central dimension of Friedman's stipulative definition of a free competitive market is its "voluntariness," such a claim is true, by definition, and is also tautological. In the real world of unequal buyers and sellers, coercion and conformity abound. The non-unionized worker who conforms to labor discipline to avoid losing his job would surely be surprised to learn that workers in the lower paid competitive sector of the American political economy are free from conformity in any of the activities which their labor market encompasses. Yet in Friedman's world, only politics and the state promote coercion and conformity; markets are harbingers of individual freedom and dignity. When evidence challenges faith, the tendency is to attribute the adverse human consequences to "imperfections" of the market rather than to recognize that the very logic of competition would entail insecurity and dislocation, even in a fictitious world in which buyers and sellers were relatively equal at the outset. This is why so many losers of competitive struggle in capitalist marketplaces have consistently turned to the state to address their plight. But in the market capitalist world of frictionless harmony brought about by free markets, the state is expected to eventually wither away.

THE ROLE OF THE STATE IN MARKET CAPITALISM

If the market is to replace politics, what legitimate role is left for the state in market capitalist political economy? If government is to be neither a direct provider of services nor a powerful instrument for symbolizing political obligation, what should it do? In Milton Friedman's view, the state ought to be a limited instrument for achieving only those goals about which citizens, *taken as individuals*, can reach consensus. Modifying Lord Acton's dictum, Friedman presumes that well-intentioned users of concentrated political power may not be corrupted by its use, but that centralized politics "will both attract and form men of a different stamp" (1962:2).

Starting from this assumption about politics, Friedman advocates two broad principles for the political organization of market capitalism – functionally limited government, and broad geographic decentralization of political authority to perform these limited functions. Friedman's ideal state is limited to four basic functions: national defense; the preservation of domestic law and order within the market framework; the enforcement of private contracts; and any additional activities that contribute to the preservation of competitive markets. Laws against fraud and monopolistic practices are examples. Beyond this, he sanctions only those collective purposes about which consensus can be reached. Of course, since he rejects majority rule as coercive and requires each person, *as an individual*, to contribute to the formation of voluntary consensus, in practice this means that only unanimously endorsed collective goals are legitimate functions of the market capitalist state. Even in such an unlikely circumstance, Friedman adds a warning. Consensual public policies should prevail only if voluntary cooperation or private enterprise have already been tried to achieve the policy objective and have failed.

Geographically, Friedman favors locating state power at the most decentralized level possible. Given his preoccupation with the potential for governmentally induced conformity, he reasons that individuals dissatisfied with state or local policies may vote with their feet if they are alienated. The possibility that citizens may exit the state or local political jurisdiction serves, in his view, as a healthy check on the arbitrariness of state and local political elites. Such a check is far more problematic at the national level because legal, language, and cultural barriers stand in the way of easy entry and exit from the nation state.

In this context of limited functions and decentralization, four "facilitative" functions are reserved for the nation state. First, the market capitalist ideal envisages a nation state devoted to the establishment of a framework of private property and contract law and custom favorable to day-to-day free economic activity among actors in the marketplace. In Friedman's utopia, this framework would constitute a set of "rules of the game" governing circumstances where freedoms conflict and mediating potential disagreements. The state would function as an *umpire*, responsible for insuring that all the actors follow the basic rules of economic civility. Second, the market capitalist state must set up some clear ground rules concerning the thorny question of "freedom to combine" (e.g. unions, trade associations) versus "freedom to compete." Third, the nation state in the market capitalist model must clearly define the parameters of property rights. Clarity is essential to avoid misunderstanding and conflict. Indeed the clarity of rights to private property is actually more important to Friedman than the actual content of the rights. In his view "the existence of a well specified and generally accepted definition of property is more important than just what the definition is" (1962:27). Fourth, the nation state should establish the framework of a monetary system within which individual rational calculations of self-interest can take place. In Friedman's view this implies a tightly controlled money policy that is predictable and hence stabilizing to market relations. He rejects the use of state power to displace the market as an allocative mechanism by using the money supply and credit structure to achieve substantive public policy goals, be they Keynesian "demand management" or more interventionist measures to promote the development of economically depressed regions.

Beyond these facilitative functions, Friedman recognizes only two legitimate positive functions of the market capitalist state. The first of these is regulatory, the second compensatory. The two "imperfections" capable of disrupting the general equilibrium of the market are: (a) the unintended positive or negative effects that accrue to third parties to market transactions, and (b) the growth of monopolies. Some of the unintended effects of economic activity, which economists term "externalities" or "neighborhood effects," may transmit positive benefits to third parties who have not paid for them (e.g. private lighting of a public sidewalk). This violates the basic market principle of distributive justice: *"To each according to his ability to pay."* Other externalities are negative, allocating unwanted costs (e.g. pollution, neighborhood visual disamenities) to innocent third parties to market transactions. This opens up a role for the state in monitoring and possibly compensating innocent third parties or in some way penalizing those guilty of causing the undesirable spillover effects.

In monitoring neighborhood or spillover effects such as air and water pollution, or reducing the scope of unintended benefits, which economists term "free rider" effects, Friedman wishes to limit government's compensatory and policing functions to a minimum. He warns that the actions of government to rectify such neighborhood effects raise three difficulties. First, because such effects are difficult to measure, the actions of government may be misdirected. Second, the compensatory actions may themselves cause neighborhood effects, unintentionally, to other innocent third parties. Third, once governments undertake activities of various kinds, they have a tendency to be permanently institutionalized. The termination of a policy is infrequent and difficult to achieve. (But see Peters and Hogwood, 1985, for an informative discussion of actual processes of policy termination.) For these reasons, he argues that the burden of proof for new government activity to compensate for market failures must rest with proponents of state action (Friedman and Friedman, 1979:32).

The preferred method among market capitalists for dealing with "free riders" is to charge user charges for distributive services heretofore regarded as public (e.g. highways and mass transportation). Friedman reasons that this sort of privatization of public services will free up tax resources that had been used to pay for the public services. These, in turn, would lead to tax cuts, which would put more disposable income in the hands of individual consumers, his ultimate desideratum. Similarly, instead of setting up governmental regulatory bodies, like the Environmental Protection Agency to guard against negative externalities like pollution, market capitalists would allow polluters to pollute, monitor the extent of their damage, and tax them for the privilege to pollute that they have freely chosen to "purchase."

Nearly all possible redistributive and regulatory activities of the national and local state are denounced by market capitalists like Friedman as "paternalistic" services unfit for free people. Lest there be any mistake about his meaning, Friedman exempts from this charge only those who are radically unfit to participate in the "free" (and, in his view humanly fulfilling) competition of civil society – namely, the insane, to whom it is legitimate to offer paternalistic forms of state financed "help." Excluded from his list of legitimate state activities are a host of public policies currently provided by federal, state, and local governments in the United States. Many of these comprise the core of regulatory, developmental, and redistributive policies affecting urban form under U.S. welfare capitalism – public housing, mortgage guarantees to encourage home ownership, the regulation of mass transportation, rent controls, minimum wage rates, and the licensing of various trades and professions. Others vitally effect the infrastructure of metropolitan areas – publicly owned toll roads, the regulation of savings deposit rates, the regulation of banking. Still others, like Medicaid and social welfare programs to low income people, form the basis of the Great Society programs enacted in the 1960s by the Johnson Administration and expanded in response to the urban protest and rebellion of that decade.

Friedman also favors privatization of distributive urban services like garbage collection and fire protection. He goes beyond the argument of market liberal E.S. Savas (1983) that competition through "contracting out" for such services will improve the efficiency of basic service delivery. He argues that such "basic" services can be disaggregated and can pay for themselves through user charges. Contending that the market can handle the matter better, Friedman also opposes rent controls on the grounds that such controls dampen housing supply because government holds rents below their market price (see Appelbaum and Gilderbloom, 1983, for contrary evidence). He even opposes the public provision of services that, because of very high capital intensity or labor intensity, could not possibly be expected to pay for themselves through user charges, e.g. public transportation, low income public housing, public works, and police services.

MARKET CAPITALISM AND MONOPOLY POWER

Milton Friedman addresses critics of the marketplace who have called attention to the adverse psychological consequences – the spirit of self-aggrandizement and mutual exploitation – attributed to the competitive ethic fostered by marketplace social relations (Tawney, 1927). For Friedman economic competition is a purely impersonal social process, free from the personal rivalries and higgling-haggling that often found their way into pre-capitalist exchange relations prior to the introduction of money economies (1979:120). In his view, exploitive social relations are also precluded by the broad dispersal of market power. In short, in competitive market situations no one can set either the prices of commodities or the terms by which others can gain access to goods or incomes. Only monopoly capitalism could be exploitive in these ways.

Acknowledging that monopoly capitalism can indeed limit voluntary exchange by unilaterally altering the terms of exchange relations, Friedman nonetheless opposes the use of state power to hold monopolies accountable to politically determined standards of social responsibility. Instead he prefers that state coercion be limited to vigorous anti-trust activities against industrial monopolies and trade unions, which he terms "labor monopolies." The state role would be to break up rather than to tame monopolistic economic power. In Friedman's limited array of policy tools, antitrust policy is a legitimate means to prevent unavoidable monopolies.

Yet some concentrations of economic power are technically necessary to perform needed productive activities. A large accumulation of capital investment is necessary, for example, to provide broadly accessible telephone service or basic utilities. In such cases Friedman prefers private monopolies to either public monopolies (e.g. an urban mass transit system) or public regulation of a private monopoly (e.g. a regulatory body to approve price increases for utilities). Although offering not a shred of historical evidence, he reasons that private monopolies will be more quick to adopt new technologies, out of fear of possible competition, than will either public or regulated monopolies. This in turn is expected to exert a downward pressure on prices, once again redounding to the benefit of Friedman's ideal-typical market consumer.

Not surprisingly, Friedman has labored tirelessly to persuade his readers that the real threat to open markets, individual liberty, and freedom of choice is trade unionism rather than corporate monopoly. His argument is ideological and unsupported by empirical evidence. Yet key elements of the ideological argument have been used to promote repressive anti-labor legislation and union-thwarting "right to work laws" in many southern states. These laws in turn have been one of the political locational incentives contributing to the accelerated pace of disinvestment in industrial production in older metropolitan areas (Perry and Watkins, 1977). Especially hard hit have been the central cities of the northeastern and midwestern regions of the United States. The mobility of capital to more politically receptive regions has contributed substantially to their current fiscal and social crises. Accordingly, this argument bears close scrutiny and critique.

In *Capitalism and Freedom,* written during the 1950s and published in 1962, Friedman cites studies ending in 1939 as the basis for his division of the economy sectorally into a state sector of 25 percent, a monopoly sector of between 11 and 19 percent, and the remainder ("perhaps as much as 85 percent of the non-state sector") as competitive. His treatment of oligopolies in which a handful of producers dominate over 50 percent of production, is oblique. He asserts that competitive sector activities such as personal services and wholesale trade are "vastly more important" components of the economy than are the communications and automobile industries. Friedman thus finesses the extent to which the private economy has become dominated by corporate power (see, for instance, Miller and Tomaskovic-Devey, 1983:20–35). He concludes that both the importance of monopoly capitalism and the extent to which technological and economic changes have promoted corporate concentration have been overestimated.

Confronting the real trend toward centralized corporate management of decentralized production for trans-national markets (see chs. 8 and 9, this volume) Friedman sees only new possibilities for increased beneficent competition. In his words: "The developments in transportation and communication . . . have *promoted* competition by reducing the importance of local regional markets and widening the scope within which competition could take place. . . ." (1962:123).

Having thus disposed of the sticky problems of corporate concentration and the internationalization of economic relations by defining them away, Friedman turns his attention to the pseudo-problem (at least in the American context of ineffectual trade unionism) of "monopoly in labor." He acknowledges that only about a quarter (now only around 15 percent) of the

American labor force is in fact unionized, and that even some unionized segments have had quite limited influence on the structure of wages in the United States. Yet for Friedman, even this limited role constitutes an unacceptable incursion on the wage rates that an unbridled free market would establish.

Successful collective bargaining by organized workers over wages is evaluated only in terms of his expectation that wage rates among the unorganized will be commensurately reduced. Interestingly, here Friedman accepts the zero-sum assumption that wage rates comprise a fixed pool, reflecting labor's overall and relatively fixed marginal productivity. Businesses and industries that make wage concessions are depicted as being forced by the very logic of capitalism to make less employment available in their firms than they otherwise would. These displaced workers would then be forced to seek work in other fields, thus increasing labor supply and driving down wage rates among unorganized labor in these other fields. Such logic ignores the possibility that the attractiveness of the wage structure won by successful bargaining might reduce worker alienation, thus driving up productivity, increasing profits, and the ability to expand production at higher wage levels. It also ignores the segmentation and stratification of labor markets (see Gordon, Edwards and Reich, 1982; Gordon, 1972; Smith and Keller, 1983) which renders it useless to conceive of the labor market as an open arena with easy entry and exit among fields and segments.

Additionally, Friedman opposes unions because they have been a leading force in the enactment of minimum wage laws and have lobbied successfully for periodic increases in the level of the minimum wage. Minimum wage legislation has placed a floor under wage rates and provided a limited protection against exploitative wage rates among the unorganized. Yet Friedman sees such laws as barriers to employment among unskilled workers. In his view, by pricing low skilled workers out of labor markets, minimum wage laws increase the level of poverty (for a critique of this argument see chapter 7, below).

Friedman's logic assumes, once again, that wages in capitalist societies are a kind of fixed amount, constrained not by the political weakness of labor vis-à-vis capital but by the marginal productivity of workers viewed as individual units of production. In the real world, rather than the abstract world of marginal productivity, the choices available to employers when wages are increased because of the political strength of labor have included options other than job reductions, such as: continuing operation at a profit/wage ratio more favorable to labor; reductions in dividends to stockholders, at least in the short run; or passing the cost of labor settlements along to the general consumer in the form of inflated prices. When such options have been chosen, increased wages resulting from collective action by organized labor have not automatically either reduced employment or increased the level of poverty. Despite the negative impact of inflationary wage settlements on industrial profits (see Kalecki, 1972) and on creditors, the poor have generally fared better during inflationary than during recessionary periods. This is because of the intercorrelation between inflation, welfare state revenues, the political strength of labor, money in circulation in the economy, and increased possibilities for absorbing a surplus population (see Hibbs and Fassbinder, 1981; Piven and Cloward, 1982:24–5).

For proponents of minimum wage laws, the absence of such laws, reflecting the political weakness of labor in general, would be an incentive to employers to offer the lowest possible wages consonant with the physical reproduction of the labor force (Smith, 1980b). Friedman acknowledges this possibility but retorts: "Insofar as the low wage rates are in fact a sign of poverty, the people who are rendered unemployed (by the minimum wage legislation) are precisely those who can least afford to give up the income they had been receiving, small as it may appear to the people voting for the minimum wage" (1962:180–181).

In addition to his opposition to labor unions in general, and to minimum wage legislation in particular, Friedman also opposes occupational licensure, affirmative action policies, and both direct engagement in economic production by state agencies, and regulation of such activities. All are viewed as unwarranted intrusions into voluntary markets which impede both the voluntariness and the efficiency of market exchange relationships.

In *Free to Choose* Friedman especially castigates municipal public service unions for draining the disposable income of taxpayers and bringing city governments to the brink of bankruptcy (1979:229–40). To address this alleged "labor monopoly" cause of urban fiscal crisis Friedman would take several extreme steps to break up union power – abolish the National Labor Relations Board, use anti-trust to dismantle unions, revoke collective bargaining elections, and do away with the right to litigate about unfair labor practices. Castigating licensure, like unionism, as a throwback to feudalism and a restraint on free trade, Friedman would do away with licensing of all vocations, even the practice of medicine (1962: ch. 9).

Not surprisingly, Friedman would also abolish all anti-discrimination legislation such as affirmative action on the ground that pure market capitalism is fundamentally incompatible with discrimination. Markets, in his view, reward merit. Unlike people, they are color blind. Rewarding the market value of labor inputs, markets are seen as the most efficient engines of economic productivity. In Friedman's words: "an impersonal market separates economic activities from political views and protects men from being discriminated against in their economic activities *for reasons that are irrelevant to productivity* – whether these reasons are associated with their views or their color" (1962:21; see also 109–10). In the place of coercive anti-discrimination laws, Friedman would substitute persuasion to end the discrimination on the basis of race and sex that currently characterizes labor markets. In taking this position he seems to equate racism and sexism with other preferences such as one's taste for particular types of consumer goods, that can be changed by rational discourse alone. To the extent that the former are deep-seated, historically rooted responses to the social world, his remedy is necessarily inadequate.

Two final *bêtes noires* in Milton Friedman's analysis of markets and politics are the government owned monopoly and the government supported monopoly. Among the former he includes the state role in highway building and municipally owned utilities. The term government monopoly is also used to designate the defense and aerospace industries in which government expenditures have financed research and development and guaranteed the industries a market for their wares. Interestingly, he argues that production by such arrangements is actually less dangerous to market arrangements than are governmentally enforced supportive cartel arrangements on behalf of politically influential private producers such as agriculture, trucking, radio and television, interstate oil and gas, and banks. The presence of the state, not the growing market concentration and political power of such interests, is his major concern. He proposes to remedy the frequently observed phenomenon of the captive regulatory agency by total deregulation of production, distribution, and exchange.

Refusing to consider possible distinctions between socially beneficial and socially undesirable regulation in terms of actual consequences, Friedman lumps together the notoriously captive Texas Railroad Commission, that has restricted oil production to keep oil prices up, with the enactment of local building codes to protect the public safety (1962:126). Noting that the latter have often become captives of local contractors and building trade unions to reduce competition in the building industry, he argues that all regulation is tantamount to a restraint on free contractual agreement. By strictly applying his logic, one would be forced to favor free contractual arrangements between builders and buyers or landlords and tenants, *in principle,* even if their practical consequences were to provide unsafe, shoddily constructed fire traps for consumers who lacked the market power to purchase safe and decent housing.

In the real world of unequal market power and imperfect information, when arrangements have enabled all who would be producers into the market (such as in the case of automobile repair shops), the actual consequences have been quite the opposite of those which Friedman and other devotees of market capitalism would predict – high prices because of the oversupply of labor and the need for each producer to charge the highest prices the market will bear to make a living under these conditions; dissatisfied consumers who feel exploited by both high prices and the lack of quality controls in the industry; and public demands for intervention of the state to redress actual and perceived injustice.

CONCLUSIONS

In the final analysis, Milton Friedman's advocacy of a minimal state is premised on a radically individualistic conception of social justice – just reward in direct proportion to individual contribution to productive output. It is assumed, a priori, that growth in economic output (Adam Smith's "wealth of the nation"), automatically serves the general welfare or common good. By this formulation, other criteria of distributive justice are altogether ignored. There is no room in this formulation for the allocation of social rewards to those, for instance, who make a special contribution to public civility, social solidarity, or active democratic citizenship. (On these issues, see the alternative views of social justice found respectively in the work of the radical individualist Nozick, 1972; the libertarian social democrat Rawls, 1971; and the structural Marxist Harvey, 1973).

Furthermore, other possible criteria of distributive justice entirely unrelated to individual input cannot even be considered in a radically individualistic formulation of the question. Thus, criteria based on need and premised on membership in society or in the political community are bound to be violated by strict application of reward in direct proportion to individual marginal productivity.

A concrete example from Friedman nicely illustrates the flaw in this radically individualist mode of thinking. Friedman's justification for allowing the state to be used to protect individual patents and copyrights is that to do otherwise will confer benefits on third parties for which writers and inventors will not be compensated. Stuck in the rut of commodified exchange relations, Friedman is required to assume that creative individuals are motivated mainly by the prospect of material compensation, and that they owe little if anything to the community that has nurtured them and provided them with the opportunities to learn to be creative. Apart from the question of actual motivation of creative people, a more fundamental problem remains.

If individuals could never be expected to undertake efforts that might confer benefits on others unless they were proportionally compensated, we would indeed have reached the ideal-typical social structure of pure market capitalism. Such a radically individualistic state of social relations would achieve a social world of truly unthinkable dimensions – atomized, impersonal, calculating egos expressing themselves only as economic actors – a world without love or hate, devoid of passion or spontaneity, with neither public life nor social responsibility; in short, a world without community (see Smith, 1979: ch. 5).

6

Market Capitalism and Urban Policy

The radical individualism and inattention to the realities of social structure characteristic of the social theory of market capitalism is nowhere more clearly apparent than in the extensive analysis of urban social services offered by market capitalists. In pursuit of an ahistorical vision of a political economy driven entirely by individual market demand, in a world where many ordinary people have little or no market power, market capitalists have proposed the use of two types of public policy tools to promote market relations. First, they have advocated the use of the tax system to provide a guaranteed minimal income to the poorest of the poor. In Milton Friedman's writings this has taken the form of a proposed "negative income tax" as a substitute for all other redistributive allocations of welfare state capitalism. Market capitalists also have advocated the use of "vouchers" to break up "municipal monopolies" such as urban public schools. The ostensible goal in both instances has been to shift ever more responsibility for allocating resources in society from state to market. It is to this key aspect of the market liberal agenda, the modification of the role of state and market in allocating income and resources, that we turn in this chapter.

MARKET CAPITALISM, THE WELFARE STATE, AND URBAN SOCIAL SERVICES

The general dislike of market capitalists for Keynesian macroeconomic policies designed to stimulate economic growth is paralleled by their objection to forms of state intervention designed to promote greater social equality – be it in the form of progressive taxation, direct social welfare measures to provide services to low income people, or universalistic public policies that remove the provision of a need from the vicissitudes of the marketplace. Their objection to such measures is argued both from principle and from perceived consequence.

As a matter of first principles, for instance, Milton Friedman has argued that using the state either to promote a more equal distribution of income or to broaden access to public services which are better left to the market violates the principle: "To each according to what he and the instruments he own produces" (1962:161–2). Thus, it follows from this principle that progressive taxation takes away the "prizes" of the competitive struggle and the incentive to compete by rewarding the losers in the game of life (1962:163). Furthermore, the norm of allocation according to productive contribution is assumed to be essential to general economic growth and national productivity, for "if what people get is determined by 'fairness' and not by what they produce, where are the prizes to come from" (1979:135).

This sort of formulation is both asociological and ahistorical. First, it ignores the actual historical patterns by which private property relations are reproduced in capitalist societies. These severely handicap some individuals, groups, and classes by advantaging those who possess capital as against labor or land as factors of production and exchange. Furthermore, the "individual" inequalities produced by these property relations tend to be socially reproduced from one generation to the next (see, for instance, Ryan, 1981; Brittain, 1977). Thus, they are often unrelated to the past productive contribution of the individual to society, the fundamental normative principle upon which the market capitalist justification of social inequality rests. This has been true, in comparative-historical context, whether the inherited resource that transmits privilege cross-generationally is inherited wealth, the prestige of a prominent family name, access to higher circles, or the political power of mandarins or a state bureaucratic elite.

Market capitalist Friedman concedes that part of the "prize" of market competition is the direct result of "initial differences in endowment, both of human capacities and of property." Yet unlike the earlier exponent of private accumulation and individualism, John Locke, who foreswore inheritance laws in order to uphold his labor theory of value, Friedman is radically unwilling to do so. Instead, he invents a proposition which allows him to posit the contradictory position that individual rewards should be directly proportionate to productive output and that laws transmitting inherited property are perfectly legitimate. This proposition is that inherited wealth and personal capacity are both forms of parental inheritance – the latter representing a choice by parents to invest in their children's future by giving them cultivation, education, and training while they are alive rather than a bundle of money when they die.

This sort of formulation is indeed very useful to those who enjoy wealth and privilege. In addition to glossing over the above contradiction, focusing analytical attention on families as the unit of analysis deflects attention from the many institutional and structural sources of unequal endowment that have little to do with family choice. Unequal "prizes" in the American political economy often have less to do with past or present personal or family initiative than with the privileged political connections of social background, preferred access to information networks, favorable neighborhood location and other manifestations of systemic class inequality. These structural biases tend to tilt the outcomes of both politics and market exchange. They often *prevent* work and personal initiative from winning prizes. They operate systematically rather than by chance. They thus make a mockery of the old Horatio Alger myth that in the end pluck and luck will lead to just distribution of reward.

Ignoring the role of wealth, status, and power in the allocation of rewards enables market liberals like Friedman to assert that current inequalities of income and wealth in America stem primarily from people's unequal contribution to marginal productivity; that the inequality so produced is no greater than that produced by other political-economic systems; and that the extent of inequality has lessened over time. The first two of these assertions fly in the face of abundant empirical evidence (see, for instance Brittain, 1977; Jencks et al., 1972; Gans, 1972; Wilensky, 1975; Heller, 1967; Ryan, 1981). The third is a more complex historical relationship and depends, significantly, on how inequality and social mobility are measured (see, for instance, Abrahamson, Mizruchi and Hornung, 1976; chs 7–10). Nevertheless, assuming for the sake of argument that Friedman is correct in asserting that inequality has lessened in capitalist societies over time, is it not the case that somewhat more equality has been achieved by the politically mediated advanced capitalist welfare state, which has expanded the size of the pie, and mildly redistributed the size of some of its slices, than by earlier competitive capitalism? Yet Friedman wants it both ways. He wants to treat capitalism per se as historically progressive, while discrediting the capitalist welfare state, the actual historical expression of the development of state structures in societies where capitalism has been the dominant form of economic organization.

This is done, as we have seen, by crediting the market in general for all advances in human liberty, equality of opportunity, creativity, and social progress while blaming all of the contradictions between these goals and actual historical practice on the emergence of a new class of technicians, government administrators, and policy analysts supported by the politically skillful and trade union elites. In this formulation it is not the market but the welfare state technocracy that is responsible for social injustice. The market is a just allocator; the state, either by means of formula allocation (e.g. social security) or by rationing need (e.g. public housing) violates the first principle of just market allocation – to each in proportion to productive output.

This logic underlies Friedman's specific opposition to the entire array of federally financed and locally administered programs to promote social welfare or alleviate poverty. The main lines of argument against each of these attempts to use public policy to allocate life chances are sketched out briefly below. The logic of the overall argument forms the basis of Friedman's defense of a "negative income tax" for the "truly needy" as a sufficient substitute for all nominally redistributive social policies of the welfare state.

Poverty and Social Welfare Policy

Milton Friedman (Friedman and Friedman, 1979:108) has identified a "ragbag of well over 100 federal programs" designed to help "the poor." Among these he lumps together both income based and general entitlements including unemployment compensation, Aid to Families with Dependent Children (AFDC), supplemental security income (SSI), food stamps, rent supplements, Medicare, Medicaid, and Social Security. His chief criticisms of these programs, as applied to income-based entitlements, have become a now familiar litany, forming part of the ideological rationale for the severe budget cuts by the Reagan administration of redistributive urban and social policies. He faults income transfer programs for duplication, waste, fraud, work disincentive, encouraging the growth of bureaucracy, and overstating poverty. He claims that the number of poor people in the United States would decrease by 50 to 75 percent if all of the in-kind income derived from housing, health care and other in-kind transfers were counted as income.

Interestingly, Friedman correctly calls attention to the frequency with which many of the programs that are perceived as progressively redistributive, in actuality benefit middle and upper income groups rather than those of lower income. His explanation for this fact reflects his essential mistrust of the political process as a means to regulate the behavior of the "new class" of policy elites that he so fears.

> The poor lack not only the skills valued in the market, but also the skills required to be successful in the political scramble for funds . . . Once well meaning reformers who may have helped get a welfare measure enacted have gone on to their next reform, the poor are left to fend for themselves and they will almost always be overpowered by the groups that have already demonstrated a greater capacity to take advantage of available opportunities (1979:118).

This logic is at the heart of Friedman's longstanding opposition to Social Security, higher educational subsidies, and direct subsidies to producer interests – that they represent transfer allocations to the politically organized who are able to help themselves while ignoring the "truly needy." While the general thrust of this argument is well taken, as we have seen above Friedman so narrowly defines the "truly needy" as to include only those physically or mentally unable to "help themselves" in the marketplace. It even excludes the aged, who in his view should be foresighted enough during their working years to provide for their own retirement by investing in private annuities (1962:188).

Housing and Urban Development Policies

Ironically, Milton Friedman's market capitalist perspective leads him to reiterate many of the criticisms of federal housing, urban renewal, and land use policies advanced by Marxist critics and often acknowledged by welfare state liberals. For example, it is true, as Friedman points out that the "federal bulldozer" (see Anderson, 1964) has caused much displacement in low income urban neighborhoods and destroyed many liveable units of moderate income housing; that public housing and subsidized housing units are often of poor quality; and that many housing subsidies go to producers rather than consumers of housing. Here the chief beneficiaries have been owners of property located in urban renewal areas, those living in the luxury housing that frequently replaced bulldozed buildings, those who developed commercial property on renewal sites, and property owners in adjacent locations whose property holdings were enhanced by publicly subsidized redevelopment (1979:111–12; 1962:179).

What Friedman fails to acknowledge is that these very same beneficiaries have also reaped most of the benefits of privately financed real estate development and neighborhood gentrification schemes (see Fainstein et al., 1983; Beauregard, 1983; Smith and Keller, 1983). This is because such uneven consequences are largely a result of the structure of private property rights to urban land in the American political economy. The sacrosanct principle of private ownership of land, politically enshrined in a recent ruling of the Reagan appointed Supreme Court (*New York Times,* June 10, 1987:1), encourages speculative investment by land-based capital fractions, whose intended purpose is to disrupt existing land uses and transform them into "higher" uses that translate into profits (see Molotch, 1976, 1979). The adverse effects – displacement of renters, "unearned" neighborhood effects, responsiveness to demands for new land uses backed up by market power – follow directly from this political-economic logic. When not *mediated* by governmentally structured subsidies and incentives, such logic is mediated by the social power and investment priorities of the key private institutions that structure the market in urban land – banks, developers, and major industrial, commercial and service users. In either case the basic political-economic logic of the "growth machine" is the underlying constant; and this constant inevitably entails a destabilizing restructuring of the built environment.

The acknowledged inability of the private market to build decent low income housing at a profit was the reason given to justify the introduction of public housing as an element of federal housing policy in the United States during the New Deal. An apparent awareness of this "market imperfection" prompts market liberals to favor cash grants or "vouchers" for low income renters over either directly provided housing or construction subsidies to builders. Yet, as we have seen in earlier chapters, in the US urban system the acquisition of housing takes place within an institutionally structured setting in which political-economic and social barriers to free access are formidable. Racism, real estate steering practices, exclusionary zoning laws, discriminatory private credit practices, and the deleterious effects of the larger scale restructuring of the built environment discussed above, all stand as major structural barriers to free choice in housing by low income consumers, particularly the low income black renters most likely to be affected by a shift from public housing to rental vouchers.

Empirical research (Hartman, Keating and LeGates, 1981; Myers, 1975; Brooks, 1981) has documented the pervasiveness and intractability of a "dual housing market" in metropolitan areas of the United States which requires more than cash or vouchers to dismantle. This dual market structure channels access to housing by segmenting the market into black and white compartments and then stratifying access to decent housing within each segment on the basis of income. In this context, if nothing else is done on a structural level, vouchers may only contribute to housing inflation for renters by adding to the amount of money in circulation at the bottom of each segment, rather than helping low income people to find decent housing. Thus, market capitalists' stated desire to help the "truly needy" through housing vouchers may well lead to consequences similar to those which have plagued the welfare state liberal housing and urban development strategy – a renewed game of musical chairs in which the rules of the game have not been restructured and the winners and losers can be predicted in advance.

Health Care Policies

Ironically, Milton Friedman's central criticism of Medicare insurance subsidies for the elderly and Medicaid payments for the poor is identical to the one I have just made with respect to housing vouchers, namely that if a policy stimulates increased demand while leaving supply-side factors unaffected, prices are likely to rise (1979:114). In the American political economy, organized physicians are protected from the market pressures of increased supply by the American Medical Association. Acting as a trade union for its members, the AMA has acted to keep supply relatively constant. Hence the infusion of new money and new categories of patients by Medicare and Medicaid funds have made physicians undeservedly wealthy while not necessarily improving either the quality of health or health care in America.

Yet, this trade union, Friedman asserts, is losing its grip on the health care delivery system: it is gradually ceding control to another "monopolistic group," government bureaucrats (1979:221). The government's expanded share of total health expenditures, reaching 42 percent in 1977, has escalated the rate of inflation in health care costs. This, in turn, has created public demand for government to regulate medical procedures to help control costs. Friedman fears that such developments may lead inexorably to socialized medicine (1979:104). Instead of greater reliance on public cost controls (which arguably could break the back of the organized providers that Friedman attacks with some justification in *Free to Choose* as predatory interests) Friedman prefers deregulation of medical licensing to increase the supply of health care providers. Once again, a renewed call for greater competition blinds Friedman both to the contradictions in his argument and to the potentially dangerous consequences of radically deregulating medical licensure.

The "Negative Income Tax"

It is against this ideological backdrop that Friedman has proposed a "negative income tax" as the central market capitalist alternative to the welfare state. He views the measure as a way to use an automatic income transfer to the very bottom of the class structure in order to avoid the appropriation of the benefits of welfare state capitalism by organized special interest groups and the state bureaucracy itself. He advocates the measure as a transitional program to cushion the blow of scrapping the welfare state while preserving work incentive. Foreshadowing the rhetoric of Reaganomics, he argues that the setting of an income floor below which no family could fall, would "assure a safety net" protecting each person and family from "dire distress" (1979:121). The floor would take the form of a cash subsidy, called a "negative income tax," allocated to all families falling below the specified amount of income beyond which those above it begin paying federal income taxes. While his actual dollar amounts have varied over the years, they have been quite low, generally approximating a cutoff point for the income floor of 50 percent of the official poverty level (George and Wilding, 1976:38) or half of the average level of allowances for welfare services, in-kind payments, and the other redistributive subsidies of the federal government (Friedman and Friedman, 1979:122). Individuals or families earning nothing would receive the entire minimally set subsidy. The subsidy would decrease gradually as income increased from zero to the specified cutoff point. Thus, for example, if 50 percent of the average federal government allowances amounted to $4,000 for a family of four, a family earning nothing would receive this amount; if a family earned $1,000, one half of the amount of money earned would be subtracted from the subsidy, for a total income of $4,500; a family earning $2,000, correspondingly, would receive a subsidy of $3,000, for a total income of $5,000; this would continue until the transfer payment reached zero for families earning over $8,000.

Ironically, then, the market liberal Friedman, a relentless critic of the "new class" of technical policy analysts, proposes a technical policy solution to poverty. This raises a number of ironic questions related to the extent to which this proposal might actually compound rather than resolve questions of administrative equity, political rationing, and the growth of bureaucracy. At a minimum, the very complexity of this policy would generate political demands for extensive monitoring. The possibilities of abuse inherent in any self-reporting tax system might well be compounded by encouraging new forms of income concealment by those just above the transfer threshold. This in turn could add to political demands for further administrative monitoring, indeed for surveillance, of the everyday lives of many ordinary citizens. Vigilant policing against possible fraud by bureaucrats, whose enforcement criteria are bound to be abstracted from the empirical circumstances in the everyday lives of the people they monitor, may add yet another dimension of meaning to the role of state administration in "regulating the poor" (Piven and Cloward, 1971). The upshot of this criticism is not to discredit income transfer policies per se, but to point out the futility of purely technical efforts to disconnect poverty from the social, political, and economic context which produces it.

As in the case of poverty, Milton Friedman's analysis of public schooling in late-capitalist America reveals a stark failure to consider the social processes through which individual wants and preferences are socially produced, economically structured, and politically mediated (see Smith, 1979; Taylor-Gooby and Dale, 1981; Lefebvre, 1973:ch. 2). Friedman regards public education in the United States as a primary institutional mechanism through which the institutions of American welfare capitalism have been reproduced. Yet his desire to replace welfare state capitalism by a return to an older set of market capitalist social relations leads him into a series of additional contradictions in his discussion of schooling. These contradictions are most clearly revealed by examining his advocacy of educational "vouchers." It is to this question which we now turn.

MARKET CAPITALISM, URBAN SCHOOLING, AND THE VOUCHER IDEA

Milton Friedman's criticism of public schooling in welfare state capitalism has virtually become one of his cottage industries. His critique is tied to his quest for a complete privatization and commodification of public education by a market-oriented educational voucher system. What does he think is wrong with public schooling in general and urban public schools in particular? How does he propose to remedy these defects through a voucher system? What other measures does he advocate to "reintroduce" market relations in the education and socialization of future generations of workers? These questions highlight the fundamental contradictions of Friedman's voucher idea.

Friedman's basic critique of US public schooling is that, despite limited competition from private, non-profit organizations, public schools are centralized, bureaucratic state monopolies, dominated by professional producer interests (i.e. by organized teachers). Both parental control of the educational process and consumer choice of the educational product have declined in direct proportion to the rising power of the producers of schooling. As an alternative to the conventional welfare state liberal argument that calls for greater investment in educational institutions as the best way to develop human resources, Friedman argues that the educational question is one of cost effectiveness rather than of too little investment in human resources. Why, he asks, are public school parents and taxpayers getting too little result per dollar spent? Teachers, he answers, are overpaid timeservers, protected by union guaranteed seniority and uniform salary schedules. These were obtained through their power in the political process that Friedman so detests. Teachers, so protected, are castigated as "dull, mediocre, and uninspiring," in contrast to the "imaginative, daring, and self-confident" few who are willing to subject themselves to the reward system of the unbridled marketplace (1962:95).

Having said this, Friedman takes the contradictory position that teachers (who have shown themselves capable of seizing the political initiative) are mere pawns of a standardized, bureaucratized curriculum which leaves them too little freedom to experiment with new ways to transmit basic skills. Thus, when it suits his ideological purposes, Friedman shifts the emphasis of his critique from "politics" to "bureaucracy." He never addresses the question why, if teachers are politically so powerful, they have been unable to dominate curricular issues. Nor does he address a further contradiction inherent in his view that the schools are both "overbureaucratized" (and, by implication, unresponsive to outside pressures) *and* overloaded with "social goals" such as increasing the degree of social mobility in society. Where, after all, do these "social goals" come from? When his protagonist is political pressure on the schools to achieve social goals ("the new class"), he conveniently chooses to forget that such goals often have been "imposed" on school systems by external *political* forces – e.g. by popular expectations that public schools should be used to introduce ladders of mobility into the prevailing system of social stratification (see Katznelson and Weir, 1985).

This selective perception and selective inattention to the actual historical processes which have produced the conditions he describes is a flaw that characterizes Milton Friedman's work more generally. Thus, for example, after describing a personal visit to a parochial school which is characterized as providing "quality education" Friedman states: "The youngsters at the school are there because their parents chose it" (1962:159). This curiously asociological formulation was clearly intended to attribute the quality of the school to the element of free choice by parents as consumers in the marketplace. Yet this example can be taken as evidence to support precisely the opposite inference. Persons who "choose" parochial education for their children generally do so because of a deep-seated, socially produced commitment to a traditional, religiously rooted belief system. This "preference" did not derive from the presence of a marketplace. Indeed, it was reinforced precisely because the parents restricted their own and seek to restrict their children's access to an arena of openness and free choice. The quality of the product may stem from the depth of their commitment to using parochial school to reproduce a traditional way of life, a way of life that in actual historical societies has been significantly undermined by the introduction of market forces into traditionally based social relations.

Even this asociological posture is occasionally abandoned by Friedman when it suits his ideological purposes. For example, in discussing the role of the public schools in providing "general education for citizenship," in *Capitalism and Freedom* (1962: 87–91), Friedman holds that such education entails political socialization into a common set of cultural values in addition to providing literacy and increasing general knowledge. True to his radical unwillingness to authorize governmental action except under the particular conditions enumerated earlier, Friedman concludes that the provision of such educational outputs constitutes a general benefit to society at large, a "neighborhood effect," that may justify a state role in basic educational service delivery. Nevertheless, the type of government involvement that he prefers is minimal. He uses the argument that the central purpose of public schooling is to disseminate general knowledge as a political weapon to justify the withdrawal of state subsidies for more explicitly vocational and professional schooling. He would require that all children receive minimal level primary and secondary education only. Furthermore, he argues that market-like arrangements should be developed to place more of the burden of financing this schooling on the parents of children who actually use the schools at the moment. This would shift a proportionate share of the burden away from the general taxpayer which, in his view, amounts to an unjustified burden on "all residents during the whole of their lives," independent of family size (1962:87). In making this argument, Friedman conveniently forgets the positive "spillover effects" that the general taxpayer might receive from a well educated citizenry in terms of possible gains in national economic productivity or enhanced capacity for effective citizen participation in political or social life. Interestingly, it is also evident here that to build political support for his preferred policy positions Friedman is willing to deviate from a radically individualist methodology and ideology to introduce particular class categories into his writings – namely, the conflicting interests of parents versus childless persons, large versus small families, and younger versus older generations in paying for public schooling.

Although he is willing to concede the legitimacy of some types of state involvement in setting minimum standards of literacy and citizen education and in financing a minimum level of education for all citizens, Friedman is radically unwilling to sanction actual direct administration of educational services by the state. This is depicted as a kind of "nationalization" or "monopolization" of the private "educational industry." Starting from this commodified view of education as a consumer product rather than a right of citizens, he advocates that publicly financed educational vouchers be issued to parents of school aged children to be used either in public or private institutions to pay for the cost of all or part of the tuition costs of each of their children's general schooling.

Friedman's voucher proposal was first introduced in what, for him, was a relatively modest form in *Capitalism and Freedom* (1962:93). There he advocated vouchers to break up the monopolistic power of the public schools. He called for a combination of public and private education at the elementary and secondary levels. Parents who chose the private option would receive a voucher equal to the estimated per pupil cost of public schooling in their localities. He hoped that such an arrangement would infuse a healthy competition among educational providers, placate parents who currently felt doubly taxed when they chose the private option, promote variety, and make teachers' salaries more responsive to market forces.

By the early 1970s, as public criticism of urban public education mounted and the "community control" movement was in full flower in many major central cities throughout the United States (see Altshuler, 1970; Fainstein and Fainstein, 1976), Friedman's rhetoric also escalated. He called urban public education "technologically backward," and argued that the market should be used to fundamentally reorganize schooling. To promote the credibility of a more extremely stated version of his voucher idea, he cast it as a "more modest reform" than his preferred alternative. This alternative was to "eliminate compulsory schooling, government operation of schools and government financing of schools except for financial assistance to the indigent" (Friedman, 1973). When compared to such a radical privatization and commodification of education, his more extreme voucher plan did indeed appear "more modest." Nevertheless, a close examination of its content reveals how emboldened Friedman had become during a period of declining economic performance and growing criticism of the welfare state and the urban crisis from both left and right.

As earlier, voucher levels would be set by the per pupil equivalent of current public school spending. Parents would continue to pay taxes. In return they would receive one voucher per school-aged child to spend on the school of their choice. The voucher could be used "anywhere," outside central city boundaries and even out-of-state.

The size of schools would be entirely determined by the size of the market they could attract. It was Friedman's hope that this would cause a hundred flowers to bloom. Indeed, "[v]oluntary organizations – ranging from the Boy Scouts to the YMCA – could set up schools and try to attract customers" (1973). Not only would Friedman create markets among schools. "Divisible vouchers" would make possible the disaggregation of market power by subject and even by course.

Vouchers could be spent, if desired, at parochial schools. Anticipating objection to this part of the plan on constitutional grounds, Friedman argued, quite asociologically, that if necessary, vouchers could be restricted to only the "secular part" of their curriculum, reserving the "religious part" for after school hours funded entirely by private tuition. This would be tantamount to requiring such schools to become schizoid, setting aside their basic motivating purpose, as if ethics and values could be entirely divorced from secular society. Once again Friedman engages in the construction of a sociologically impracticable legal fiction. It is radically unlikely that even to gain public financial support in the form of vouchers, parochial schools would be willing to set aside their core religious beliefs and assumptions when teaching such "secular" subjects as contemporary social issues, the history of war, the biology of conception, or the sociology of marriage and the family.

As in this instance, so also in the case of his anticipated effect of vouchers on the American class structure, Friedman seems to believe that market forces can break up any social structure, no matter how enmeshed in cultural belief or how supported by asymmetrical networks of social stratification. He predicts that vouchers would open up such currently jurisdictionally sheltered suburban public schools as Beverly Hills, California; Lake Forest, Illinois; and Scarsdale, New York to possible class diversity. Ignoring the existing practice of educational tracking, which amounts to a form of class segregation *within* even large "magnet" schools (see Bowles, 1971), Friedman further predicts that schools would be encouraged to excel in particular programs by his "divisible vouchers" and would thereby attract a more hetero-geneous clientele. This would help to reduce race and class segregation in American life. Once again, this formulation conveniently ignores the subsidy his plan would give to those at the upper reaches of the class structure to create new exclusive enclaves if the ones they are already intentionally using to reproduce their power and privilege were suddenly integrated by race and class. Friedman further overlooks the incentive such a plan would create to fraudulent educational enterprises to set up shop in low and moderate income areas, where real or imagined consumer gullibility about the economic returns of particular forms of post-primary education has prompted such market behavior even without a voucher system. (See, for example, *Boston Globe,* 1974; *New Orleans Times Picayune-States Item,* 1985.)

Friedman has consistently argued that his proposals would benefit the urban poor because an educational voucher would be used to enable needy families to exercise the same "free choice" now open to those who have the financial means to send their children to the suburban school of their choice. Lost in this formulation is any willingness to acknowledge that in a class stratified society, equal access to a voucher is not the same as equal access to a school. This is because access to the information needed to make effective use of the voucher is itself socially stratified (see Olivas, 1981).

Studies of the information networks used by poor and disadvantaged population groups reveal that although the dissemi-nation of program information is a crucial element of effective service delivery, "poor persons use informal, oral, familial networks and are less likely to have access to information resources than are more advantaged populations" (Olivas, 1981). Olivas

(1981:140), a close student of class based information inequities, concludes that rather than increasing the chances of low income consumer sovereignty, "a complex voucher system would more likely decrease the participation of low income families, as oral information and informal networks would be inadequate to convey complicated data on school characteristics or parental prerogatives to organize and establish new schools."

Schools in a metropolitan area, after all, as complex organizations, are more difficult to compare, even for sophisticated consumers, than food in a supermarket, radios in an appliance store, or even individual housing units (see, for instance DeGregori, 1974). Formal efforts to breach this class-based information gap are only likely to further advantage those information rich strata of the population most used to dealing with formalized channels of information and communication flows, thereby leading to even greater inequality of result than otherwise exists. In sum, poor people lack the experience, skills and positive relationship to bureaucratic intermediaries that might make the voucher an effective consumer tool.

In his more recent work *Free to Choose* (1979:161, emphasis added) Friedman goes a step further with his voucher idea, arguing that "parents should be permitted to use the vouchers . . . not only at schools in their own district, city or state, but at *any* school that is willing to accept their child. That would give . . . every parent greater opportunity to choose." Who, however, can be expected to know about such wider alternatives? Would not this global expansion of the voucher idea merely amount to a subsidy to the wealthy to send their children to expensive out of-state private schools well know within elite social circles, less known in middle-class communities, and virtually unheard of in urban ghettos? It is not paternalism but realism to recognize the limits that class inequality places on some people's freedom to choose.

In each of Friedman's plans there would be a state role in the process of setting minimal standards for the individual educational enterprise and certifying these standards. This raises the socio-political question of the risks posed by state certification of sectarian or church related schools. Friedman has been evasive and contradictory in addressing this question.

On the one hand, in responding to secular liberal critics of his voucher plan who have argued that it would violate the principle of separation of church and state, Friedman actually mirrors an essential facet of the neo-Marxist criticism of the functions of schooling in capitalist societies (see, for instance, Bowles and Gintis, 1976). He states:

> Public schools teach religion too – not formal theistic religion, but a set of values and beliefs that constitute a religion in all but name. The present arrangements abridge the ... freedom of those who do not accept the religion taught by the public schools yet are forced to pay to have their children indoctrinated with it, and to pay still more to have their children escape indoctrination (Friedman, 1979:164).

On the other hand, having thus distracted attention from the issue by upholding sectarian schools as sources of cultural pluralism, he also argues that if market forces are allowed to work their magic, "bad products," including religious schools which inhibit free thought will be driven from the marketplace. He speculates that as competition among schools expands choices and efficiently meets consumer demand, "the final result may ... be that parochial schools would decline rather than grow in importance." Once again, this conjecture ignores the fact that such schools have survived and even prospered in a secular culture because demand for their traditional, religiously based "wares" has been institutionally socialized. If this were not so, we would expect to see many Lutherans and Jews, for instance, already choosing to send their children to high quality Catholic parochial schools (and vice versa) available in the "educational marketplace" rather than making financial sacrifices to maintain schools of their own.

A fear that a voucher system would undermine the ability of the state to socialize citizens into the dominant secular-liberal ideology of welfare state capitalism (the secular religion alluded to in Friedman's earlier statement) has prompted opposition to Friedman's voucher idea. Characteristically, in responding to these sorts of criticisms Friedman again shifts gears. He holds that vouchers would not undermine public education as a "unifying force" in society because existing social arrangements already have undermined the effectiveness of schools as agencies of political socialization. In his words (1962:92): "Under present arrangements, stratification of residential areas effectively restricts the intermingling of children from decidedly different backgrounds. In addition, parents are not now prevented from sending their children to private schools. Only a highly limited class can or does so, parochial schools aside, thus producing further stratification."

This statement represents a recognition by Friedman of the realities of class stratification and of unequal access to "cultural capital" (Bourdieu and Passeron, 1977). Yet Friedman is unwilling to see that his very critique of welfare capitalist social arrangements undermines his radically individualistic assumptions about the potentially beneficent effects of commodified education by means of educational vouchers.

Class and subcultural segregation and stratification currently limit the patterns of social intercourse in American society. The social milieus in which differently situated classes, strata, and subcultures live their everyday lives are both enabling and constraining social worlds (see Smith, 1979: chs. 5–6). They enable marginal subcultures to reproduce values that are unavailable in other milieus while constraining particular classes or strata from acquiring access to the structures of opportunity available to more privileged classes. The class-specific milieus of everyday life are limited, partial, particularistic social worlds. People acquire much of the information on which they act in their everyday life from other people found within their own social networks. To the extent that this is so, the nature and quality of the information provided within a person's social milieu vitally effects his or her "consumer choices." If key sources of information and networks of referral are not normally part of one's everyday world, one is forced to "choose" from a fairly narrow range of options, sometimes from alternatives which are not really choices at all.

For example, in the everyday life of the black urban ghettos of America, the ghetto dweller's consumer choices are restricted to one among many price inflated stores found in a segregated neighborhood; medical care available through state subsidized medical care may be limited to treatment in an emergency room of a public hospital; the choice of schools, even with the availability of state subsidized vouchers, is limited to the schools, usually public, which are familiar to the other members of his or her social network.

Despite these realities of social structure, partially acknowledged in the previous quotation, Friedman shies away from the obvious implication of structured inequality for the effectiveness of his voucher idea. In a context of class structured inequalities in access to information, the means of mobility, and awareness of options falling considerably outside one's immediate everyday milieu, opening up a marketplace to rational choices among consumer-parents is unlikely to reduce race and class inequality (unless, of course, specific measures are also undertaken to eliminate these systemic inequalities). Indeed, the voucher formula proposed by Friedman may even exacerbate these inequalities, because it would make a per capita voucher available to all, regardless of income. This, in turn, would allow more affluent parents to "top-up" their vouchers to send their children to the school of their choice. In this way, affluent parents who currently send their children to exclusive private schools, entirely at their own expense, would actually receive a state subsidized voucher to supplement their private expenditure. Having previously paid both taxes for public schools and tuitions for private schools, affluent recipients of educational vouchers could use their voucher as a cash transfer either to reduce their personal contribution to private tuition or to afford even more exclusive private schooling.

If nothing is done to restructure social class inequality (or, at minimum, to structure access to information about the quality and links to social mobility of present educational alternatives) the voucher idea can be expected to reinforce the reproduction of unequal class relations instead of ushering in a new era of consumer sovereignty. It may even worsen the situation by subsidizing affluent parents and rewarding those institutions most adept at salesmanship. While doing this, it may add yet another dimension of ideological legitimation to the system which produces these unequal outcomes by causing winners to attribute the outcomes to the wisdom of their "consumer choice" in the apolitical marketplace and losers to blame themselves for their misjudgment.

POLITICS REVISITED

The error of Keynesian "fine-tuning" was to abstract the technical stimulation of economic demand from the political demands and expectations which disrupted administration of "the economy" by technocrats and fueled prolonged inflation. The error of Friedman's proposed technical interventions to eliminate deficient urban public schools, poverty, inadequate housing, and inequalities in health care is that public policy analysis cannot be abstracted from the admixture of conflicting political demands, bureaucratic interests, and the changing balance of class forces that are crystallized in the formulation and modification of public policies over historical time. There simply is no technical "quick-fix" for social conditions that have been structurally produced, bureaucratically mediated, and modified in time and space by the changing organization of political demand in the advanced societies. The social and political power relations embodied in this demand differentially express the interests of segments of capital and labor, state officials, geographic localities, and the particularistic groupings that comprise actual civil societies.

Perhaps it is this detachment from real historical time, this ahistoricity, which accounts for Friedman's misstatements of fact and misinterpretation of history on those occasions when he cites historical evidence to buttress his theoretical arguments. Thus, for instance, Friedman has attributed the rapid economic growth of the United States in the 19th century and America's current world agricultural leadership (1979:3–4) to its ascendancy as a free market society. Such an attribution flies in the face of abundant historical evidence (McConnell, 1966; Wolfe, 1977; Tyler, 1980) that protectionist national government policies contributed most to 19th century American economic growth. From 1828 to 1914 the United States government erected ever higher protectionist walls to protect developing American industry. At times, tariff rates were set so high as to not merely discourage foreign competition but to virtually eliminate it.

Furthermore, despite the popular stereotype that 19th century America was a laissez faire society, in reality American state and local governments played an important role in supporting the development of commercial capitalism by subsidizing the modernization of transportation and commercially useful infra-structure — turnpikes, canals, and some railroads. As a result of interregional rivalries that led to a sectional division of the national legislature, the national state's role was at that time relatively limited, but state governments and particular cities engaged in active competition to develop their respective economies by political means. This meant that other local public services were often quite limited because the public costs of economic promotionalism often ran quite high.

Likewise, in the 20th century the United States has not become the world's agricultural leader by dint of market forces, but because of strong federal government support for the development of agricultural technology, land grant colleges and universities, price supports to large agricultural landholders, and various other subsidy policies. The upshot has been an increasingly economically concentrated agricultural sector, the very opposite of the free market ideal.

As with the United States, so also with Britain, Friedman attributes rapid economic growth to the beneficence of market liberalism. He argues (1979) that from the early to the late 19th century the government share of national income in Britain decreased, while economic growth expanded rapidly, and the standard of living of the ordinary citizen improved dramatically. Apart from the fact that the condition of the "ordinary citizens" of the working class districts of 19th century Manchester (see Engels, 1844; Marcus, 1974) fit this characterization only when compared to the marginal condition of subsistence peasants of a pre-industrial age, a more fundamental analytical weakness flaws this argument. Friedman compares an early 19th century society, when government spending was around 25 percent of national income, with the end of the century when it was around 10 percent. But in several respects these two periods are not comparable. First, the dominant mode of production in each period was radically different. Early 19th century Britain was an admixture of agrarian and mercantilist commercial capitalism. By the end of the century *industrial* capital's hegemonic rise had radically transformed the mode of production and geometrically expanded the gross national income. It had done so in all of the industrializing societies, to varying degree, regardless of whether interventionist public policies promoted laissez faire liberalism, as, for a time, they did in Britain, or whether state intervention promoted other models of industrial development, as in the protectionist United States or in the shifting relations between state, capital, and the emergent working class which shaped continental European political economies. In short, industrialization, not the market or a noninterventionist state, accounted for the growth in national income. And the political state was used in different ways by national industrialists to insure their "lion's share" of the new growth. The greatly expanded national income left many things for the state to do with resources that, in absolute terms, greatly exceeded state resources in the pre-industrial age a century earlier.

CONCLUSIONS

A central question of urban political economy thus becomes whose interests become crystallized in state policy at what level in given historical periods and to what purposes are national, state, and local governments put. Before the emergence of political parties and trade unions to pursue strategies of collective action few interests of ordinary working people were crystallized in state policy at any level. Now that they have been partially incorporated in various public policies, forces on the political right have adopted the rhetoric of market capitalism to attack precisely those elements of the political structure of welfare state capitalism that have protected working people from the worst excesses of the necessarily unequal exchange between buyers and sellers of labor power in the productive sphere.

For without some channels of access to the political state, ordinary people, Adam Smith's "necessitous" classes, are not free to choose. They must consent to the unequal exchange relationship between buyers and sellers of labor power or go hungry. Industries are free to locate their activities in necessitous communities and regions. Those who have only their labor to sell are not equally free to bargain with employers who can hold out longer or move, if it suits their interest.

In this context, we would do well to reflect on the insightful observation of market liberalism's mentor Adam Smith (1976:84). "Masters [employers] are always and everywhere in a sort of tacit but constant and uniform combination, not to raise the wages above their natural level [i.e., the level of physical reproduction of labor as a factor of production]. . . . We seldom hear of this combination because it is the usual . . . state of things which nobody even hears of."

When the state is not consciously used to modify the domination of allocative resources by the social relations of wage labor, state officials operate in a context which necessarily tilts toward capitalistic "imperatives" (Lindblom, 1977; Giddens, 1981). This is because, in the capitalistic societies, state revenues, like ordinary people's employment, are dependent on the activities of employers of wage labor. Thus, in the absence of "pressures from below," the public policy outputs of the state are likely to adapt ordinary people to the requirements of capitalistic employers. With politically conscious efforts to use the state to modify these "requirements," to offset the narrow blindness of "market justice," to free people from absolute dependence on wage labor for survival, and to redistribute the political experience necessary to do so, there is at least the chance that the state will partially embody those elements which stand in contradictory relation to the accumulation needs of capital.

7
Reaganomics and Urban Development

The economic historian Brebner (1948:60) has shown that in the first half of the 19th century in Britain, when laissez faire ideology was in full flower:

> [as] the state took its fingers off commerce ... it simultaneously put them on industry and its accompaniments; and ... industry, having by 1850 used its slogan with considerable success against the landed oligarchy, promptly directed it, with some Spencerian and Darwinian trimmings, against its allies, the laborers, who were becoming convinced that the vote was a natural right of man.

These uses of state power were the results of political struggle. Industrial capitalists and their utilitarian allies initially promoted public policies opposed to the use of state power to subsidize the landed aristocracy. Then, landed interests, at times before 1848, with working class allies, used state power (justified on humanitarian, anti-industrial grounds) to intervene in the emergent industrial economy with reformist legislation. This use of state power was the forerunner of British "Tory Planning." After the working class political uprisings of 1848, all forms of property, defending their common class interest against developing democratic tendencies, seized upon various rationales for Social Darwinism. Confronting a more politicized labor movement, propertied interests converged around an ideology of extreme laissez faire. Labor, in its turn, demanded state intervention by a democratically responsive state.

This example illustrates that demands for both laissez faire and for state intervention constitute pressures for state policies to be used to structure access to life chances. The dynamics of the political struggle to obtain governmental protections or market privileges have always depended on the current balance of power among the principal contending interests. As Brebner (1948) explains:

> These interests strove to be the state, to use state power for economic and social ends. Occasionally one or the other triumphed with considerable purity, but never for long, and usually the political enactments represented compromises among them. In the large power passed from the land to other forms of wealth and from them to the people, but as it did so, and as these three political-economic elements moved in and out of the possible combinations of two against one, there was an astonishingly constant inclination to resort to the Benthamite formula for state intervention.

State interventions into civil society as a result of this politically driven dynamic have been cumulative. Politics has been the agency used by groups, classes, and class segments to improve their market advantages or compensate for their disadvantages. State policy has become an essential element in shaping the character of the advanced capitalist societies. Various segments of capital have extracted new services, new subsidies, and new forms of "license" from the state; those adversely affected by the development of this state-mediated political-economic order have likewise sought new forms of support and protection from the state. As a result, the cumulative contradictions of societal development have come to be embodied in the frequently contradictory public policies constituting modern welfare states.

As we have seen in previous chapters, the development of the American variant of welfare capitalism has been mediated by historically specific political structures which are important elements in shaping the particular forms that both the urban crisis and state responses to it have taken. Institutional aspects of the American political structure, such as fiscal federalism and the relative autonomy of the local government have been "exceptionalist" dimensions of the representation of interests central to understanding the urban fiscal crisis in the United States. Moreover, both the ways in which the major US political parties have come to overrepresent business interests and the particular forms that working class self-organization has taken in pursuit of state policies (see McConnell, 1966; Skocpol and Inkelberry 1983; Ginsberg, 1984) are additional aspects of the uniqueness by which non-capitalist interests have been incorporated into US urban policies. In the American political economy working-class political action has traditionally been fragmented by ethnic, geographic, and sectional differentiation. No working-class political parties have developed. The non-capitalist beneficiaries of public policies have generally been categorically "needy" segments of the working class. "Need" has been politically defined by such practices as the periodic popular mobilizations, the labelling of "need" by reformist professionals, and the political interests of presidential candidates in search of reliable voting blocks.

The uneven distributional effects of federal entitlement programs have created new social divisions among the working class. Combined with the further decomposition of the working class through the operation of the uneven distributional effects of the "fiscal welfare" state, these state policies have served to undermine the New Deal public philosophy of interest group pluralism. This public philosophy previously served to legitimate the contradictory distributional effects of US welfare capitalism (Lowi, 1969). The legitimation deficit faced by welfare state liberal economic and social policies, exacerbated by declining economic performance and fiscal crises, has prompted an effort by forces on the political right to develop an alternative legitimating political-economic ideology. At the level of national policy making, the resurgent ideology of "market liberalism," originally rendered ineffective by the twin realities of the Great Depression and growing corporate economic concentration, has proven useful once again as an alternative rationale for a renewed quest for a higher rate of economic growth to be achieved by a lowered social wage, chastened workers, weaker unions, and more accommodative communities. In the previous two chapters the theoretical weaknesses of this "market liberal" effort to disconnect economics from politics and people from their social context were explored. In this chapter the urban consequences of the effort by the Reagan administration to re-enshrine market capitalism as a "new" public philosophy are assessed. The chapter explores the socioeconomic and political implications of this approach for the future course of American cities and the people living in them.

THE IDEOLOGY OF THE MARKET: "URBAN ENTERPRISE ZONES"

The Reagan administration has sought to legitimate an urban policy of "enterprise zones" on the ground that "relief of taxes, regulations, and other government burdens [would] spur the formation of new business activity, which [would] create employment opportunities in designated areas" (GAO, 1982: 1). Reagan's proposal was a variant of a bill originally proposed by Congress-persons Kemp and Garcia, who represent the declining Snowbelt urban areas of Buffalo and the South Bronx. The Kemp–Garcia proposal combined extensive business tax incentives with "regulatory relief" designed to attract new firms to locate in designated "depressed areas." Because of strong opposition from labor and environmentalist organizations at the national level to the deregulation proposals, the modified Reagan "enterprise zone" proposal focused instead on offering a package of tax exemptions and shelters to lure business to declining locations.

Businesses agreeing to locate in "enterprise zones" would gain the elimination of their capital gains taxes and the sheltering of one-half of their earned income. If they were designated as "free trade zones" they also would be exempt from tariff and import duties. Employers hiring "disadvantaged workers" in the zones would receive additional tax credits for each such person employed. Creditors granting loans to firms agreeing to locate in designated zones would be allowed to shelter one-half of the interest income earned from their loans. In late 1983 these tax provision changes were estimated by the Treasury Department to amount to a $1 billion annual loss of tax revenues.

Although "enterprise zones" was originally justified as an "urban" policy that would recentralize investment in decaying inner cities, the modified Reagan proposal made eligible nearly 2,000 depressed areas, including rural pockets of poverty and Indian reservations. State and local governments were to nominate areas for possible designation. While this might seem to create an opening for a wide variety of possible political "winners," local governments offering nominations would be required to offer additional indicators of "local commitment" such as local tax breaks and regulatory concessions to business interests or "privatization" of (i.e., "contracting out" to private businesses for) public service delivery before they would be considered for designation as an "enterprise zone" by Reagan's Department of Housing and Urban Development (see Goldsmith, 1982a, and b).

Because Democrats have not wished to allow Ronald Reagan to claim credit for a policy symbolizing concern for urban problems, national "enterprise zone" legislation has not been passed by the Democratic controlled House Ways and Means Committee, whose chairman has called the proposal a "gimmick." Despite the absence of national legislation however, 19 state governments concerned about capital flight have activated such zones or passed zone legislation. Ten other states have passed zone legislation, but have not yet designated any zones. As of late 1982, over 60 related bills were pending in other states (for a fuller discussion of state and local policy responses to capital flight see chapter 9 below).

Based on experience with similar policies in Great Britain, Italy and Puerto Rico, critics have questioned the ability of the policy to create new jobs at stable wage levels in depressed urban areas (see Walton, 1982; Massey, 1982; Goldsmith, 1982a and b; Aronowitz and Goodman, 1981; Malone, 1982; Harrison, 1982; Stewart, 1981; Aronowitz, 1981). Moreover, Reagan's extension of the zone concept to rural areas to garner political support is likely to offset any recentralizing effect the policy might have if limited to distressed central cities. More importantly, the very logic of the policy is to heighten the intense competition for business investment among fiscally distressed local governments and to compound their immediate revenue shortages in exchange for an elusive promise of stable jobs and future tax revenues generated by economic growth.

The stated goal of the "enterprise zone" policy is to achieve a high rate of growth of new, small, labor-intensive enterprises within the zones. But as Walton (1982) and Harrison (1982) have shown, new firms do not generally show much profit earlier than their first four to seven years of operation. Thus, tax breaks are of very little use to such new firms.

For this reason, unless a publicly financed capital pool were made available for the explicit purpose of starting up new businesses in depressed urban areas, the main beneficiaries of the incentives contained in existing and proposed "enterprise zone" legislation would be existing large firms that make enough profits to benefit from the various tax shelter and capital gains tax breaks. Located in the primary labor market, such employers (e.g. producers of business and professional services) are unlikely to create new employment opportunities for the relatively unskilled workers living in declining urban areas. In fact, because of the dynamics of real estate speculation, they may even further reduce employment opportunities among this strata. If an "enterprise zone" underwent rapid redevelopment as the result of the incentives we have been discussing, this would create pressures to inflate land values and rents within the area, triggering the process of "gentrification," and thus threatening to drive out many longstanding smaller firms renting buildings in the area, which often employ local labor. Eventually, this dynamic also might put a brake on further investment, as inflated land prices and rents began to offset the returns from tax incentives to even large investors (see Stewart, 1981:6).

THE REALITIES OF POWER: FISCAL AND MILITARY KEYNESIANISM

Although Ronald Reagan has advocated the creation of "enterprise zones" as a symbolic market liberal policy for revitalizing declining central city areas like the South Bronx, the basic logic of his larger blueprint for economic recovery was destined to overshadow any impact, good or ill, that such a policy might have. Reagan's taxing and spending policies further eroded the economic foundations of many distressed industrial cities, while creating new problems for the already overburdened physical infrastructure of growing Sunbelt cities.

The Reagan tax cut proposals for individual taxpayers were sold to Congress and the public as an effort to shift power from a bloated centralized government to individual citizens at the grassroots. It was further claimed that those who received a substantial tax cut would save or invest it in economic development rather than spend it. This has not happened. Following Reagan's initial "supply-side" tax cuts, plant investment within the United States actually declined by 5 percent in 1982 (Yago, 1983:127). Furthermore, by the third year of the Reagan Administration, when cyclical recovery proceeded at a pace that exceeded most economists' expectations, it had become clear, ironically, that affluent taxpayers had spent most of their tax windfall on consumption, thus producing an unintended massive dose of Keynesian aggregate demand stimulation to the depressed economy (Kilborn, 1983).

Because Reagan was unable politically to cut social programs significantly further than his first round of severe cuts, his massive tax cuts were combined with deficit financing of the huge military buildup. Both factors gave a stimulus to the weak economy; but the reasons for the stimulus were not those predicted by supply side theorists. Instead of saving their tax cut, consumers spent it. The savings rate actually went down. Thus by the second quarter of 1983 the economy began a swing upward. This accelerated throughout 1983 as more disposable income was channeled into consumer spending instead of savings or investment. This fostered a consumer led recovery and a mild decline in general unemployment. Defense spending fostered new rounds of growth in those localities and regions best situated to benefit from this shift in federal spending priorities.

Furthermore, because the previously discussed "recapitalization" strategy has combined high profits with weakened labor resistance, inflation was significantly reduced. As one commentator has said (Kilborn, 1983:29): "Consumers took the tax cut and spent it. People started buying houses and automobiles, and businesses accelerated production so the economy boomed. Profits soared, relieving industry of pressure to raise prices, and some companies, such as Greyhound . . . dug in their heels against wage increases, so inflation abated."

Yet the beneficial impacts of this "recovery" have been distributed very unevenly by place, class, and economic sector. Many central city political economies continue to be structurally distressed islands in a sea of general cyclical recovery. This is particularly true of those cities highly dependent on heavy industry which is moving to Third World production sites as part of the unfolding internationalization of production. The upshot of this development is a growing crisis of disinvestment in specific sectors and localities. The inequalities produced by the differential corporate economic investment pattern have been compounded by key public policy priorities of the current national ruling political elites.

Thus, for instance, a second aspect of Reagan's economic recovery strategy, the rapid increase of defense expenditures, has added to the structural crisis in many distressed older industrial cities. Reagan's increases over and above Carter's sizable expansion of the defense budget have expanded employment in defense-related industries. But as a long-term byproduct of patterns of defense-related industrial investment, military procurement policies, and the distribution of power in congressional committees, the lion's share of most major defense industries, as well as defense installations themselves, are located in suburbs and Sunbelt states. Thus, a shift from domestic spending for social programs to defense spending has actually worsened the plight of many of the Snowbelt cities that have been hardest hit by structural job shifts, decaying industrial facilities, and fiscal crises.

Under Reagan the regional distribution of Federal funds to state and local governments shifted even further in the direction of growing Sunbelt states. In part this was due to previous economic and demographic changes reflected in new census figures used in formula grants. In part, also, however, Reagan's shift in priorities to defense and highway spending and away from employment, mass transit, and environmental grant programs has tilted the regional distribution toward the southwest and Rocky Mountain states and away from declining industrial cities and states (Herbers, 1983a:1).

In view of these effects, central city political leaders in declining cities and states have experienced a multidimensional crisis of major proportions. The Reagan fiscal policies have cut subsidies for their ailing infrastructures, mass transit systems, social welfare programs and neighborhood development programs. Comprehensive Employment Training (CETA) programs, which despite some abuses, produced training, employment, and workers to deliver basic city services, were no longer available to cushion the stress of economic decline. In return, local leaders were initially reassured that untargeted tax provisions to allow business more rapid depreciation for investment in new buildings and equipment offered a "new beginning" to declining industrial cities. Yet as in the past, these tax expenditures only served to accelerate corporate disinvestment from many declining industrial cities to "new" and more profitable forms of investment like real estate and more "flexible" points of production where the political power of workers was weaker.

THE URBAN IMPACTS OF BUDGET CUTS

Richard Nathan and his associates (1983) recently completed a very useful study of the impact of the Reagan cuts on cities like Boston, Newark, Cleveland, Phoenix, Chicago, St Louis, Houston, Los Angeles, Seattle, and Rochester (New York), Orlando (Florida), Jackson (Mississippi), Tulsa (Oklahoma), and Sioux Falls (South Dakota). These researchers found that:

1 The adverse impact was greatest for larger cities which were obligated to provide housing and services to those cut from welfare rolls at a time of local fiscal crises exacerbated by the recession.

2 The coincidence of the cuts with changes in aid formulas as a result of employment and demographic shifts meant that the adverse impact was far more severe in the case of older cities like St Louis and Cleveland, whose more mobile residents had left with the economic crisis, leaving behind an immobile, dependent, virtually unemployable poor population with pressing service needs.

3 The increased authority given to state governments under several Reagan program shifts led to a shifting of funds for various community services from cities to electorally more powerful suburbs and surrounding counties; thus, many community agencies that had provided assistance to inner-city residents in localities where "have not" interests were politically represented were forced to close.

4 The inequities of public service delivery packages and local levels of spending produced by these political changes (already considerable prior to the Reagan presidency for reasons spelled out in chapter 1) increased the sectoral, state and city unevenness.

Compounding these imbalances has been the uneven social class impact of the fact that approximately $6 in every $10 cut by the Reagan administration in support for state and local governments was obtained from programs for low income people *(New York Times,* February 28, 1982:19). Furthermore, grants-in-aid to states and localities dropped by $9 billion dollars between 1981 and 1982 and by $13 billion in the following year. This has meant that most major central cities have been forced by the new fiscal realities to reduce many service programs. Most recent research has indicated that collective consumption or "human service" expenditures have suffered the most adverse cutbacks as a result of this forced fiscal austerity (Judd and Mosqueda, 1982). Let us consider in detail the impacts of New Right changes in two major "human services" programs.

SOCIAL CLASSES AND NEW RIGHT HOUSING
POLICIES

The class bias of Reagan's housing policies was evident from the outset of his presidency. The $30 billion previously authorized for public housing and rent supplements for low and moderate income people was reduced by $12 billion. The number of planned new units of such housing was cut by 39 percent from 254,000 to 154,000 units. Rent supplements were also reduced for those who received such benefits. Low income recipients of subsidized housing were required to pay 30 percent rather than 25 percent of their adjusted income for rent. Initially, physical development programs like Community Development Block Grants (CDBG) and Urban Development Action Grants (UDAG) fared better. The former was cut marginally from $3.9 billion to $3.6 billion; the latter from $650 million to $500 million (*New York Times*, March 20 1983:E3; Pear, 1983:9).

To reduce the scope of housing support for low and moderate income renters, eligibility requirements were changed so that only those earning 50 percent or less of the regional median income could qualify for rent supplements. Previously the maximum income of eligible recipients could be as high as 80 percent of the median income (Oser, 1983:14). These changes were justified as restricting public subsidies only to the "truly needy," thus making rental subsidies nominally more redistributive to a smaller number of eligibles. This has been a classic Republican party strategy for cutting public spending for social programs while offering benefits to those at the very bottom of the social structure.

In contrast, to these tightened restrictions for direct supplements for renters, no limitations were placed on indirect subsidies to homeowners though the tax code. Therefore, the impact of this policy change was to increase further the already existing bias in public subsidies away from renters, cities, and economically and more socially integrated housing toward homeowners, suburbs, and more class segregated housing.

Mortgage interest tax deductions not only have no ceilings, they also apply to second homes. Policy recommendations to set a limit or "cap" on the amount that any taxpayer can deduct for housing interest or to restrict the benefits to people's primary residence have not been treated as feasible options in public discussion. Even when forced to the surface by the fiscal crisis of the federal government precipitated by Reagan tax cuts and expansionary defense spending policies, these sacrosanct subsidies for home ownership were retained while other tax expenditures fared less well in the 1986 congressional debate on comprehensive tax reform. This is not surprising – both the real estate industry and a sizable segment of the population now benefit from the inflation prone dual housing subsidy system.

To address the inability of many renters to afford prevailing market rents, the Reagan administration's proposed housing voucher program would expand an existing limited experimental voucher program, while eliminating all other low to moderate income housing programs, such as the Section 8 rent subsidy program. Reagan's housing voucher proposal would target only the very poor. Furthermore, as in the case of public housing policy changes, the voucher scheme would require the "beneficiaries" of vouchers to pay a larger share of their meager incomes for their rent than they previously were required to pay under existing housing policies.

A 1982 study of the probable impact of this housing voucher program on low-income families in New York City, conducted by the Pratt Institute Center for Community Development, found that because of its restrictive scope of beneficiaries, its use as a substitute for all other housing aid programs, and the limited funds to be made available under it, the Reagan housing voucher program would have a "devastating" impact on the ability of low income New Yorkers to find adequate shelter. Not only would it directly produce a net loss in federal housing aid to low income renters, it also would indirectly reduce complementary private sector housing investment by $281 million over a five year period and eliminate the 7,000 housing related jobs the existing government housing aid programs would have stimulated (Daniels, 1981:73).

The Pratt Institute study pointed out that the program had three additional deficiencies: (1) It failed to take into consideration supply-side factors in metropolitan housing markets such as the very low vacancy rate of 2.13 percent in inhabitable private rental housing in New York. (2) It failed to take into account that avoiding the targeting of available funds to declining neighborhoods could lead to "wholesale abandonment" of such neighborhoods, as remaining inhabitants gave up hope of reversing decline. (3) It ignored the special problems of the "working poor," of minorities, and of larger poor families, which studies have shown must spend the largest percent of their income for housing.

REAGANOMICS LABOR POLICIES

Several policy changes, all having important implications for working-class Americans, also have had significant adverse impacts on living conditions in declining industrial cities. Consider the following dimensions of what might collectively be regarded as federal "employment policy," under the regime of Reaganomics.

The public service employment component of the CETA program, which, despite some abuses, generated jobs for its beneficiaries at relatively low cost per worker, has been terminated. Not only the direct employment loss by workers but also the indirect loss of public services provided to local governments by people with CETA jobs must be considered a key adverse urban impact of eliminating this program. In Rochester, New York, for example, CETA workers had repaired streets and sidewalks, and performed clerical work in the police department to allow more officers to walk their beat (*New York Times,* March 25, 1981:10). Eliminating the program for the CETA workers also eliminated these services for the general working population.

Reagan's revision of Trade Adjustment Assistance benefits which had paid cash benefits to industrial workers who had lost jobs because of import competition, drastically cut income maintenance benefits to people living in declining industrial cities in favor of much cheaper relocation assistance subsidies (Pear, 1983:8). This reduced the capital in circulation in declining industrial cities and encouraged further outmigration from such areas. The number of beneficiaries of the restructured program dropped from over a half million in 1980 to under 30,000 in 1982 (Pear 1981:8).

The impact of the Reagan administration's budget cuts on the "working poor," disproportionately concentrated in central cities, was devastating. A study conducted by the Center of Welfare Policy at the University of Chicago, for instance, found that a working poor mother of two school-aged children in New York City would lose 15 percent of her monthly disposable income as a result of the Reagan social welfare cuts (Rosenbaum, 1981a:11). Cuts in eligibility for need-based income supplement programs like AFDC also has meant ineligibility for in-kind benefits like Medicaid.

In 1982, at the height of national unemployment in the postwar period, of the 11.5 million unemployed workers 55 percent had been without work for so long they had exhausted all of their unemployment benefits (*New York Times*, November 18, 1982:16). Yet the Reagan administration actually proposed taxing the benefits of those still receiving unemployment compensation to pay for job training programs for the remainder of the unemployed. Negative public reaction to this proposal prompted its early withdrawal.

By 1984, the Reagan Administration had replaced the CETA program with a scaled down job training program known as the "Job Training Partnership Act." In the last year of the Carter administration CETA had been funded at nearly $6 billion. Four years later, in the face of massive industrial restructuring and manufacturing job loss, the principal job training policy of the Reagan presidency was a much smaller $2.8 billion program to be administered by state and local governments. To gain federal funds, local governments participating in the Job Training Partnership program were required to incorporate "private industry councils" into their public planning process as yet another form of public–private partnership (Boyd, 1984:12). As in the past, persons participating in training programs were not guaranteed a job at the end of their training. Yet the new program eliminated the income support guarantees which had induced unemployed people to participate in the replaced training program despite the lack of a guaranteed job. This meant that the beneficiaries of the new program could not include trainees who lacked the resources to support themselves during training or retraining. In this way, the weakened program not only reduced the level of state funding for employment training, it also insured that those who did benefit from state policy were those best able to have obtained employment training without governmental support.

Another employment policy advocated by the Reagan administration has called for a lower minimum wage restricted to teenage workers. It has been argued that currently very high unemployment rates among black teenagers in urban ghetto areas will thereby be lowered. Debate on this issue has centered on the likelihood that a lower minimum wage would achieve these objectives. For instance, opponents have argued that there are now too few jobs in the ghetto to enable a wage differential for teenagers to work; that racial discrimination would continue to restrict job opportunities for unskilled blacks; and that the great distance between jobs and housing would remain a barrier to employment opportunities. Proponents have dismissed these arguments, citing employer surveys and data concerning increases in unemployment rates following past increases in the minimum wage.

But few analysts have considered the possible spillover effects that a lower minimum wage might cause even if it succeeded in achieving its stated objectives. Let us consider some of the unintended consequences that might well occur even if proponents of the lower minimum wage for teenagers are correct in their immediate policy expectations.

If the goal is to pay low-valued, unskilled labor the price it deserves, in strictly market terms, the unskilled employee in many central cities is likely to be dragged well below the poverty level by such wage reductions. Moreover, the gap between skilled and unskilled wages would then surely widen. Employers of skilled labor would have an even greater incentive to replace skilled workers by the sorts of technological automation and work miniaturization that could enable the unskilled to perform tasks now done by the skilled. The wider the differential between skilled and unskilled wages, the greater this incentive becomes. The long-term consequences of these developments would be lower rates of unemployment among the unskilled; higher rates of unemployment for displaced skilled workers; more alienating work; reduced living standards for the employed; and greater long-run profits for employers.

If the unskilled are motivated to seek skills, but lack the money, time, or information to acquire effective training, they may fail and become even more alienated from society than they already are. On the other hand, if despite the considerable odds, they succeed through education and training in moving into a skilled sector of the economy, this would increase the supply of skilled labor. This, in turn, could enable employers to lower wages for skilled work, at least among non-unionized skilled workers (which constitute an increasing segment of workers in the service sector). The upshot would then be a long-term reduction in the total share of surplus profit allocated to labor as a factor of production.

If minimum wages were lowered only for teenagers, the result would be to institutionalize rather than remedy a dual labor market. A permanently cheap supply of unskilled teenage workers would create incentives for employers to redistribute the burden of unemployment to the older work force. This is because, given profit incentives, it is reasonable to expect that with a dual wage structure in effect it would be cheaper for employers to fire workers when they turned 20, replacing them with teenagers who would work for the lower wage scale. Not only could employers pay lower wages, they also could thereby avoid any longer-term commitments such as fringe benefits and greater pension rights to employees who had passed into the higher wage bracket.

The upshot of these developments would mean substantial cost-savings for employers; increased reliance on apprentice labor (arguably, accompanied by less effective service to customers); a transferral upward of high unemployment rates from teenagers, most of whom do not have families to support, to those between 20 and 25 years old, who often do; and, most disturbingly, the further institutionalization of the dual labor market structure that has become such a prominent feature of "restructured" American cities (Smith, 1980a:14).

BLOCK GRANTS AND THE ANTI-POVERTY NETWORK

A shift under Reagan to greater reliance on block grants to state and local governments rather than categorical federal social programs has undermined the past political influence of what has been termed the "anti-poverty network" or "social industrial complex." This service delivery and political communication network is composed of program administrators, social and community service professionals, local political elites, and service recipient clientele groups. The network has supported the continuation of a flow of federal resources for the provision of social services to low-income people (Roberts, 1981:17). A particular target of Reagan's cuts has been the programs of the Legal Services and Community Services Administrations which first politically organized as voices for the urban poor in the Great Society era.

An indirect effect of Reagan's actual cuts in poverty programs and his symbolic victory over the poverty network has been the discouragement of many eligible recipients from even applying for social welfare benefits to which they are entitled. For example, in the summer of 1982, amidst the recession with the highest level of unemployment since the Great Depression, the *New York Times* reported that "the growth of welfare and food stamp rolls has been halted" (Pear, 1982). This occurred even while the Census Bureau was reporting a two-million person increase in the official number of people living in poverty (see Pear, 1984).

RURAL DEVELOPMENT: WINNERS AND LOSERS

Despite the Reagan administration's espoused free market ideology, the most expensive agricultural subsidy programs for dairy and tobacco farmers were continued while food stamp and school lunch program eligibility requirements were raised, thereby cutting out many low to moderate income people. In the dairy price support program, half the estimated $2 billion program in 1981 went to the richest 15 percent of dairy farmers. In contrast, in 1982, 90 percent of food stamp recipients had incomes at or below the $9,862 official poverty level for a family of four (*New York Times*, October 31, 1983:13).

The Reagan administration did attempt to slow down, to a limited extent, but did not eliminate the rapid rate of growth in the loan and loan-guarantee programs of the Farmers Home Administration. This agency, which issued $45 billion in credit between 1977 and 1981 alone, was originally intended to support the credit needs of farmers and rural residents. In the 1970s, however, the Farmers Home Administration's resources were greatly expanded and its mandate broadened to encompass "rural development." Under this rubric the public treasury was virtually raided by rural real estate developers, thereby further accelerating the investment, employment and population decline of central cities. For example, its new mandate enabled the Agency "to finance rural water and sewer systems and to guarantee loans to businesses and developers promising to locate in rural areas" (Crittenden, 1981:8). The major beneficiaries of this federal largesse have included condominium builders, industrial corporations, and developers of rural communities, who received below market loan rates.

The program has been criticized not only for its adverse urban impacts but also for political favoritism and abuse by loan recipients. Not surprisingly, the cuts achieved in this agency's direct loan powers are most likely to effect weaker political interests. According to the Congressional Budget Office, the greatest losers will be low income and beginning small farmers who, unlike industrial, real estate development, and recreation interests, will be unlikely to find credit elsewhere (Crittenden, 1981).

REAGANOMICS AND URBAN FISCAL CRISIS

Since the Reagan cutbacks in intergovernmental fiscal assistance, state and local governments have generally been unable or unwilling to restore federal cuts in human services administered by local governments. This illustrates both the relative independence of the policies of the regional state (i.e., state governments) from the national government and their dependence upon external contextual factors which shape the options they may pursue.

While there has been much variation from state to state, even states inclined toward general restoration of the Reagan cuts, like New York, have been able to restore only 15 to 20 percent of the reductions (Herbers, 1983b). Many of those states ideologically most inclined to make restorations, like northeastern states with a long-standing tradition of social welfare spending, have been among those least able to do so, because of the impact that sectoral and interregional shifts in economic activity have had on their governmental revenue base.

By early 1983 many state governments were particularly hard pressed for revenues to meet operating expenses. High unemployment and reduced sales tax revenues caused by the recession of the early 1980s and reduced gasoline tax revenues, because of reduced automobile use and improved fuel efficiency, combined to produce this fiscal bind. Sunbelt and Snowbelt states alike were both affected by these conditions. As we have seen in chapter 4, many of the former began for the first time to experience symptoms of fiscal stress once thought to be unique to the political economies of Snowbelt states (Pear, 1983:12).

Yet ironically, by the end of 1983 some states which had been retrenching or adding taxes to cope with their revenue crises suddenly found themselves with unexpectedly sizable surpluses. This dramatic turnaround was produced by extrinsic politically produced factors such as the consumer-demand led recovery in the last three quarters of 1983 and the rapid defense buildup which produced an uneven boom benefiting states like California whose economics were buttressed by defense industries. Thus, in the short run, many state governments unexpectedly found themselves in a position to decide the extent to which they would assist their cities to cope with their public service crises, or repair their crumbling infrastructures, or simply cut back on the new taxes they enacted to cope with their previous revenue crises.

Yet the state governments' capacity to address urban fiscal and social problems varied greatly among the states. The extreme unevenness of the Reagan "recovery" from state to state and sector to sector well illustrates the embeddedness of the local and regional state in developments at the level of the overall national political economy. Both tax stimulated "recovery" and high defense spending have selectively induced revenue windfalls that have affected the states very unevenly. While diversified and defense-industry-rich states like California have experienced a dramatic turnaround in fiscal fortunes, states highly dependent on "civilian" heavy industry (e.g. Illinois) have not "recovered." Likewise states heavily dependent on currently slumping sectors, like energy production (e.g. Oklahoma and Louisiana) face large fiscal deficits rather than surpluses. Moreover, the virtually rollercoaster reversal of fiscal fortunes has left all state governments with a highly uncertain environment. This, in turn, has made long-term policy planning very difficult. As Herbers (1983a:1) has succinctly described this predicament:

> The States in recent years have been on a rags-to-riches roller coaster as the Federal Government has withdrawn assistance that once helped stabilize state treasuries and as state tax revenues have become increasingly sensitive to

fluctuations in the economy. This has led to rampant uncertainty in planning a wide range of public services and capital improvement.

CONCLUSIONS

Robert Lekachman (1983:18) has correctly pointed out that if "industrial policy" means nothing more than state sector influence on the location, type, and quantity of capital investment, we already have an abundance of such public policies, which in the aggregate channel a good bit of investment. These policies include, but are not limited to: IRS incentives favoring capital over labor intensive work and foreign over domestic investment; low taxation of banks, giving bankers more resources to channel into still other investment (see Table 2.3, p. 49); and subsidies to the agricultural sector which favor large over smaller producers. Reaganomics did little to alter these state policies while weakening the policy networks within the state structure that have been most supportive of the interests of workers, older industrial cities, minorities, and the poor.

To these must be added Reagan's continued support for state policies channeling the extraordinary amount of investment of productive resources into the construction of suburban single family homes at the expense of rental housing in cities; the uneven interregional locational and investment impacts of his greatly expanded defense spending; the long-term investment impact of the continuing massive subsidies and transfers to the medical-industrial-complex (whose centrally located but tax-exempt hospital facilities often compound the urban fiscal crisis); and the array of tax policies that continue to underwrite the commodification of leisure in subsidized urban sports arenas, shopping malls, luxury hotels, and rural retirement and recreation enclaves.

An alternative strategy for real economic recovery is needed that offers more promise of effectiveness. First of all, we must abandon the current premise that all government spending for social welfare policy entails "unproductive" consumption. Many such social policies have "percolate up" effects that contribute to productivity (Thurow, 1980). Federal support for education, for instance, is actually a long-term social investment in upgrading the quality of labor, a vital factor of production that has been sorely neglected in the current debate on "capital shortage." This weakens the case for across the board cuts in social services. If cuts in public expenditure are to be justified to increase aggregate social productivity, it makes sense to target the most socially wasteful and regressive subsidy programs which benefit the politically influential few, but contribute little to real long term productivity – tobacco price supports, uncapped home ownership interest deductions, rapid increases in the level of expenditures available to uncompetitive military procurement practices, and unconditional bailouts of unproductive corporations.

The withdrawal of state power from those policies incorporating weaker interests into public policy networks has been justified by reliance on the ideology of the market. As we have seen in the case of the subminimum wage, even if Reaganomics had represented a return to market allocation of life chances rather than representing, as it does, a shift in the structure of interests embodied in state policy, the interests which Reagan purposively excluded would have fared little better. As shown in chapters 5 and 6, in the real world, labor, consumer, and real estate markets do not operate according to the textbook model of open market information, a multiplicity of small scale production and consumption units, autonomous consumer tastes, and free mobility of labor and capital leading to an efficient equilibrium. Rather, in reality, distortions, disequilibrium, and imperfections characterize economic life in contemporary American society. Secrecy, high information costs, and socially structured accessibility to information about jobs, products, and services abound. Monopoly and oligopoly are common. Workers are attached to people, places and cultures. They are often bound by past investments in particular work abilities. Thus they cannot move as freely as can multilocational capital. Even many workers who are psychologically, socially, or technologically free to move must incur significant real economic costs to do so.

Consumer tastes are socially produced. Individual market preferences are influenced by personal social networks and by elite trend setting and mass media advertising. The autonomous individual consumer, like the fully mobile worker, the open consumer information market, and the deconcentrated production process is a potent myth which distorts the unequal exchange actually characterizing producer–consumer relations in the era of monopoly capitalism. As previous arguments have made clear, there is little reason to expect that the transfer of such a mythical model to the arena of public service provision would lead to fewer imperfections, distortions, or inequalities. In both instances the structure of consumption reflects the demands of those who have the power to make their demands effective.

Part IV

The Global Economy and Local Politics

8
Global Capital Restructuring and Community Change

The task of analyzing urban politics in the 1980s is compounded by new global conditions affecting the economic and political development of local communities. As noted earlier, these conditions include the increased concentration and fluidity of investment capital, intensified international competition, intensified interregional and international labor migration, and capital restructuring by multinational corporations to maintain profitability in an increasingly uncertain environment.

In the United States, during the past decade, attempts by agents of American multinational capital and by national political elites to restructure capital and the state have taken the form of a state-capital alliance to promote "recapitalization" by decreasing corporate tax burdens and promoting fiscal retrenchment in social policy (Miller and Tomaskovic-Devey, 1983). Ironically, this has served to accelerate sectoral and spatial shifts of investment both within the USA and globally by channeling more resources from tax breaks into the hands of big capital sectors whose operations are increasingly delocalized.

In the current period, multilocational industries have concentrated investment in some cities and regions of the advanced capitalist societies at the expense of others and have shifted investment to peripheral locations globally to combine relatively advanced technologies with cheaper and more politically controllable labor (Portes and Walton, 1981; Smith and Feagin, 1987). This sectoral shift is a key dimension of the decline of older industrial areas which have suffered rapid disinvestment (Perry, 1987). The ongoing sectoral shift has provoked locality crises in places experiencing underinvestment, disinvestment, or excessively rapid growth.

In the US urban system, locality crises are especially pronounced in the Snowbelt, the declining older manufacturing centers of the northeastern and midwestern regions. The other developed capitalist societies, facing similar global conditions, have experienced a similar series of local crises (Urry, 1981; Morgan, 1982; Body-Gendrot, 1987). Local crises, however, are not limited to older manufacturing cities. As we have seen in earlier chapters, the presumed prosperity of the Sunbelt is a myth. Both rapid metropolitan growth and industrial decline have characterized the Sunbelt's development. This uneven development also has engendered local political crisis conditions. Sunbelt urban growth has attracted both people from the declining Snowbelt and immigrants from the Third World, most of whom have fled economic and political conditions related to the global reorganization of capitalism (Portes and Walton, 1981; Sassen-Koob, 1983, 1984; Feagin and Smith, 1987). The resulting population boom in growing Sunbelt cities has intensified pressures on municipal budgets (Firestine, 1977; Lupsha and Siembieda, 1977; Fainstein et al., 1983). This has occurred at precisely the time that the region's own manufacturing sector, a major potential source of employment for the new migrants, has undergone rapid decline. The internationalization of capital brought foreign competition for markets; postwar plants were shut down as US manufacturers channeled capital from profits and tax cuts into consolidations and mergers, diversification, real estate ventures, and financial markets rather than investing in further modernization of domestic plants.

Our understanding of the dynamics of the new international political economy and its impact on localities is still incomplete. (Compare, for instance, Frobel, Heinrichs and Kreye, 1980; Portes and Walton, 1981.) Nevertheless, it has become clear that global capital restructuring by multinational enterprises and state responses to it have produced a new global-local interplay (see Smith and Feagin, 1987). Local communities, including local political and social structures and prevailing political alliances are increasingly affected by changes in the pattern of international trade and investment, trends in the organization and control of production under conditions of increased uncertainty, and trends of labor migration.

What impact has global economic restructuring had on the everyday lives of people living in impacted communities in the

United States? What have been its implications for the class structure of US cities? What implications do global economic restructuring and the current state response to it have for the future economic and political development of US cities? These questions form the basis of this chapter and chapter 9.

PLANT CLOSURES AND COMMUNITY CHANGE

In 1983 the management of the US Steel Corporation decided to close down the Johnstown Works in Johnstown, Pennsylvania, following a decade of gradual job loss through reduced production. The plant closure, announced two days after Christmas, 1983, meant that at the depths of the most recent "recession" Johnstown had the highest official urban unemployment rate in the United States – 25.9 percent. Overlaid upon the long-term decline in this community's industrial base (from 38,000 to 12,000 jobs in the two-county area surrounding Johnstown between 1950 and 1980) was a precipitous decline in employment in steel production of 50 percent between 1980 and the 1983 plant closure.

Despite strenuous local efforts to adapt from a goods producing to a service producing local economy, Johnstown had been dependent for so long on coal and steel to provide jobs for its people that it has been unable to generate enough new service jobs to even begin to offset its manufacturing job decline.

As a result of the global restructuring of production, "family problems" in Johnstown are on the rise. The president of a community organization called the Wives Action Committee has enumerated these "family" problems. They include increased domestic disputes, increased domestic violence by emasculated unemployed male "breadwinners," reliance on public welfare to support the families of unionized industrial workers who have no place to work, and listlessness and anxiety among children in affected families (*New Orleans Times-Picayune/States-Item*, January 2, 1984:24).

Displaced workers in other cities are belatedly beginning to comprehend that the causes of their current plight are structural rather than family centered. For instance, before closing down Chicago's massive South Side Steel Works, US Steel had held forth the promise of building a new $225 million high technology steel mill in Chicago if workers agreed to both pay cuts and more restrictive work rules. Unionized workers resisted this proposal, perceiving it as part of a larger effort by American corporations to weaken the labor movement as a whole (Serrin, 1983b:9). After twice previously agreeing to concessions to save jobs that ultimately disappeared anyway, union leaders in Chicago refused the initial concession demands. Instead, they expressed a willingness to discuss modifications of local work rules. US Steel, whose current accumulation strategy has been to diversify into a multi-national holding company which increasingly channels its capital investment into finance, real estate and energy development, quickly rejected this proposal to bargain and decided to shut down most of the South Works operation rather than open the new plant.

US Steel's plant closing policies directly eliminated over 15,000 jobs in 13 states in the early 1980s. The indirect effect of these closures has been far greater than job loss. The very economic foundation of community life was virtually removed in industrial suburbs surrounding Cleveland and Pittsburgh, as well as in smaller industrial cities like Elmira, New York, Trenton, New Jersey, and Ambridge, Pennsylvania. Only four month's notice was given to displaced workers in these communities. Because of the weakness of working-class political organizations in the US state structure, these displaced workers enjoyed none of the protections from and compensations for job displacement which characterize the political mediation of plant closures in Europe (see, for instance, Body-Gendrot, 1987; Mayer, 1987). The latitude given to corporations to enter and exit local communities in the US urban system is correspondingly greater.

In adversely affected industrial cities in all regions, the job loss produced by plant closures is more than an economic problem; it affects not just work life but the material basis of the residential communities where working-class life has been reproduced (see Nash, 1987). Because of the high degree of class segregation of everyday life in the US urban system, relatively autonomous local working-class cultures have persisted despite rapid social and economic changes in the society as a whole. The continued reproduction of these local cultures is now severely threatened by capital flight of multinational industrial capital to new global points of production.

The connection between work life and community life has been close in people's actual material and cultural existence, despite the distorting ideological perception in advanced capitalism that "the home" and the "neighborhood" are retreats from the worlds of work, production and market exchange (see Sennett, 1970; Katznelson, 1981). This connection has been well captured by Serrin (1983b:9). Commenting on the working class culture of South Side Chicago, which developed out of informal workplace social relations at the South Works Steel complex, Serrin notes that:

The South Works is an epochal American story that started a century ago with the construction on wild prairie lands of one of the world's massive industrial centers. It is a story of the immigration here of tens of thousands of workers and of the special communities they built. It is a story today of the decimation of the lives of those workers and their communities, of vast change in American industry ... a story, ultimately, of a time and place that soon may be no more ... Houses and shops were thrown up and soon the area was a thick stew of Irish, Swedes, Poles, Germans, Serbians, Croats, Hungarians, Italians, and more recently, blacks and Mexicans. This, while in Chicago, was a separate place. Distinct communities grew up, South Chicago, the East Side, South Deering, Hegewisch, the Bush, Slag Valley. Churches like St. Michael's Roman Catholic Church rivaled in size the mills and the skyscrapers downtown. . . In World War II, 18,000 workers were employed at the works, which stretches for three and a half miles between 79th and 89th streets. As recently as the late 1970s, the plant had several thousand workers. The plant today employs 1,150, and much of the mill and the workers' neighborhoods, houses, taverns, grocery stores, shops, have been knocked down, leaving gaps like lost teeth in an old face. . . A special poignancy exists because steel work is often performed in teams. Steel workers often call each other "my partner." They might have a beer or two together after work or go fishing or to a White Sox game together. . . The decline of the South Works brings a wrenching end to these relationships.

As this story suggests, the deepest but least noted social cost of the current global restructuring of industrial production has been

Table 8.1 Manufacturing, services, and government employment in the United States as percentages of total employment

Year	Manufacturing employment (000)	%	Services employment (000)	%	Government employment (000)	%
1940	10,985	33.9	3,665	11.3	4,202	13.0
1945	15,524	38.4	4,222	10.4	5,944	14.7
1950	15,241	33.7	5,357	11.8	6,026	13.3
1955	16,882	33.3	6,240	12.3	9,914	13.6
1960	16,796	31.0	7,378	13.6	8,353	15.4
1965	18,062	29.7	9,036	14.9	10,074	16.6
1970	19,367	27.3	11,548	16.3	12,554	17.7
1975	18,323	23.8	13,892	18.0	14,686	19.1
1980	20,285	22.4	17,890	19.8	16,241	18.0
1981	20,173	22.1	18,592	20.4	16,024	17.6
1982	18,848	21.0	19,001	21.2	15,788	17.6

Source: Adapted from Sternlieb, Burchell and Wilhelm (1983).

the undermining of the urban working-class cultures for which factory work provided a material and social base for enduring social relationships in residential communities.

JOB RESTRUCTURING AND CLASS RESTRUCTURING

As industrial employment declined and industrial capital shifted resources to Third World production facilities, trade union membership in the USA declined from nearly a third of the labor force in the 1950s to only 18 percent in 1980. The decline in unionization intensified during the 1980s. By 1983 only 15 percent of Americans belonged to unions (Lipset, 1983:1). This decline reflects the fact that four decades ago nearly 40 percent of the labor force was employed in manufacturing while today only 21 percent are so employed (Table 8.1). In the past decade alone membership in the steel, auto, rubber, and mining unions has declined by a third. Recent trends in the global economy suggest a continuation and intensification of this long-term trend.

US Steel's current accumulation strategy in the global political economy of becoming less integrated and more specialized by closing factories like the South Works parallels the strategy now being followed by all of the large domestic steel producers in the United States (Greenhouse, 1983b:32). Industrial economists predict even more plant closures because of the combination of growing labor resistance to further cost saving measures and the reluctance of US-based multinational steel corporations to pay the price of full modernization of their domestic plants, choosing instead to purchase semi-finished products from specific Third World countries while demanding general protectionism from the state (Greenhouse, 1983b:32).

Moreover, the global restructuring of steel can no longer be viewed as simply an interregional disinvestment process. Bethlehem Steel, for example, has closed not only its older mills in New York and Pennsylvania, but also its more modern mill in Los Angeles (Greenhouse, 1983a). In California over 100,000 jobs were permanently lost in the industrial sector when 979 manufacturing plants closed between 1980 and 1982 (*New York Times*, October 27, 1982:12). Likewise, the industrial boom experienced by a host of non-metropolitan communities in the US South from the 1950s until the mid-1970s abruptly ended in the early 1980s, as hundreds of shoe factories, textile mills, automobile parts and electric motor assembly plants all closed their doors, unable to compete with more cheaply produced imported goods, even in low wage, nonunionized southern states and communities (Schmidt, 1984:1, 21; 1985:1, 12).

Industrial employment and trade union membership in the USA both declined throughout the 1970s and 1980s because of global economic restructuring and the movement of industry to Third World production and assembly sites. As a result, the number of involuntary part-time workers in the US labor force increased dramatically. From 1970 to 1982 the number of part-time workers rose from 11.5 to 18.3 million, an increase of 57.9 percent. The lion's share of this increase came from the involuntary segment of part-time workers, which grew from 2,198,000 to 5,852,000, a 66 percent increase in the 12-year period (*New York Times*, August 14, 1983:22). This meant that in 1982, when 10.6 million workers were officially classified as unemployed, an additional 5.8 million workers were involuntarily working part-time. Another 1.5 million "discouraged" workers had given up looking for work

(*New York Times*, August 14, 1983:22). Because these latter two categories of workers are not counted in official unemployment figures, the human consequences of the last major recession were significantly understated. If discouraged and involuntary part-time workers were added to the unemployment figures, the national unemployment rate in 1982 would have increased by 75 percent, encompassing 18 percent of the employed work force.

Popular periodicals frequently stress the extent to which the availability of part-time work allows many families the flexibility to raise children and pursue careers. For upper-middle income professional families this doubtless is true. But this social construction of "part-time work" overlooks the fact that much of the new pattern of job creation is the result of involuntary displacement of people from full-time work in the primary labor market to part-time work in the secondary sector. The case of Mr and Mrs Bell Passafiume well illustrates this other face of the rising tide of part-time work (Serrin, 1982:1):

> At his last full time job, at the United States Steel Corporation's plant at Homestead, Pennsylvania, Mr Passafiume, a 39-year-old welder, made $14 an hour, plus benefits that probably amounted to $10 more an hour.
>
> Today Mr Passafiume has a part-time job, three or four days a week, cleaning up a Pittsburgh movie house. He makes the minimum wage, $3.35 an hour. He receives no benefits. He has not worked full time since he was laid off by US Steel in 1981. To help bring in cash, his wife also works part-time, answering telephone calls at a Pittsburgh banking house. She is there from 10 a.m. to 2 p.m., three to five days a week. Mrs Passafiume also makes the minimum wage and receives no benefits. They have two children and no health insurance.

The experience of the Passafiume family suggests some of the reasons why global economic restructuring has included so much part-time employment. Because part-time workers generally do not receive the fringe benefits that unionized full-time workers have won from employers in past decades – i.e., politically produced occupational benefits in the form of hospital insurance, sick pay, paid vacations, and retirement pensions – labor costs for employers using part-time workers have been greatly reduced.

Moreover, part-time work may enable employers to induce more intensified work performances during the shorter durations worked by part-time workers. This is illustrated in the case of the MacDonald fast food chain, which has relied extensively on part-time young workers for intensified work performances during peak dining hours (*New York Times*, August 14, 1983:22). Third, the use of part-time workers, possessing neither fringe benefits nor career ladders, and thus lacking meaningful identification with their work, also thwarts efforts by unions to organize this low-paying end of the sector of the labor force employing service workers.

The decline in middle income, unionized industrial jobs in the US urban system has been accompanied by a rapid increase in the number of both high and low paying jobs in this growing "service sector" (Sassen-Koob, 1984). Between 1979 and 1984, while manufacturing, construction, and mining employment shrank by 2.4 million jobs, the number of jobs in personal, financial, and business services, and in wholesale and retail trade increased by over 4 million (Harrison & Bluestone, 1984:A27). It was this restructuring of employment rather than industrial recovery which resulted in decreased US unemployment between the early and mid-1980s.

CLASS RESTRUCTURING AND URBAN RESTRUCTURING

What are the implications of this pattern of job restructuring for the economic and political development of US cities? Where is the economic restructuring taking place? Is it likely to have a positive or negative impact on the economic base of declining central cities? Is it likely to reverse or accelerate the four-decade long trend in the US urban system toward metropolitan deconcentration and suburban sprawl? The answers to these questions are complex and contradictory.

In 1977, producer services accounted for 20 percent of GNP in the United States. This segment of the "service sector" has experienced the greatest growth rate in the past decade. Some other segments of the "service sector" like public service, and consumer and distributive services have actually levelled off since the late 1960s (Sassen-Koob, 1983:6; Stanbeck, 1979:16–22).

The major producer services, such as banking, accounting, advertising, and communications, are not dependent on proximity to consumer markets. As services operating to serve institutional clients on a global scale, some of these financial and business services have concentrated in a limited number of large cities.

Sassen-Koob (1983) has shown that in the US urban system, the growth of the business service sector has not paralleled the locational pattern of manufacturing disinvestment. In fact, it has operated, in part, to offset industrial job shifts. Thus, for instance, 60 percent of direct German, Swiss, and English investment in the USA from 1978 to 1980 took place in the deindustrializing northeastern cities. Sassen-Koob's explanation for this investment pattern rests on political logic. In her view: "The crisis in the manufacturing sector has created the conditions for renewed profitable investment in the form of a defeated and weakened working class and the willingness of local governments to make major concessions in order to draw investment."

Empirical support for the proposition that some previously declining major industrial cities have successfully "converted" to new forms and functions is found in the examples of New York, Boston, Chicago, Minneapolis, Pittsburgh, San Francisco, and Milwaukee (Fainstein and Fainstein, 1981; Sassen-Koob, 1984). "Public–private" central city growth coalitions having stakes in the urban land market have competed intensely to lure some of the new growth sector firms to declining central city cores by offering investors large direct or indirect public subsidies on a project-by-project basis. The tools of attempted "conversion" have included convention centers, sports arenas, office complexes, government headquarters, hotels, shops and restaurants, resurrected historical districts, and waterfront commercial development (Fainstein and Fainstein, 1981:6; Smith and Keller, 1983; Fainstein et al., 1983). The contours of each successful project have served the political and economic needs of local pro-growth coalitions, which have carved out entire sections of major "converting" central cities for the work, residential, commercial, and recreational needs of the professional business strata (Hill, 1984).

Those cities blessed by waterfronts have been especially successful in attracting national development capitalists interested in catering to the tourist trade as well as the new urban professional strata. Thus, for example, waterfront conversion projects are now either completed, underway, or planned in Boston, New York,

Baltimore, San Francisco, Philadelphia, New Orleans, Los Angeles, Cincinnati, Seattle, and St Louis. Older industrial, shipping, and warehouse districts, once a key element in these cities' local economies and cultures, have declined as employment sources in the late capitalist service economy. As land values on urban waterfronts dropped, they became prime targets of development corporations, such as the Rouse Company, seeking to convert them into upmarket shopping, entertainment, office, and luxury residential complexes. The primordial human fascination with moving water has thus become a central component of these newly commodified urban spaces.

In these new urban spaces, where the political rationale for meeting the urban crisis has become defined as identical to the goals and interests of financial capital and the producers of these newly commodified marketplaces, the "successful" public–private partnerships have displaced the economic foundations of old working class cultural communities and created new elite engendered uses of urban space. In the process, densely lived urban life is reduced to the act of shopping in a preplanned, risk-free, self-contained ensemble of stimuli, designed to induce the regime of individualized consumption under the illusion of participation in the urban crowd.

Where the process of central city conversion from industrial to corporate-professional urban space has been successful, a major result in some cities (e.g. St Paul and San Francisco) has been "private" gentrification of nearby residential neighborhoods and geographic displacement of the lower classes from the urban core to more peripheral urban districts. Where this has occurred, race and class inequality have not decreased. Rather, the spatial location of the unequal and uneven development of these successfully "converted" American cities has simply shifted around. As well stated by the Fainsteins (1981:14): "Large scale accumulation in new service production facilities combines with gentrification to establish a revalorized and vibrant urban core .... Working and lower class populations are forced to the periphery. Class inequality in no sense diminishes yet its physical manifestations alter sharply."

Furthermore, the movement of young urban professionals into previously low income neighborhoods in major cities which have expanded their business service sector has reduced the supply of affordable rental housing units (see Gilderbloom and Appelbaum,

1987). As we have seen in chapter 2, the processes of "gen-trification" and condominium conversions alter housing supply, thus driving up rents. These interrelated processes have been significantly abetted by the taxation policies of American local governments which view gentrification as a solution to rather than an expression of the urban crisis.

Despite these spatial transformations, the movement of the old urban working and lower classes to the periphery has not taken place in all converting cities (e.g. black neighborhoods remain quite close to the core CBD in Boston, Philadelphia, New Orleans, and Atlanta). By and large, gentrification has not succeeded in insulating the newly created "yuppie city" from visible manifestations of *old* patterns of uneven development at the core. Moreover, alongside the emergent urban form of the "postindustrial" city *new* patterns of low-paying employment and new lower-working class residential neighborhoods have developed in precisely those cities experiencing successful conversion and robust employment growth.

Why have new patterns of inequality emerged in cities experiencing rapid economic growth? In part, this is because the demand for low paid personal, commercial and clerical service workers has grown in such places as a kind of "multiplier effect" of the conversion of these core cities to tourist, professional service, and restaurant and entertainment meccas (see Sassen-Koob, 1984). Thus, for example, in the successfully converted city of New York "more than 60 percent of the service jobs pay salaries below the Bureau of Labor Statistics' living standard for a low income family of four, while 25 percent of full-time service workers earn less than the poverty level" (McGahey, 1983:23).

These low-paid service workers are taking their place alongside a growing number of poorly paid *industrial* workers from the Third World who account for another major US central city employment growth sector in the past decade – the new immigrant "sweatshop." The past decade has witnessed a fourth great urban migration wave to US cities (Erie, 1985). This wave is driven by political and economic conditions in Latin America, the Caribbean Basin, and the Pacific Rim, and drawn to large cities in the US (e.g. New York, Los Angeles, San Francisco, Chicago) which are undergoing conversion to new patterns of employment growth. The new immigrants, who often have migrated illegally, constitute a large pool of inexpensive and politically weak labor. Their concentration in "converting" core city residential enclaves is both a medium and an outcome of the growth there of thousands of small workplaces in both low tech areas such as textile manufacturing and hightech areas such as microcomputer assembly. Such competitive businesses are able to survive in the global marketplace by overexploiting this highly vulnerable labor force of new urban immigrants. These new sweatshops commonly violate existing labor laws, minimum wage requirements, and occupational health and safety regulations. Furthermore, the use of new sweatshops is not limited to competitive economic sectors. In the monopoly sector, unionized manufacturers frequently contract out to small assembly shops that employ non-union workers. This enables them to take advantage of the latter's cheaper wages, limited regulations, and dependent labor force.

Many of the new immigrants working in the new sweatshops have entered the United States illegally, and thus currently lack even the basic right of citizenship as a political resource for resisting these conditions. The new sweatshops tend to be located within or close to new immigrant neighborhoods in core cities. They constitute a key dimension of the growing concentration of *polarized* job opportunities in many of today's fastest growing urban cores. This development has aptly been termed "the peripheralization of the core" (Sassen-Koob, 1983).

As we have seen in earlier chapters, the trend toward greater income polarization observable in the 1980s as a result of the changing occupational structure has been compounded by the fact that transfer payments to low and moderate income families have been significantly reduced by state budget cuts in social policy expenditures. Even before the Reagan administration's sharp cuts in federal expenditures for social welfare, the overall purchasing power of such benefits decreased by nearly one-third between 1969 and 1980, as fiscally hard-pressed state and local government officials refused to raise means-tested entitlements to keep pace with high inflation (Wald, 1980:1; Pear, 1983:13). The political power relations underlying the consolidation of middle-class benefits while eroding low income entitlements thus have contributed significantly to the increased income polarization now plaguing many large American cities undergoing economic restructuring.

CONCLUSIONS

When these labor market and political restructurings are combined with the continuing decline in well-paying manufacturing employment, it becomes apparent that dire predictions of increased urban poverty and increased class polarization are already beginning to materialize in some major US central cities. Intraclass conflict among segments of the secondary labor market is a real possibility as already marginalized occupational groups such as women and minorities face intensified competition from newly displaced manufacturing workers. Another is the prospect of heightened conflict between primary and secondary workers in new employment growth sectors like high technology and services where new jobs are characterized by extreme disparities in pay (Sassen-Koob, 1984; Smith and Judd; 1984; McGahey, 1983; Nash, 1983).

Having said this, it must be noted that the increased velocity and portability of high tech and business service investment in the current epoch suggest a cautionary note. Some leading large older cities have successfully converted to corporate professional cities, and some of these have displayed signs of class polarization. Nevertheless, it should not be assumed that this developmental pattern is likely to become the general pattern of urban development in contemporary American society. Sternlieb, Burchell and Wilhelm (1983) have carefully documented a long-term trend toward metropolitan deconcentration of employment opportunities. Their research provides statistical evidence supporting the conclusion that, despite notable exceptions like New York and Los Angeles, overall "the central city share of the new dynamic clearly is inadequate to provide real economic regeneration" of older industrial cities (Sternlieb, Burchell and Wilhelm, 1983). As Tables 8.1 through 8.4, adapted from their study, illustrate, manufacturing employment in the United States has been relatively stagnant since 1965. This has had particularly harsh consequences for those cities dependent on manufacturing (e.g. Detroit, Buffalo, Gary, Indiana, and Youngstown, Ohio) which have been unable to attract new business and service investment. America's current stagnant domestic industrial base is now located primarily in *newer* points of production in suburbs, rural areas, and the Southwest. As we have seen, even these currently preferred industrial locations are now threatened by the internationalization

Table 8.2   Declining manufacturing industries

The following industries decreased in the 1970 to 198⸢ decade:

Industry	Change in employment 1970–80
Non-durable goods	−0.7
Paper and allied products	−1.8
Miscellaneous manufacturing	−1.8
Food and kindred products	−4.4
Apparel and other textile products	−7.4
Primary metal industry	−9.4
Textile mill products	−13.0
Tobacco products	−16.9
Leather and leather products	−27.1

Source: Adapted from Sternleib, Burchell and Wilhelm (1983).

Table 8.3   Leading growth sectors in services

Industry	Percentage change in employment 1970–80
Banking	+137.3
Legal services	+110.9
Social services	+105.2 (72–80)
Business servics	+84.5
Credit agencies, other than banks	+58.4
Holding and other investment services (72–80)	+57.6
Insurance agents, brokers and service	+57.0
Miscellaneous services	+56.6
Miscellaneous repairs	+53.0
Amusement and recreation	+51.4 (72–80)
Real estate	+48.5
Finance, insurance and real estate	+41.6

Source: Adapted from Exhibit 8 in Sternleib, Burchell and Wilhelm (1983).

Table 8.4 Service employment distribution, 1965–82

Year	Total service employment (in millions)	Percent personal service employment[a]	Percent business service employment[b]	Percent health service employment	Percent educational service employment	Percent all other services employment[c]
1965	9.036	10.9	12.6	23.0	8.5	44.9
1970	11.548	8.6	14.5	26.4	8.1	42.4
1975	13.892	6.2	14.7	29.8	7.2	31.7
1980	17.890	5.0	17.3	29.5	6.4	33.2
1981	18.592	4.9	17.5	29.9	6.3	33.2
1982	19.001	4.9	17.4	30.4	6.2	33.1

[a] Includes laundry, cleaning, beauty shops and funeral services.
[b] Includes advertising, credit reporting and collection, mailing, reproduction, etc., building services, and computer and data processing services
[c] Includes motels, auto repair services, miscellaneous repair services, motion pictures, amusement and recreation services, engineering and architectural services, and accounting, auditing and bookkeeping services.
Source: Adapted from Sternleib, Burchell and Wilhelm (1983).

of production relations, capital flight, and deindustrialization.

Furthermore, the rapid rise in service sector employment has not generally produced a rapid increase in such employment in older central cities. Data derived from Sternlieb's study, presented in Table 8.4, indicate that the robust growth of business services has not been sufficient to maintain the previous employment base of most of America's large central cities. There is evidence, instead, of a tendency toward continuing dispersion of these activities to suburban office-parks and even to very remote locations (Sternlieb, Burchell and Wilhelm, 1983).

In late capitalist America, the increased concentration, portability, and global reach of capital investment offers multilocational corporations engaged in business, high tech and communication services wide latitude to leave areas that may have disadvantages, from the standpoint of capital, such as politically conscious workers and citizens. This suggests a locational advantage for new business service growth in relatively remote places, which lack a previous history of labor-management relations. Some signs of this urban disinvestment trend are already apparent. For example, The American Express Corporation's traveler's check operations have recently been moved from New York City to a remote location in Utah. Citicorp has moved its credit card operations to South Dakota (Pollack, 1983:30). According to a recent Congressional Joint Economic Committee survey of US business leaders, it is the perception of a negative "business climate" in large northern cities which stands in the way of conversion of more of that region's declining industrial cities into office parks for the corporate-professional strata (Muller, 1981:38).

These examples suggest that even those cities currently enjoying growth in highly mobile segments of the advanced services sector could experience rapid outmigration in the future if corporate capital were to develop an unfavorable impression of their political "business climate." Just as factories were once shifted from central city locations to suburban satellite communities or company towns in response to actual and anticipated labor militancy (Gordon, 1977), the socially constructed political climate of today's urban cores remains a key variable affecting the ability of the current urban "winners" to retain their new economic functions.

9
Global Restructuring and the New Urban Politics

James O'Connor (1981) has defined the current economic crisis of world capitalism as an "interruption in the accumulation of capital" brought about by changed environmental conditions. To cope with this crisis a central strategy of big capital sectors within the advanced societies has been global capital restructuring. According to O'Connor, capital restructuring may prevent, postpone, or displace the current economic crisis. He does not entertain the possibility that capital restructuring may also compound and thus prolong the crisis. It is the premise of this final chapter that the very unfolding of global capital restructuring creates profoundly destabilizing conditions of everyday life in the localities most immediately affected. Accordingly, we must turn to the realm of urban politics, as it intersects with the changing global economy, to comprehend the real consequences of capital restructuring.

What have been the local political responses to global capital restructuring? The forms of resistance or accommodation to local crises of disinvestment or unregulated rapid growth have varied from nation to nation and place to place. Where popular opposition to locality crises has occurred, its form, development, and effectiveness have depended on the channels available for expressing discontent; the character of existing or emergent forms of local political organization connecting affected individuals, households, and social networks to the political process; the prevailing structure and culture of local politics; and class and political alignments at the local and national scales in the affected societies.

This chapter examines both the policy responses of the "local state" and the actions of grassroots political movements in US cities linked to the restructuring of the global economy. The aim of the analysis is to assess the political implications of four complexly interrelated phenomena: the call by American state and local government officials for more fiscal welfare in the form of "enterprise zones," tax abatements and "public-private partnerships" to restore the employment base of declining US cities and regions; the spread of new immigration and new sweatshops in a number of large US cities; the expansion there of the "informal" economy; and the changing character of urban political mobilization in contemporary America.

THE USES OF "ENTERPRISE ZONES" AND "PUBLIC–PRIVATE PARTNERSHIPS"

In their quest to reverse local and regional economic decline, both the Reagan administration and state and local government officials from distressed cities and regions have proposed the establishment of a variety of incentives to attract new capital investment. Specific items on the agenda of state and local governments have included measures to lower or remove property taxes, to suspend zoning and building regulations, to deregulate environmental and health and safety regulations, to allow sub-minimum wages for all workers or for youth, and to pass additional "right to work" laws to weaken union power. The most frequently proposed solutions to the problem of capital flight have been two local forms of fiscal welfare – urban "enterprise zones" and "public–private partnerships."

John Walton (1982:12–13) points out that the model for creating "enterprise zones" in declining cities in the USA is the practice of multilocational capital investment in such export-processing and free-trade zones as Hong Kong, Puerto Rico, and the Mexican border. These places are characterized by low wages, widespread poverty, sweatshop working conditions, and, in many instances, renewed capital flight to new points of production. These characteristics raise the question of what kind of working and living conditions in declining American cities would be needed to render firms that locate in "enterprise zones" competitive in the global marketplace.

For reasons previously discussed in chapter 7 "enterprise zones" are unlikely to create new jobs, at stable wage levels, in depressed urban areas (see Aronowitz, 1981; Aronowitz and Goodman, 1981; Walton, 1982; Massey, 1982; Goldsmith, 1982a and b; Malone, 1982). Places like the South Bronx, ravaged by disinvestment, abandonment, arson, and high levels of welfare dependency, have become prototypes of the sort of older inner city area the policy is nominally intended to revitalize. Critics point out that the policy does nothing about key features of the urban ghetto context, like low skill levels and high insurance rates, due to actual or perceived high crime rates, which currently are impediments to inner city investment. More importantly, the very logic of the enterprise zone heightens the destructive competition for new capital investment among local governments. Interlocal competition for new investment is already eroding state and local tax bases and may further undermine workers' already beleaguered protections under the regime of Reaganomics by encouraging the elimination of health and safety protections and organizing rights.

In the context of the global reorganization of capitalism, the creation of tax havens to lure "footloose firms" and "runaway plants" as envisaged in enterprise zone policies, is unlikely to generate net gains in employment in the overall national economy. The world capitalist economy has already been sufficiently restructured to enable large multinational corporations to plan and control global networks of economic activity with production facilities spanning the globe in the quest for cheaper, more flexible, and more controllable labor pools. To the extent that enterprise zones might prove an effective lure (and it is by no means clear that they could offset labor cost and political control factors in countries like Korea, Taiwan, and parts of Latin America) they are simply likely to encourage the moving around of existing jobs within and among metropolitan areas, regions, and even nation states, playing one set of workers off against another, to the overall political benefit of the big capital sectors of the advanced societies. This sort of "substitution effect" is especially likely during periods of limited economic growth.

Evidence from Britain (Massey, 1982) suggests that many firms within metropolitan areas have simply moved short distances to designated zones at minimal cost to themselves and no net gain in employment in depressed older metropolitan areas. This is not an accidental outcome; it is an inherent feature of the logic of the policy within the evolving global economy. In the absence of politically effective constraints on capital flows, and as long as there are more exploitable points of production, the intensified competition for employment among cities, states, and national economies will continue to bode ill for the living standards of working people in both the core and the periphery.

Enterprise zone policies actually legitimate the process of capital flight from localities where production costs, including labor costs entailing decent living standards, render the areas "uncompetitive" in the global political economy. Goldsmith (1982b:23) and Aronowitz (1981) have shown that the decline in living standards has been precisely the fate of the once booming and now declining economy of Puerto Rico, whose once highly touted enterprise zone policy "Operation Bootstrap," has been discredited. The policy's inner contradiction, reflecting the inner contradiction of global competition in late capitalism, has been nicely stated by Goldsmith (1982b:23): "To the extent that 'Operation Bootstrap' succeeded, thereby raising wages, it reduced the attraction for investors, and (eventually) failed."

An equally contradictory policy mechanism relied upon increasingly by local governments in the face of the accelerated movement of capital investment on the global scale in the past decade has been the "public–private partnership." A multitude of alliances have been forged at the state and local levels of government between public officials and various business interests to promote new local business investment. These "public–private partnerships," are forms of local corporatism. They have played a key role in exacerbating the uneven economic development pattern we have been discussing.

Another expression of the rise of the US tax state, public–private partnerships have become the primary tool used to extract material resources from society and to build symbolic support for the goals of the local networks of economic and political elites that Molotch (1976) has aptly termed the "growth machine." Public subsidies to private development provided through public–private partnerships have included tax abatements, tax exempt industrial revenue bonds, property tax holidays and rollbacks, sales tax exemptions, lease financing, and state and local income tax reductions (see Smith, Ready and Judd, 1985). The relatively low visibility of these policies, their tendency to "contract out" additional bits and pieces of state sovereignty to private interests, and their lack of public accountability are all manifestations of the unique and highly amorphous character of the US tax state.

Public–private partnerships are institutionally managed by non-profit, quasi-public development organizations variously called Downtown Development Authorities, Economic Development Corporations, and Local Development Corporations. These institutions legitimate and organize an overt alliance between the local state and particular capital fractions under the rubric of "partnership." They usually implement their decisions without referenda or legislative approval of specific projects. They have a great deal of discretion over the use of public funds and the granting of tax concessions. Perhaps because of this flexibility, they are fast becoming the primary means through which local political jurisdictions attempt to foster new economic growth.

When viewed in isolation, the achievements of these organizational networks have been significant in revitalizing declining downtowns in successfully "converting" central cities. Their principal achievement has been the proliferation of development projects which have leveraged additional capital investment for downtown convention centers, hotels, shopping malls, sports arenas, and luxury housing development. Despite these achievements, public–private partnerships have been less successful in attracting new industrial investment to declining industrial communities? Why has this been the case?

The tax incentive schemes used by the local public–private partnerships are politically legitimated to the general public and to non-capitalist interests by incessant reiteration of the underlying assumptions of neo-classical economic location theory. Yet in purely economic terms, the tax incentives currently in use have been shown to be extremely marginal in effect, as a cost related factor of production (see Smith, Ready and Judd, 1985). Most analysts agree that *labor* is the most important factor influencing business location in most industries (see Vaughan, 1979; Moriarity et al., 1980; Daniels, 1982). Labor accounts for nearly two-thirds of each dollar of value added cost for the average industry. Service industries are even more labor intensive (Daniels, 1982:59). Firms are most often influenced by such labor force characteristics as its size, unemployment rate, skill level, and degree of unionization (Moriarity, 1980).

Furthermore, the internationalization of the world political economy has made it extremely difficult for declining US cities and states, with high unemployment rates, to outbid emerging

Third World industrial location sites by tax incentives alone. This is because both the low wage structures and the forms of political domination in late industrializing countries more than offset possible US tax incentive effects. (On the latter, see Feagin and Smith, 1987.)

Despite their ineffectiveness as selective economic incentives for generating stable employment, the cumulative political effect of state and local tax incentive policies has been a dramatic shift in the burden of governmental revenue production from corporations to households. In 1950, businesses paid 20 percent of all state and local property taxes. By the late 1970s their share had declined to 12 percent (Friedland, 1983a). Moreover, since the location of new business investment necessarily entails increased demands on the infrastructure, police, fire protection, and the environment, the public costs of state and local public–private partnership projects are increasingly being borne by individual households (or, if you will, by "labor in the community").

Given their dubious worth as stable job creation strategies, why are enterprise zones and public–private partnerships so prominently placed on the political agenda of US cities? What factors underlie their treatment as serious policy tools? Walton (1982:14–16) has interpreted them as a strategy of urban political elites to deflect criticism for their inaction on the "urban crisis" front, while simultaneously serving the interests of those "who would align themselves with a continued redistribution of income [to capital] and tax burdens [to households and wage earners] for other political purposes." Walton does not specify what these other purposes might be. Yet if we ask the question, "Who benefits?" several winners are clearly discernible. These include:

1 Republican party elites and their supporters in the world of corporate and finance capital, who currently are seeking to establish a new ideological hegemony to replace New Deal liberalism with a more limited "social wage" and a new social contract more favorable to business interests;

2 state and local politicians in both major political parties, whose campaign coffers remain full and whose political support among business interests widens as they define the urban crisis increasingly in terms of the "problems" of "inadequate capital formation" and "population migration" rather than in terms of capital flight, structurally segmented

housing and labor markets, or past public policies which
have contributed to urban deterioration, deconcentration,
disinvestment, and decline;

3   industrial capitalists who underinvested in the upgrading of
domestic plant and equipment for decades, diversified into
real estate speculation, built new production and assembly
facilities in the Third World, and now seek various public
subsidies for "reindustrialization" within a new context of
weakened labor unions, chastened workers, and supportive
politicians;

4   suburban, southern, and western congressional representatives of both major political parties, who view their growing
influence in the recently reapportioned Congress as an
opportunity to turn yet another economic development
policy to their own regional advantage. As Herbers (1980:4E)
has said of past practice:

(T)he tendency has almost always been to bring in so many
areas for help that the plan was rendered ineffective. Just as
. . . rural areas received Model Cities money, with political
power shifting to the South and West, anyone who has
watched Congress in action can envision enterprise zones in
the vast suburban expanses where economic growth has been
underway, drawing jobs ˉaway from the most distressed
central cities. . . .

Despite their ineffectiveness in attracting industrial development,
their capture by downtown real estate interests, and their adverse
distributional consequences for residential households, state and
local tax concessions remain in use because they serve these
political interests. The use of these types of fiscal welfare policy
has expanded because state and local political elites in both major
political parties are caught in a political bind. At a time when
the national capture of state power by the Republican Right has
ushered in a new ideological climate in which capital accumulation
has become its own legitimation (Smith and Judd, 1984), local
jurisdictions cannot act unilaterally to resist the practice of tax
concessions without communicating to both corporate elites and
their own citizens the threatening message of an unfavorable
political climate for business investment. Fearing capital flight,
and unable to manage the popular reactions to local economic

crises, state and local officials have discovered that the path of least resistance lies in symbolically placating the citizenry with promises of future economic growth.

Because state and local governments in the United States are dependent on private investment to generate jobs and future revenues, but are expected by their populations to act autonomously, tax concessions offer a way out of an impossible contradiction. With limited resources at their disposal to insure stable employment in a globalized economy, state and local officials have seized upon the rhetoric of "tax incentives" to symbolize their active initiative in local economic development. In this way state and local officials mask their political weakness, deflect criticisms from overburdened taxpaying households, point with pride to whatever investment has been lured by the salesmanship of public–private partnerships, and escape their obligation to mediate conflicting political interests, by pretending that growth policies have no losers, but benefit the "community-as-a-whole." (For extended criticisms of this conception of politics see Smith, 1979, 1983; Swanstrom, 1985.) This is yet another use of the US tax state, its use by the direct beneficiaries of tax expenditures to foster the illusion that no one pays when "the economy" is unleashed from its political fetters through tax incentives.

In an effort to manufacture this illusion, scores of corporate elites have argued before congressional subcommittees that tax incentives do make a major economic difference in their locational decisions. For example, the debate over the use of industrial Revenue Bonds (IRBs), a form of fiscal welfare offered to state and local governments by the federal government, reveals much about the institutions which promote and benefit most from their use. Most of the support for IRBs comes from the quasi-public economic development agencies which coordinate public–private partnerships and from the large corporations which benefit most from the fiscal welfare state. Spokespersons for these interests have argued that IRBs should be retained as an effective supply-side capital investment stimulus which will generate jobs and, eventually, local, state, and federal tax revenues. Testimony before various congressional subcommittees reveals a virtually united front among corporate elites, insisting that IRBs are valuable locational incentives that benefit communities through their "multiplier effect" (see Subcommittee on Oversight, 1981).

When confronted with the evidence that tax incentives make little difference in locational decision-making, proponents assert that these incentives are important "signs" of a favorable "business climate" in a city or region. For corporate elites, a key measure of a locality's climate for "doing business" is its willingness to grant tax incentives. Such concessions thus are taken very seriously by large corporations less as a measure of economic cost reduction than as a symbol of political domination. Any local government which does not subordinate itself to this essentially political logic can expect little in the way of new corporate capital investment. In sum, despite their marginal economic significance, "tax incentives" have become a potent symbolic weapon. They have come to signify the willingness of state and local political elites to defer to the reprivatization of "the economy" as a separate container which business is entitled to manage.

THE NEW IMMIGRATION AND THE NEW SWEATSHOPS

Critics of enterprise zone proposals and related tax incentive schemes have aptly characterized them as a method which, if they did "work" in core cities, would accelerate the spread of new immigrant sweatshops there (Glickman, 1981; Goldsmith 1982a). The specter of "bringing the Third World home" is already haunting some core cities in the United States, as the globalization of economic sectors such as textiles and electronics assembly fosters the employment of cheap and politically quiescent illegal immigrant labor. Meanwhile, the threat of further capital flight in primary sector manufacturing reduces the bargaining power of remaining middle income workers, keeps wage structures lower than they otherwise would be, and contributes to income polarization in core cities. Thus, even without national enterprise zone legislation, key conditions anticipated by their critics are already emerging (see Sassen-Koob, 1984; Smith and Judd, 1984).

As we have seen in chapter 8, in contrast to the affluence of technical and scientific professionals, the vast majority of the new "service" jobs in US cities are very poorly paid. In light of the decline of US trade unionism, organizing the low paid clerical and service work force through traditional unionization is a limited strategy for driving up wages to maintain middle-class living standards. The supply of surplus workers is being swelled by the displacement of unionized industrial workers and by the inflow of migrant labor at precisely a time the new technologies are giving high tech companies the option of moving jobs overseas (Serrin, 1983a). For instance, in 1983 Atari announced its intention to move 1,700 assembly jobs from California to Asia to assemble home computers and video games for the world market. It joined other high technology corporations like Intel, Apple, and Wang which had already begun to locate assembly plants in Asian countries. The quest for politically mediated wages as low as $4.00 a day prompted this investment shift to the Pacific basin and Mexico. This shift was a sign that not only attempts to restructure the Snowbelt economy but also the process of Sunbelt development are vulnerable to new rounds of capital flight.

To be sure, assembly of high tech products like computers still remains largely within the USA. Nevertheless, "as the price of more sophisticated personal computers declines, and as profit margins erode, these manufacturers may also move overseas" (*New York Times*, March 19, 1983:1, 21). In such circumstances, those firms that remain in the United States have increasingly begun to resemble the new sweatshops that have sprung up in many US cities in textile manufacturing, another highly competitive global industry.

Decline of stable markets due to intensified international competition in the textile sector has recreated the classical conditions of overexploitation portrayed by early 20th century social reformers like Jacob Riis and Lewis Hine. Production in the new sweatshops is organized within the new immigrant enclaves in US cities to make the firms more competitive globally. Thousands of small garment factories have been established in many major urban centers in the past decade. Chicago, Boston, New York, Los Angeles, and other Sunbelt cities with large Hispanic labor pools have hundreds of sweatshops. New York is estimated to house over 3,000 (Malone, 1982:28; see also Portes, 1983).

The spread of these new sweatshops can be traced to two key dimensions of the new global political economy. First, as certain manufacturing sectors like textiles become globalized, foreign produced clothing, relying on inexpensive, politically weak Third World labor, accounts for an increasing share of the American market. For example, reliable estimates indicate that in 1983 nearly 50 percent of women's clothing was produced abroad. Intensified global competition has forced American clothing manufacturers, operating in an already competitive domestic environment of thousands of small, undercapitalized firms, to further cut costs by relying on sweatshops whenever possible. Second, the dramatic rise in illegal immigration to the United States has made such overexploitive conditions increasingly possible in core cities, for it concentrates there a steady supply of cheap and politically manageable labor.

Just how exploitative these conditions are was recently revealed in a series of articles by Serrin (1983a) dealing with "new" labor conditions in the garment industry in New York City. Beyond describing working conditions as "hot, bleak, unsanitary, and unsafe," Serrin documents the depressed pay and virtual absence of benefits.

> In many cases, the minimum wage, $3.35 an hour, is ignored. Employers, particularly in nonunion shops, pay few benefits, and often no overtime. Holiday pay is often late or is not given to workers. Sweatshops can be union or nonunion shops. The union label, while it generally means that garments that carry it have been sewn in shops with better working conditions than have clothes that do not, is no guarantee that government or contractual wage, hour, and workplace standards have been met. Workers can make $5 an hour, particularly in union shops, although wages can run as low as $1 an hour or, for a time, as high as $9 an hour, because of the complicated piecework wage system that has almost always existed in the industry. The industry and the union consider this system efficient . . . although some critics and some workers say that it makes the workers both slave driver and slave.

Thus we see that far from transforming the politics of production, US trade unions, weakened by both New Right state policies and the new internationalization of production, have actually colluded in preserving some of the most exploitative features of the "new" productive relations.

It is important to realize that neither sweatshop-like organization of production nor trade union vulnerability is limited to the most competitive sectors. In less competitive industrial sectors, unionized manufacturers frequently contract out to small assembly shops that employ non-union workers. This practice enables large corporations to take advantage of the latter's cheaper wages, limited regulations, and dependent labor force. Not surprisingly, the response of US trade unions has been defensive and ineffectual (Portes and Walton, 1981).

Given the vulnerability of US trade unions and the virtual lack of working class representation in the American political party system historically, what other channels are currently available for people experiencing declining living conditions stemming from "recapitalization" and global capital restructuring? Historically, two basic modes of response by popular classes to worsening economic conditions have been: (a) the pooling of resources by households through informal support networks; and (b) the collective mobilization of demands by adversely affected communities directed at agencies of the state. What have been the responses of households and communities in the US to the new conditions ushered in by the internationalization of production and the fiscal crisis of the welfare state? What are the major political consequences of the growing reliance by households on the "informal economy" to survive in the face of declining social welfare services and decreased opportunities for making a living through formal wage labor? How are the prospects for grassroots political mobilization affected by the globalization of production relations, the crisis of the welfare state, the rise of new sweatshops, the spread of the informal economy, and the movement of the fourth great wave of immigrants to the service based economies of the growing cities of the Sunbelt?

THE INFORMAL ECONOMY

Integral to the analysis of the interplay between the global restructuring of capital and urban politics is the spread of the "informal economy." Portes (1983:159) defines the informal economy as "the sum total of income-producing activities in which members of a household engage, *excluding* income from contractual and legally regulated employment." This includes a broad range of activities such as direct subsistence, the production and exchange of goods or services by the self-employed, and the employment of unprotected wage labor (Portes, 1983:159–61;

see also Mingione, 1983). In the USA, the provision of personal services, labor exchange, and industrial subcontracting are examples of such "informal" activity.

The growth of informal production of this sort as a household "survival strategy" (Mingione, 1983) in the face of global economic restructuring and the crisis of the welfare state has several important political implications. Like fiscal welfare, informalization reduces the ability of the welfare state to deliver services by weakening the state's capacity to tax "in respect to the real volume of goods and services . . . produced" (Mingione, 1983:320). Because the entire burden of state expenditures falls upon the formal sector, firms in this sector, in turn, seek to avoid the increasing tax burden by intensifying political pressures upon the state for tax breaks and informalizing parts of their operations through subcontracting, capital flight, and the like.

The growing informal sector also puts pressure on the national and local state in the form of deepening fiscal crises. These intertwined processes, by reducing both public revenues and formal job opportunities, intensify the need for more and more workers to enter the informal economy as a survival strategy in the face of state revenue and service cutbacks and deindustrialization. As household barter, labor exchange, and self-production come to substitute for public services and purchased goods and services as means for reproducing households, more and more time is subtracted from the available supply of wage labor. Ironically, this situation complicates the possibilities for labor exploitation and capital accumulation in the US urban system by reducing the scope of the basic form of worker exploitation under capitalism – wage labor. (See Mingione, 1983:323 for a discussion of other dimensions of reduced availability of labor time as a result of growing informalization in other countries.)

Consider the following example from California's Silicon Valley. Employment restructuring in Silicon Valley has placed the blue collar work force, particularly immigrants and women, in a structurally disadvantaged position. Nevertheless, Katz and Kemnitzer (1983:334) have identified the many ways by which individuals and households knowingly take advantage of the contradictions of their situation. For example, they extract free time and obviate the need for paid day-care services by working at nominally lower paid industrial homework; they increase their income beyond wages available inside factories by subcontracting, job-hopping, and moonlighting; and they supplement their income derived from wage labor by such informal activities. In these ways, individuals and households are not merely passive objects of social change. Rather, in the face of economic and political restructuring people "make choices for themselves that allow not only survival, but assertion of self and flexibility in the arrangement of their work, compatible with their life situation and with their definition and understanding of it."

These practices, of course, are double-edged phenomena. On the one hand, informalization enables particular individuals and households to survive outside the regulative controls of wage labor. On the other, the growing informal sector undermines the already weakened fiscal basis of the social wage paid by the welfare state because of the lost tax revenues that it engenders (Mingione, 1983). Informalization also reduces the need for capitalist employers in the mainstream economy to pay direct and indirect wages sufficient to reproduce labor power. Indeed, as Wolpe (1975:247) has pointed out: "The most important condition enabling capitalism to pay for labor power below its cost of reproduction . . . is the availability of a supply of labor power which is produced and reproduced outside the capitalist mode of production."

The growing prevalence of informal household labor outside formal wage labor arrangements also has implications for how working people are likely to interact with political institutions. Wage labor in the formal sector remains connected to political life through trade unionism, whereas labor in the informal sector is more likely to be connected to the political system through community organization.

Several conditions underlie the connection of informal workers to political life through residential community. To begin with, informal workers often engage in petty commodity production and piecework within places of residence (Mingione, 1983; Portes, 1983). Furthermore, they often are concentrated in immigrant communities which lack services, amenities, and access to institutions of the wider city and society. In addition, many informal sector workers are women, whose traditional responsibility for social reproduction makes them especially concerned about issues relating to the quality of everyday life in their residential communities (see Castells, 1984). Finally, beleaguered US trade unions have made little effort to organize these new workers, who lack citizen rights and are not concentrated in large workplaces. Thus we see that the residential community has become the shopfloor of workers in the informal sector.

COMMUNITY MOBILIZATION AND THE LOCAL STATE

During earlier periods of mass immigration to US cities, white ethnic groups from Europe and black migrants from the rural South caused problems of social control for local political elites. Political mobilization of these popular classes over issues of employment, public service, and the quality of community life led to the development of political relations, first between white ethnics and urban political machines, and later between blacks and public bureaucracies. The purpose of these relations was to coopt opposition and to confer legitimacy on the political system.

The past decade's migration to US cities has created different problems for local political elites. Consisting largely of illegal workers from Latin America and Asia, the new migrants have not been directly connected to either the mainstream economy or the political system. Nevertheless, the very concentration of large numbers of illegal migrants in core cities has compounded the political management problems of local public officials. It has done so by contributing to the growth of the informal economy, thereby reducing the capacity of urban governments to tax and provide public services through revenue sharing. The growth of informal work thus has contributed to the deepening of the urban fiscal crisis. In the wider context of national fiscal retrenchment, alliances between local officials and mainstream constituencies have been threatened by the erosion of the fiscal base for cementing such relations.

It follows that the growing numbers of illegal migrants in US cities may eventually provoke political discontent among *other* social groups. One possibility is that as migrants compete with other lower income citizens for "off-the-books" jobs, the latter workers will rebel, as apparently occurred in the 1980 revolt in Miami's black ghetto. For these reasons, what at first glance appears to be a minor problem for urban political elites may prove to be a problematic situation, fraught with considerable potential for mass mobilization and political instability.

The class structure of US cities increasingly reflects the sectoral and spatial crises of the national and global political economies. In the Snowbelt, "growth coalitions" of business and government leadership have coopted some segments of organized labor (Friedland, 1983b) but still face the institutionalized political leverage of mobilized grassroots neighborhood organizations (Mollenkopf, 1983; Smith, 1987). In the Sunbelt, where a growing segment of the workforce lacks the basic right of citizenship, investors and government officials appear at first glance to face much weaker pressures from below (Mollenkopf, 1983; Davis, 1984; Sassen-Koob, 1984).

In addition to lack of political rights, other dimensions of the social, cultural, and political structures of Sunbelt cities may be regarded as barriers to the grassroots political mobilization of the new urban immigrants. The widespread poverty and low level of education among Mexican-American immigrants, and their past history of alienation from the political arena, inhibit political participation (Bloomberg and Martinez-Sandoval, 1982:122). The privatistic ethos of southerners and new southern white migrants favors good basic local government services but opposes local public expenditures for social and human services (Lupsha and Siembieda, 1977). The scale and forms of "return migration" as a survival strategy among Hispanic migrants retards the creation of channels for local political influence within Sunbelt cities, as it once did for Italian immigrants to the USA in the early 20th century (Erie, 1985). The prevalence of "reformed" local political institutions like at-large and non-partisan elections impedes neighborhood-based political mobilization. Urban patronage and social policy bureaucracies, the traditional mechanisms linking older waves of ethnic migrants to the political system (Erie, 1985) are no longer available in the current period of fiscal austerity. The more limited functions assumed by Sunbelt city governments limit the use of public sector jobs as both a target of political mobilization and a mechanism of political integration (Lupsha and Siembieda, 1977; Bloomberg, 1979; Erie, 1985).

Despite these unfavorable conditions, grassroots mobilization at the neighborhood level has become an instrumental political force in many Sunbelt cities. The emergent style of neighborhood politics in these cities has included: the rise of neighborhood associations as interest groups; the use of spatial concentration by both the new professional stratum and racial and ethnic minorities as a political resource; the creation of smaller city council districts to express the place-based interests of neighborhoods; and the proliferation of community organizations as mechanisms to connect individuals and households to the apparatus of the local state (Abbott, 1981:212).

Ironically, the mounting social costs of unregulated urban growth in Sunbelt cities has produced the defection of a growing segment of the "yuppie" stratum from the pro-growth coalitions and pro-business development taxation policies which initially created their jobs. The call for an improved "quality of life" has become the rallying cry of the new neighborhood movement in Sunbelt cities. The urban upper-middle class segment of the new neighborhood movement has resisted traffic congestion, highway expansion and commercial encroachment into residential neighborhoods. According to a major study of the new movement (Abbott, 1981:213): "Their concerns also support efforts to preserve and rehabilitate old housing and old neighborhoods, to slow the rapid turnover in population, and to promote stable racial integration." The movement has forcefully raised the issue of who should pay for the mounting environmental costs of publicly subsidized rapid growth. An anti-growth oriented "quality of life" movement has recently emerged as an effective political force even in traditionally growth-oriented Los Angeles (Higbee, 1987:3).

What can be said of the black and Hispanic segments of the new neighborhood movement? In several Sunbelt cities (as in older American cities in other regions) there has been a shift in political alliances by racial and ethnic groups away from growth-oriented toward neighborhood-oriented whites (Abbott, 1981:214). Abandoning the older pattern of making deals with pro-growth forces in exchange for city jobs, favors, and marginal increases in public housing, black and Hispanic neighborhood leaders have discovered that neighborhood-based local government electoral forms and neighborhood targeting of community improvement funds can be used to improve conditions in the ghettos and barrios as well as in gentrified urban neighborhoods. As a result of this political shift, ward-based voting has been adopted in Atlanta, San Antonio, Richmond, Fort Worth, Albuquerque, and, for a time, in San Francisco. Hispanic mayors have been elected in Denver and San Antonio, an anti-growth activist has been elected to the Los Angeles city council, and a "managed growth" oriented woman now heads Houston's city government. Black mayors have been elected in New Orleans and Atlanta, though in these instances by maintaining a delicate balance between pro-growth and "managed growth" forces (see Smith and Keller, 1983; Higbee, 1987).

It must be cautioned, however, that the resilience of the new neighborhood oriented urban political coalitions may prove increasingly precarious because the emergent terrain of the new urban politics includes other potentially divisive issues. Such emerging issues as the need for jobs, the form and content of community economic development, the enforcement of immigration laws, and citizen rights for new immigrants, for example, may prove divisive to loosely linked multi-class coalitions of neighborhood groups united around an agenda of "managed growth," a better "quality of life," and improved neighborhood services.

Whatever the fate of these coalitions, Hispanic interests are likely to become a more powerful element in Sunbelt politics. In some Sunbelt cities – San Antonio, El Paso, and Los Angeles – Hispanics already approach 50 percent of the population. While many of them are not yet citizens, "the sons and daughters of undocumented aliens born in the United States are citizens and thus ultimately will be eligible voters" (Erie, 1985). Most undocumented aliens are Mexican; and since the average age of Mexican-Americans is 18 – compared to age 30 for Anglos – they will undoubtedly become a crucial electoral force. This is especially true in the leading cities of California and Texas, where 85 percent of Mexican-Americans and undocumented Mexicans live. Their growing electoral influence in these two states is all the more important given that California and Texas now command nearly one-fourth of the votes in the presidential electoral college (Erie, 1985).

It is nonetheless true that the connection between this demographic trend and political mobilization and influence has not yet crystallized into predictable patterns. Although the concentrated numbers of Mexican-Americans in specific cities and neighborhoods has become a political resource in some Sunbelt cities (e.g. San Antonio), their growing numbers have not been translated into political power in others (e.g. Houston). Moreover, the pronounced residential segregation among Chicanos may enable local government officials to channel the limited benefits they do have at their disposal so as to reinforce the political isolation of

Mexican-Americans. This possibility may impede the formation of wider political alliances, just as the anti-poverty program of the 1960s politically isolated blacks (see Cloward and Piven, 1974, 1978).

CONCLUSIONS

Three interrelated political-economic realities, the rise of the fiscal welfare state, the proliferation of public-private partnerships to promote urban revitalization, and the growing informal economy, have significantly shaped the US urban system. The political consequences of these developments should not be taken lightly. These consequences start with the reduced capacity of the state to tax the actual volume of economic transactions. This, in turn, makes the delivery of adequate public services increasingly difficult to achieve. The inadequacy of public services in turn has political ramifications for urban politics.

The twin forces of national political restructuring under Reagan and global economic restructuring have weakened the political leverage of US trade unions. In the current period unions have been displaced as channels for representing political interests by the growing importance of community-based movements for improved services and living conditions. Community organizations have emerged as an increasingly important channel of popular pressure on local governments. In declining parts of the Snowbelt local political elites have responded to local pressures for job creation with calls for enterprise zones. In rapidly growing parts of the Sunbelt local officials are responding to public pressures occasioned by rapid growth with proposals to control land use and manage growth's adverse environmental effects. In both instances, the policies are indicators of shifting balances of political power.

The creation of enterprise zones and public–private partnerships to stem the outflow of capital is a sign of a shifting balance of power in favor of corporate business interests in regions of previous labor strength. Thus, such proposals cannot be expected to slow the continued growth of the domestic informal sector, which has drawn capital abroad and now attracts it to new peripheries within the core (Sassen-Koob, 1983).

The growth of grassroots political mobilizations in Sunbelt

cities is an important development because the former political quiescence of the region was a factor attracting new investment there (Mollenkopf, 1983). Thus, ironically, the interplay of the new immigration, informalization, the fiscal crisis of urban services, and the spread of neighborhood political mobilization in Sunbelt cities is contributing to the erosion of the quiescent and privatistic style of local politics that was once a key dimension of Sunbelt growth.

In the short run, the reliance by new immigrant households on self-help and the informal economy to survive the twin onslaught of declining social services and disappearing industrial jobs has had conservative political implications. These have included the reduced costs to capital of reproducing labor power, the individualism of "household" rather than "community" responses to crisis, and the willingness of marginalized people to engage in additional personal labor rather than working to transform the relations of production and politics through collective action. Likewise the immediate effects of the rise of Reaganomics nationally and the spread of the fiscal welfare approach to public policy from the federal government to the local state have been conservative – the weakening of the social wage, the "privatization" of public services, and the consolidation of capitalist hegemony in the productive sphere.

In the long run, however, the contradictions of these socially constructed realities have sown the seeds of new forms of local crisis – joblessness in declining cities, inadequate services in growing cities, and generalized neglect of the urban infrastructure. The active social base supporting the fiscal welfare state nationally has compounded these locality crises by reducing the level of federal government support for local public services. Ironically, as the social costs of the rise of the tax state have become increasingly apparent locally, cracks have begun to appear in the social base of support for fiscal welfare. This has taken the form of grassroots movements which include middle strata opposition to extending business tax breaks which impoverish local public services. The structure of the American political system allows for the representation of social discontent at the level of the local state. The new grassroots political mobilization in Sunbelt cities is an encouraging sign that the restructuring of the state, capital, labor, and communities may yet produce new forms of popular resistance to elite restructuring.

References

Abbott, Carl (1981) *The New Urban America: Growth and Politics in Sunbelt Cities*. Chapel Hill: University of North Carolina Press.

Abrahamson, Mark, Ephraim Mizruchi and Carlton Hornung (1976) *Stratification and Mobility*. New York: Macmillan.

Alclay, R. and D. Mermelstein (eds.) (1977) *The Fiscal Crisis of American Cities*. New York: Vintage.

Alperovitz, Gar and Jeff Faux (1984) *Rebuilding America*. New York: Pantheon Books.

Altshuler, Alan (1970) *Community Control: The Black Demand for Participation in Large American Cities*. New York: Pegasus.

Anderson, Karen (1981) "The Quiet Repeal of the Corporate Income Tax," *New York Times* (August 2): Sec. 3: 1, 20.

Anderson, Martin (1964) *The Federal Bulldozer*. Cambridge, MA: MIT Press.

Appelbaum, Richard and John I. Gilderbloom (1983) "Housing Supply and Regulation: A Study of the Rental Housing Market," *Journal of Applied Behavioral Science,* 19(1): 1–18.

Arenson, Karen (1982) "The 25% of 'Expenditures' Washington Never Sees," *New York Times* (February 7): 4E.

Aronowitz, Stanley (1981) *South Bronx Revitalization Program and Development Guide. A Critique*. New York: Urban Research and Strategy Center.

Aronowitz, Stanley and C. Goodman (1981) "Ghetto Enterprise Zones: A Walk on the Supply Side," *The Nation* (February 21): 207–208.

Arroyo, Enrique (1981) "Federal Urban Nonpolicy," *New York Times* (January 16): 27.

Bachrach, Peter, and Morton Baratz (1962) "Two Faces of Power," *American Political Science Review* 56 (December): 947–952.

Bachrach, Peter and Morton Baratz, (1963) "Decisions and Nondecisions: An Analytical Framework," *American Political Science Review, 57* (September): 632–642.

Bachrach, Peter and Morton Baratz (1970) *Power and Poverty: Theory and Practice*. New York: Oxford University Press.

Banfield, Edward (1970) *Unheavenly City*. Boston: Little, Brown.

Banfield, Edward (1974) *Unheavenly City Revisited*. Boston: Little, Brown.

Barnekov, Timothy K., Daniel Rich and Robert Warren (1981) "The New Privatism, Federalism, and the Future of Urban Governance: National Urban Policy in the 1980s," *Journal of Urban Affairs* 3 (Fall): 1–15.

Barros, Steven M. (1978) *The Urban Impacts of Federal Policies*, Vol. 3, *Fiscal Conditions*, Rand: Santa Monica.

Beauregard, Robert A. (1983) "Structural Analysis and Urban Redevelopment," *Comparative Urban Research*, 9(2): 47–52.

Bendick, Marc (1983) "Workers Dislocated by Economic Change," *The Urban Institute Policy and Research Report*, 13(3) (Fall): 1-4.

Bernard, Richard M. and Bradley R. Rice (eds.) (1983) *Sunbelt Cities: Politics and Growth Since World War II*. Austin: University of Texas Press.

Best, Michael H. and William Connolly (1982) *The Politicized Economy*. Lexington, MA: D.C. Heath.

Birkhead, Jesse (1975) "The Political Economy of Urban America: National Urban Policy Revisited." In G. Gappert and H. Rose (eds.), *The Social Economy of Cities*, Urban Affairs Annual Review 19. Beverly Hills: Sage.

Blair, John P. and David Nachmias (1979) "Urban Policy in the Lean Society," pp. 1–29 in John Blair and David Nachmias (eds.), *Fiscal Retrenchment and Urban Policy*. Beverly Hills: Sage:

Block, Fred (1981) "The Fiscal Crisis of the Capitalist State," *Annual Review of Sociology*, 7: 1–27.

Bloomberg, Warner (1979) "Anglo Retrenchment and Hispanic Renaissance: A View from the Southwest." In J.P. Blair and D. Nachmias (eds.), *Fiscal Retrenchment and Urban Policy*. Beverly Hills: Sage.

Bloomberg, Warner and Rodrigo Martinez-Sandoval (1982) "The Hispanic-American Urban Order: A Border Perspective," pp. 112–132 in Gary Gappert and Richard Knight (eds.), *Cities in the 21st Century*. Beverly Hills: Sage.

Bluestone, Barry and Bennett Harrison (1982) *The Deindustrialization of America*. New York: Basic Books.

Body-Gendrot, Sophie (1987) "Plant Closures in Socialist France," pp. 237–51 in Michael Peter Smith and Joe R. Feagin (Eds.), *The Capitalist City: Global Restructuring and Community Politics*. Oxford: Basil Blackwell.

Boston Globe (March 25–31, May 30, 1974): 1ff.

Bourdieu, Pierre and Jean-Claude Passeron (1977) *Reproduction in Education, Society and Culture*. Beverly Hills: Sage.

Bowles, Samuel (1971) "Unequal Education and the Reproduction of the Social Division of Labor," *Review of Radical Political Economics*, 3(4).

Bowles, Samuel and Herbert Gintis (1976) *Schooling in Capitalist America: Educational Reforms and the Contradictions of Economic Life*. New York: Basic Books.

Boyd, Gerald (1984) "Vouchers – Key to Housing the Poor?" *New York Times* (February 19): 4E.

Bradford, Calvin P. and Leonard F. Rubinowitz (1975) "The Urban-Suburban Investment Disinvestment Process," pp. 77–86 in *American Academy of Political and Social Science*, Annals, 422.

Brebner, J.B. (1948) "Laissez Faire and State Intervention in Nineteenth-Century Britain," *Journal of Economic History*: 59–73.

Brittain, John (1977) *The Inheritance of Economic Status*. Washington, DC: Brookings Institution.

Brooks, J. Michael (1981) "Dual Housing Markets: Applications of Theory and Research," Paper presented at the Annual Meeting of the Southern Sociological Society, (April).

Buchanan, James and Gordon Tullock (1962) *The Calculus of Consent: Logical Foundations of Constitutional Democracy.* Ann Arbor: University of Michigan Press.

Business Week (1981) "State and Local Government in Trouble," (October 26): 135–181.

Butler, Stuart (1981) *Enterprise Zones: Greenlining the Inner Cities.* New York: Universe Books.

Campbell, Allen K., Roy Bahl and David Greylack (1974) *Taxes, Expenditures and the Economic Base.* New York: Praeger.

Castells, Manuel (1975) "Urban Sociology and Urban Politics: From a Critique to New Trends of Research," *Comparative Urban Research* 3(1):7–13.

Castells, Manuel (1976a) "Theoretical Propositions for an Experimental Study of Urban Social Movements," pp. 147–173 in C.G. Pickvance (ed.), *Urban Sociology: Critical Essays.* London: Tavistock Publications.

Castells, Manuel (1976b) "Theory and Ideology in Urban Sociology," pp. 60–84 in C.G. Pickvance (ed.), *Urban Sociology: Critical Essays.* London: Tavistock Publications.

Castells, Manuel (1977) *The Urban Question.* Cambridge, MA: M.I.T. Press.

Castells, Manuel (1978) *City, Class, and Power.* New York: St Martin's.

Castells, Manuel (1983) *The City and the Grassroots.* Berkeley: University of California Press.

Castells, Manuel (1984) "Space and Society: Managing the New Historical Relationships," pp. 235–260 in Michael Peter Smith (ed.), *Cities in Transformation.* Beverly Hills: Sage.

Castells, Manuel (ed.) (1985) *High Technology, Space and Society.* Beverly Hills: Sage.

Chase-Dunn, Christopher (1984) "Urbanization in the World System: New Directions for Research," pp. 111–120 in Michael Peter Smith (ed.), *Cities in Transformation: Class, Capital and the State.* Beverly Hills: Sage.

Cho, Yong Hyo and David Puryear (1980) "Distressed Cities: Targeting HUD Programs," pp. 191–210 in Donald B. Rosenthal (ed.), *Urban Revitalization.* Beverly Hills: Sage.

Choate, Pat and Susan Walter (1981a) *America in Ruins.* Council of State Planning Agencies.

Choate, Pat and Susan Walter (1981b) "Public Facilities: Key to Economic Revival," *American Federationist* (August): 9–14.

Cloward, Richard A. and Frances Fox Piven (1974) *The Politics of Turmoil.* New York: Pantheon.

Cloward, Richard and Frances Fox Piven (1978) *Poor People's Movements: Why They Succeed? How They Fail?* New York: Vintage.

Cockburn, Cynthia (1977) "The Local State: Management of Cities and People," *Race and Class,* 18(4): 363–376.

Coleman, James (1976) "Liberty and Equality in School Desegregation," *Social Policy,* 6: 9–13.

Cowley, John (1977) "The Politics of Community Organising." pp. 222–242 in John Cowley et al. (eds.), *Community or Class Struggle?* London: Stage 1.

Crenson, Matthew (1971) *The UnPolitics of Air Pollution.* Baltimore: Johns Hopkins.

Crittenden, Ann (1981) "Reagan's Agricultural Policy Emerges as Lobbies and Budget Cutters Clash," *New York Times* (April 10): 8.

Cuomo, Mario (1974) *Forest Hills Diary*. New York: Random House.

Dahl, Robert (1961) *Who Governs? Democracy and Power in an American City*. New Haven: Yale University Press.

Daniels, B. (1982) "Capital is Only Part of the Problem," pp. 53–76 in P.J. Bearse (ed.), *Mobilizing Capital*. New York: Elsevier Science Publishing Co.

Daniels, Lee (1981) "New York Assails Reagan Proposal on Public Housing," (November 15): 1, 21.

Danziger, Sheldon, Robert Haveman, and Robert Plotnick (1980) "Retrenchment or Reorientation: Options for Income Support Policy," *Public Policy* 23(4): (Fall).

Davis, Mike (1984) "The Political Economy of Late Imperial America," *New Left Review*, 143: 6–38.

Davis, Mike (1986) *Prisoners of the American Dream*. London: Verso.

DeGregori, Thomas R. (1974) "Caveat Emptor: A Critique of the Emerging Paradigm of Public Choice," *Administration and Society*, 6(2) (August): 205–228.

Devine, Joel (1983) "Fiscal Policy and Class Income Inequality: The Distributional Consequences of Governmental Revenues and Expenditures in the US 1949–1976," *American Sociological Review*, 48: 606–622.

Dunleavy, P. (1980) *Urban Political Analysis*. London: Macmillan.

Engels, Friedrich (1844) "The Condition of the Working Class in England in 1844."

Erie, Steven P. (1985) "Rainbow's End: From the Old to the New Urban Ethnic Politics," pp. 249–275 in J.W. Moore and L.A. Maldonado (eds.), *Urban Ethnicity in the United States*. Beverly Hills: Sage.

Esping-Anderson, Gøsta (1985) *Politics Against Markets: The Social Democratic Road to Power*. Princeton: Princeton University Press.

Fainstein, Norman and Susan Fainstein (1976) "The Future of Community Control," *American Political Science Review* (September): 905–923.

Fainstein, Susan S. and Norman I. Fainstein (1981) "Production and Welfare in American Cities: Changing Functions and their Consequences for Inequality." Paper presented at the Conference on Urban Political Economy, Department of Economics, the American University, Washington, D.C.

Fainstein, Susan S., Norman I. Fainstein, Richard Child Hill, Dennis Judd and Michael Peter Smith (1983) *Restructuring the City: The Political Economy of Urban Redevelopment*. New York: Longman.

Feagin, Joe R. (1983) *The Urban Real Estate Game*. Englewood Cliffs, NJ: Prentice Hall.

Feagin, Joe R. (1984) "The Socioeconomic Base of Urban Growth: The Case of Houston and the Oil Industry." Unpublished manuscript.

Feagin, Joe R. (1985) "The Global and State Context of Urban Growth: Houston and the Oil Industry," *American Journal of Sociology*, 90 (May): 1204–31.

Feagin, Joe R. and Michael Peter Smith (1987) "Cities and the New International Division of Labor: An Overview," pp. 3–34 in Michael Peter Smith and Joe R. Feagin (eds.), *The Capitalist City: Global Restructuring and Community Politics*. Oxford and New York: Basil Blackwell.

Firestine, Robert (1977) "Economic Growth and Inequality: Demographic Change and the Public Sector Response," pp. 191–210 in David Perry and Alfred Watkins (eds.), *The Rise of the Sunbelt Cities*. Beverly Hills: Sage.

Fligstein, Neil (1981) *Going North: Migration of Blacks and Whites from the South, 1900–1950*. New York: Academic Press.

Friedland, Roger (1983a) "The Politics of Profit and the Geography of Growth," *Urban Affairs Quarterly, 19*(1) (September): 41–54.

Friedland, Roger (1983b) *Power and Crisis in the City*. New York: Schoken.

Friedland, Roger, Frances Fox Piven, and Robert Alford (1977) "Political Conflict, Urban Structure, and Fiscal Crisis." In Douglas Ashford (ed.), *Comparative Public Policy*. Beverly Hills: Sage.

Friedman, Milton (1962) *Capitalism and Freedom*. Chicago: University of Chicago Press.

Friedman, Milton (1973) "The Voucher Idea," *New York Times Magazine* (September 23): 22 ff.

Friedman, Milton and Rose Friedman (1979) *Free to Choose: A Personal Statement*. New York: Harcourt Brace Jovanovich.

Frobel, Folker, Jurgen Heinrichs, and Otto Kreye (1980) *The New International Division of Labor*. Cambridge: Cambridge University Press.

Galbraith, John Kenneth (1969) *The New Industrial State*. Boston: Houghton Mifflin.

Galbraith, John Kenneth (1973) *Economics and the Public Purpose*. Boston: Houghton Mifflin.

Galbraith, John Kenneth (1981) "The Conservative Onslaught," *New York Review of Books* (January): 30–36.

Gans, Herbert (1972) *More Equality*. New York: Random House.

GAO Report (1982) "Revitalizing Distressed Areas through Enterprise Zones: Many Uncertainties Exist." Report by the Comptroller General to the Congress of the United Sates, US General Accounting Office (July 15).

Gappert, Gary and Harold Rose (eds.) (1975) *The Social Economy of Cities*. Beverly Hills: Sage.

George, Vic and Paul Wilding (1976) *Ideology and Social Welfare*. London: Routledge & Kegan Paul.

Giddens, Anthony (1981) *A Contemporary Critique of Historical Materialism*. London: Macmillan.

Gilderbloom, John I. and Richard P. Appelbaum (1987) *America's Rental Housing Crisis*. Philadelphia: Temple University Press.

Ginsberg, Benjamin (1984) "Money and Power: The New Political Economy of American Elections." In Thomas Ferguson and Joel Rogers (eds.), *The Political Economy: Readings in the Politics and Economics of American Public Policy*. New York: M.E. Sharpe.

Gist, John (1980) "Urban Development Action Grants: Design and Implementation," pp. 237–252 in Donald B. Rosenthal (ed.), *Urban Revitalization*. Beverly Hills: Sage.

Glickman, Norman J. (1981) "Emerging Urban Policies in a Slow Growth Economy: Conservative Initiatives and Progressive Responses in the United States," *International Journal of Urban and Regional Research, 5*(4): 492–527.

Goetz, Rolf (1981a) "The Housing Bubble," *Working Papers* (January-February): 44–52.

Goetz, Rolf (1981b) "Housing, Inflation and Taxes," *New York Times* (March 18).

Goldsmith, William (1982a) "Enterprise Zones: If They Work We're in Trouble," *International Journal of Urban and Regional Research* 6(3): 435–442.

Goldsmith, William (1982b) "Enterprise Zones," *New York Times* (February 8): 23.

Goodman, Robert (1979) *The Last Entrepreneurs: America's Regional Wars for Jobs and Dollars*. Boston: South End Press.

Goodwin, Leonard (1972) *Do the Poor Want to Work?* Washington, DC: Brookings.

Gordon, David M. (1972) *Theories of Poverty and Underemployment*. Lexington, MA: D.C. Heath.

Gordon, David (1977) "Class Struggle and the Stages of Urban Development," pp.55–82 in David Perry and Al Watkins (eds.), *The Rise of the Sunbelt Cities*. Beverly Hills: Sage.

Gordon, David M., Richard Edwards, and Michael Reich (1982) *Segmented Work, Divided Workers*. Cambridge: Cambridge University Press.

Gorz, Andre (1982) *Farewell to the Working Class*. Boston: South End Press.

Gottdiener, M. (1985) *The Social Production of Urban Space*. Austin: University of Texas Press.

Gough, Ian (1979) *The Political Economy of the Welfare State*. London: Macmillan.

Gramsci, Antonio (1971) *Prison Notebooks*. New York: International Publishers.

Greenhouse, Steven (1983a) "Searching for Profits at Bethlehem," *New York Times* (December 25): Section 3: 1, 19.

Greenhouse, Steven (1983b) "US Steel's Closings Reflect a Strategy," *New York Times* (December 29): 32.

Habermas, Jürgen (1973) *Legitimation Crisis*. Boston: Beacon Press.

Harris, Patricia (1981) "Economic Scene: A New Burden for Business," *New York Times* (August 12): D2.

Harrison, Bennett (1982) "The Politics and Economics of the Urban Enterprise Zone Proposal: A Critique," *International Journal of Urban and Regional Research*, 6(3): 422–428.

Harrison, Bennett and Barry Bluestone (1984) "More Jobs, Lower Wages," *New York Times* (June 19): A27.

Hartman, Chester, Dennis Keating and LeGates (1981) *Displacement: How to Fight It*. Berkeley, CA: National Housing Law Project.

Harvey, David (1973) *Social Justice and the City*. Baltimore: Johns Hopkins University Press.

Harvey, David (1975a) "Class-Monopoly Rent, Finance Capital and the Urban Revolution." In Stephen Gale and Eric Moore (eds.), *The Manipulated City: Perspectives on Spatial Structure and Social Issues in Urban America*. Chicago: Maaroufa Press.

Harvey, David (1975b) "The Political Economy of Urbanization in Advanced Capitalist Societies: The Case of the US," pp. 119–163 in Gary Gappert and Harold M. Rose (eds.), *The Social Economy of Cities*. Beverly Hills: Sage.

Harvey, David (1976) "Labor, Capital, and Class Struggle Around the Built Environment in Advanced Capitalist Societies," *Politics and Society* 6(3): 265–295.

Harvey, David (1982) *The Limits to Capital.* Chicago: University of Chicago Press.

Harvey, David (1985) *The Urbanization of Capital.* Oxford: Basil Blackwell.

Heady, Bruce (1978) *Housing Policy in the Developed Economy.* New York: St Martin's Press.

Heidenheimer, Arnold, Hugh Heclo, and Carolyn Adams (1975) *Comparative Public Policy.* New York: St. Martin's Press.

Heller, Walter (1967) *New Dimensions of Political Economy.* Cambridge: Harvard University Press.

Herbers, John (1972) "Federal Agencies Press Inquiry on Housing Frauds in Big Cities," *New York Times* (May 8): 28.

Herbers, John (1975) "After New York: The Need for a Federal Help-the-Cities Policy," *New York Times* (December 7): 7.

Herbers, John (1980) "Private Incentives: A New Tonic for Tired Old Cities?" *New York Times* (December 28): 4E.

Herbers, John (1982) "Congress Survey Finds Cities Using Property Tax to Absorb Losses in Aid," *New York Times* (October 17): 12.

Herbers, John (1983a) "Census Data Reveal 70s Legacy: Poor Cities and Richer Suburbs," *New York Times* (February 27): 1, 14.

Herbers, John (1983b) "Industrial Flight in Minnesota," *New York Times* (April 12): 33, 38.

Hibbs, Doug and Heino Fassbender (eds) (1981) *Contemporary Political Economy: Studies in the Interdependence of Politics and Economics.* New York: North-Holland Publishing Co.

Higbee, Arthur (1987) "Urban Growth is Slowed In L.A.," *International Herald Tribune* (June 29).

Hill, Richard Child (1974) "Separate and Unequal: Governmental Inequality in the Metropolis," *American Political Science Review, 68* (December): 1557–1568.

Hill, Richard Child (1978) "Fiscal Collapse and Political Struggle in Decaying Central Cities in the United States," pp. 213–240 in William K. Tabb and Larry Sawers (eds.), *Marxism and the Metropolis.* New York: Oxford.

Hill, Richard Child (1983) "Crisis in the Motor City: The Politics of Economic Development in Detroit," pp. 80–125 in Susan S. Fainstein, et al, *Restructuring the City.* New York: Longman.

Hill, Richard Child (1984) "Fiscal Crisis, Austerity Politics, and Alternative Urban Policies," pp. 298–322 in William K. Tabb and Larry Sawers (eds.), *Marxism and the Metropolis.* New York: Oxford University Press.

Hill, Richard Child and Joe R. Feagin (1987) "Detroit and Houston: Two Cities in Global Perspective," pp. 155–177 in Joe R. Feagin and Michael Peter Smith (eds.), *The Capitalist City: Global Restructuring and Community Politics.* Oxford and New York: Basil Blackwell Ltd.

Hirsch, Arnold R. (1983) *Making the Second Ghetto: Race and Housing in Chicago, 1940–1960.* Cambridge: Cambridge University Press.

Hirsh, Joachim (1981) "The Apparatus of the State, the Reproduction of Capital and Urban Conflicts," pp. 155–177 in Michael Dear and Allen J. Scott (eds.), *Urbanization and Urban Planning in Capitalist Society.* London: Methuen.

Hogwood, Bryan and Guy Peters (1985) *The Pathology of Public Policy.* New York: Oxford University Press.

Hunter, Floyd (1953) *Community Power Structure: a Study of Decision Makers.* Chapel Hill: University of North Carolina Press.

James, Dorothy (1972) *Poverty, Politics, and Change.* Englewood Cliffs, NJ: Prentice Hall.

Jencks, Christopher et al. (1972) *Inequality.* New York: Basic Books.

Jessop, Bob (1982) *The Capitalist State.* New York and London: New York University Press.

Johnson, David R., John A. Booth, and Richard J. Harris (eds.) (1983) *The Politics of San Antonio: Community, Progress, and Power.* Lincoln and London: University of Nebraska Press.

Judd, Dennis R. (1983) "From Cowtown to Sunbelt City: Boosterism and Economic Growth in Denver," pp. 167–201 in Susan S. Fainstein et al., *Restructuring the City: The Political Economy of Urban Redevelopment.* New York: Longman.

Judd, Dennis (1984) *The Politics of American Cities: Private Power and Public Policy.* Boston: Little Brown.

Judd, Dennis and Lawrence Mosqueda (1982) "Trickle-Down Theory as Urban Policy." Paper prepared for the Annual Meeting of the Association of Collegiate Schools of Planning, Chicago.

Kalecki, Michal (1972) "Political Aspects of Full Employment," pp. 75–85 in Michal Kalecki, *The Last Phase in the Development of Capitalism.* New York: Monthly Review Press.

Kasarda, John D. (1980) "The Implications of Contemporary Redistributional Trends for National Urban Policy," *Social Science Quarterly, 16*(3 and 4) (December): 373–400.

Kasarda, John D.(1981) "Spatial Redistribution Trends and Public Policy: Prescriptions and Proscriptions," *American Planning Association Journal, 47*(3) (July): 340–345.

Katz, N. and D. S. Kemnitzer (1983) "Fast Forward: The Internationalization of Silicon Valley," pp. 332–345 in June Nash and Maria Patricia Fernandez-Kelly (eds.), *Women, Men and the New International Division of Labor.* Albany: State University of New York Press.

Katznelson, Ira (1976a) "Class Capacity and Social Cohesion in American Cities," pp. 19–36 in Louis Masotti and Robert Lineberry (eds.), *The New Urban Politics.* Cambridge, MA: Ballinger.

Katznelson, Ira (1976b) "The Crisis of the Capitalist City: Urban Politics and Social Control." In Willis Hawley, et al. (eds.), *Theoretical Perspectives on Urban Politics.* Englewood Cliffs: Prentice-Hall.

Katznelson, Ira (1981) *City Trenches: Urban Politics and the Patterning of Class in the US.* New York: Pantheon Books.

Katznelson, Ira and Margaret Weir (1985) *Schooling for All: Class, Race and the Decline of the Democratic Ideal.* New York: Basic Books.

Kay, Adah and Mike Thompson (1977) "The Class Basis of Planning," pp. 101–107 in John Cowley et al. *Community or Class Struggle?* London: Stage 1.

Kennedy, Michael D. (1983) "Urban Fiscal Crisis and Forms of Expenditure: An Empirical Evaluation of Structuralist Urban Theory," *Comparative Urban Research, 9*(2): 28–33.

Kennedy, Michael D. (1984) "The Fiscal Crisis of the City," pp. 91–110 in Michael Peter Smith (ed.), *Cities in Transformation.* Beverly Hills: Sage.

Kilborn, Peter (1983) "Why Prognosticators Strayed: Tax Cut Used for Spending." *New York Times* (December 16): 29.

Kirby, Andrew (1985) "The Politics of Location: An Examination of Conflict and the Local State." Paper presented at the annual meeting of the

American Political Science Association, New Orleans, LA (August-September).

Lefebvre, Henri (1973) *The Survival of Capitalism*. London: Allison and Busby.

Lekachman, Robert (1983) "Review of Robert Reich, The New American Frontier," *New York Times Book Review* (April 26): 1, 18.

Levin, Jeffrey (1985) "Redevelopment and the Local State." Department of City and Regional Planning, U.C. Berkeley, unpublished manuscript.

Lindblom, Charles E. (1977) *Politics and Markets*. New York: Basic Books.

Lipset, Seymour M. (1983) "America's Changing Unions," *New York Times Book Review* (December 11): 1.

Lowi, Theodore J. (1969) *The End of Liberalism: Ideology, Policy, and the Crisis of Public Authority*. New York: W.W. Norton.

Lukes, Steven (1974) *Power: A Radical View*. London: Macmillan.

Lupo, Alan, Frank Colcord and Edmund Fowler (1971) *Rites of Way: The Politics of Transportation in Boston and the US City*. Boston: Little Brown.

Lupsha, Peter A. and William J. Siembieda (1977) "The Poverty of Public Services in the Land of Plenty," pp. 169–190 in D. Perry and A. Watkins (eds.), *The Rise of the Sunbelt Cities*. Beverly Hills: Sage.

Malone, J. H. (1982) "The Questionable Promise of Enterprise Zones: Lessons from England and Italy," *Urban Affairs Quarterly*, 18(1): 19–30.

Marcus, Steven (1974) *Engels, Manchester and the Working Class*. New York: Random House.

Marcuse, Peter (1981) "The Targeted Crisis: On the Ideology of Urban Fiscal Crisis and its Uses," *International Journal of Urban and Regional Research*, 5(3): 330–355.

Marks, Carole (1985) "Black Labor Migration: 1910–1920," *Insurgent Sociologist*, 12(4) (Winter): 5–24.

Markusen, Ann (1979) "The Urban Impact Statement: A Critical Forecast," Working Paper No. 302, Institute of Urban & Regional Development (March), Berkeley: University of California.

Markusen, Ann (1984) "Class and Urban Social Expenditure: A Marxist Theory of Metropolitan Government." In William K. Tabb and Larry Sawers (eds.), *Marxism and the Metropolis: New Perspectives in Urban Political Economy*. New York: Oxford University Press.

Markusen, Ann (1987) *Regions: The Economics and Politics of Territory*. Totowa, NJ: Rowman and Littlefield.

Markusen, Ann and D. Wilmoth (1982) "The Political Economy of National Urban Policy in the USA 1976–81," *Canadian Journal of Regional Science* (Summer).

Marshall, T.H. (1972) "Value Problem of Welfare Capitalism," *Journal of Social Policy* (January): 15–32.

Massey, Doreen (1982) "Enterprise Zones: A Political Issue," *International Journal of Urban and Regional Research*, 6(3): 429–434.

Mayer, Margit (1987) "Restructuring and Popular Opposition in West German Cities," pp. 343–363 in Michael Peter Smith and Joe R. Feagin (eds.), *The Capitalist City: Global Restructuring and Community Politics*. Oxford and New York: Basil Blackwell.

McConnell, Grant (1966) *Private Power and American Democracy*. New York: Alfred Knopf.

McGahey, R. (1981) "In Search of the Undeserving Poor," *Working Papers* (November/ December): 62–64.

McGahey, R. (1983) "High Tech, Low Hopes," *New York Times* (May 15): 23.

Meehan, Eugene (1980) "Urban Development: An Alternative Strategy," pp. 279–301 in Donald B. Rosenthal (ed.), *Urban Revitalization*. Beverly Hills: Sage.

Miller, S.M. (1978) "The Recapitalization of Capitalism," *International Journal of Urban and Regional Research*, 2(2) (June): 202–212.

Miller, S.M. and Donald Tomaskovic-Devey (1983) *Recapitalizing America: Alternatives to the Corporate Distortion of National Policy*. London: Routledge and Kegan Paul.

Mingione, Enzo (1983) "Informalization, Restructuring, and the Survival Strategies of the Working Class," *International Journal of Urban and Regional Research*, 7(3): 311–339.

Minsky, Hyman (1981–82) "The Breakdown of the 1960s Policy Synthesis," *Telos #50* (Winter): 49–58.

Mishra, Ramesh (1977) *Society and Social Policy*. London: Macmillan.

Mollenkopf, John (1975) "The Post War Politics of Urban Development," *Politics and Society* 5(3): 247–296.

Mollenkopf, John (1983) *The Contested City*. Princeton: Princeton University Press.

Molotch, Harvey (1976) "The City as Growth Machine," *American Journal of Sociology, 82* (September): 309–332.

Molotch, Harvey (1979) "Capital and Neighborhood in the US," *Urban Affairs Quarterly*, 289–312.

Molotch, Harvey and John Logan (1980) "Tensions in the Growth Machine: Overcoming Resistance to Value-Free Development," *Social Problems, 31*(5): 483–499.

Morgan, Kevin (1982) "Restructuring Steel: The Crisis of Labor and Locality in Britain," *Working Paper 30, Urban and Regional Studies*, University of Sussex, U.K. (July).

Moriarty, B.M. et al. (1980) *Industrial Location and Community Development*. Chapel Hill: University of North Carolina Press.

Muller, Thomas (1981) "Regional-Urban Policy: Should the Government Intervene?" *The Urban Institute Policy and Research Report, 2*(2) (Summer): 11–14.

Myers, Dowell (1975) "Housing Allowances, Submarket Relationships and the Filtering Process," *Urban Affairs Quarterly, 11*(2) (December): 215–239.

Nash, June (1983) "The Impact of the Changing International Division of Labor on Different Sectors of the Labor Force." In June Nash and Maria Patricia Fernandez-Kelly (eds.), *Women, Men, and the New International Division of Labor*. Albany: State University of New York Press.

Nash, June (1987) "Community and Corporations in the Restructuring of Industry," pp. 275–295 in Michael Peter Smith and Joe R. Feagin (eds.), *The Capitalist City: Global Restructuring and Community Politics*. Oxford: Basil Blackwell.

Nash, June and Maria Patricia Fernandez-Kelly (eds) (1983) *Women, Men, and the New International Division of Labor*. Albany: State University of New York Press.

Nathan, Richard (1983) Cited in John Herbers "Study Tells ..." *New York Times* (May 8).

National Urban Policy Collective (1978) "Carter's National Urban Policy," Berkeley: University of California, Department of City and Regional Planning.

Navarro, Vicente (1985) "The 1984 Election and the New Deal: An Alternative Interpretation," *Social Policy*, 16(1) (Summer): 7–17.

Neiman, Max (1975) *Metropology: Toward a More Constructive Research Agenda*. Beverly Hills: Sage.

Nelson, Joan (1979) *Access to Power*. Princeton: Princeton University Press.

New Orleans Times Picayune/States Item (1983) "Blacks Have Made Major Gains but Economic Equality is Elusive," (June 5): Sec. 1: 16.

New Orleans Times Picayune/States Item (January 2, 1984): 24.

New Orleans Times Picayune/States Item (1985) "Reagan's '87 Plan Includes Selling FHA," (December 14): A1, A5.

New York Times (September 20, 1974): 1, 14.

New York Times (October 7, 1975): 18.

New York Times (November 2, 1975): 6.

New York Times (December 2, 1975): 64.

New York Times (December 4, 1975): 35.

New York Times (February 1, 1978): 1, 38.

New York Times (April 2, 1978): Sec 4: 1.

New York Times (May 15, 1980): A23.

New York Times (January 5–6, 1981): 7.

New York Times (March 25, 1981): 10.

New York Times (November 12, 1981): 12.

New York Times (February 28, 1982): 19.

New York Times (October 27, 1982): 1, 12.

New York Times (November 18, 1982): 16.

New York Times (March 19, 1983): 1, 21.

New York Times (March 20, 1983): E3.

New York Times (August 14, 1983): 22.

New York Times (October 31, 1983): 13.

New York Times (January 29, 1986): 12.

New York Times (March 24, 1986).

New York Times (June 10, 1987): 1.

Newton, Kenneth (1975) "American Urban Politics: Social Class, Political Structure and Public Goods," *Urban Affairs Quarterly*, 11 (December): 241–264.

Newton, Kenneth (1976) "Feeble Governments and Private Power," pp. 37–58 in Louis Masotti and Robert Lineberry (eds.), *The New Urban Politics*. Cambridge, MA: Ballinger.

Niskanen, William (1971) *Bureaucracy and Representative Government*. Chicago: Aldine Atherton.

Nozick, Robert (1974) *Anarchy, State and Utopia*. New York: Basic Books.

O'Connor, James (1973) *The Fiscal Crisis of the State*. New York: St Martin's.

O'Connor, James (1981) "The Meaning of Crises," *International Journal of Urban and Regional Research*. 5(3): 301–329.

O'Connor, James (1984) *Accumulation Crisis*. Oxford: Basil Blackwell.

Okun, Arthur (1977) "Equality and Efficiency: The Big Tradeoff." In David M. Gordon (ed.), *Problems in Political Economy: An Urban Perspective*.

Lexington, Mass.: D.C. Heath: 28–33.

Olivas, Michael A. (1981) "Information Inequities: A Fatal Flaw in Parochaid Plans," pp. 133–149, in Edward M. Gaffney, Jr. (ed.), *Private Schools and The Public Good: Policy Alternatives for the 1980s*. Notre Dame and London: University of Notre Dame Press.

Oser, Alan (1983) "New Federal Rent Rules Will Have Wide Impact," *New York Times* (June 24): 14.

Pahl, Ray (1975) *Whose City?* Harmondsworth: Penguin.

Palen, John J. and Bruce London (eds.) (1984) *Gentrification, Displacement and Neighborhood Revitalization*. Albany: State University of New York Press.

Palloix, C. (1975) *L'Internationalisation du Capital*. Paris: Maspero.

Parkinson, Michael (1985) *Liverpool on the Brink*. Berks: Policy Journals.

Pear, Robert (1981) *New York Times* (March 25): 10.

Pear, Robert (1982) "Reagan's Social Impact," *New York Times* (August 25): 1, 14.

Pear, Robert (1983) "Middle Class Shrinking as More Families Sink into Poverty, Two Studies Find," *New York Times* (December 11): 13.

Pear, Robert (1984) "Rise in Poverty from '79 to '82 is Found in US," *New York Times* (February 24): 1.

Pechman, Joseph A. (1975) "Business Doesn't Need Any More Tax Breaks," *New York Times* (July 20): 12.

Peet, Richard (ed.) (1987) *International Capitalism and Industrial Restructuring*. Boston: Allen and Unwin.

Perry, David C. (1987) "The Politics of Dependency in Deindustrializing America: The Case of Buffalo, New York," pp. 113–137 in Michael Peter Smith and Joe R. Feagin (eds.), *The Capitalist City: Global Restructuring and Community Politics*. Oxford and New York: Basil Blackwell.

Perry, David and Alfred Watkins (eds.) (1977) *The Rise of the Sunbelt Cities*. Beverly Hills: Sage.

Peterson, George (1977) "Shaping – and Misshaping – the Metropolis," *Search, a Report from the Urban Institute*, 7(1) (Spring): 4–8.

Peterson, George (1980) "The Impact of Federal Fiscal Policies on Urban Economic Development." Urban Consortium Information Bulletin, US Department of Commerce, Washington, DC: The Urban Institute (September).

Pickvance, Chris (1976a) "Historical Materialist Approaches to Urban Sociology," pp. 1–32 in C.G. Pickvance (ed.), *Urban Sociology: Critical Essays*. London: Tavistock Publications.

Pickvance, Chris (1976b) "Housing: Reproduction of Capital and Reproduction of Labor Power," pp. 271–289 in John Walton and Louis Masotti (eds.), *The City in Comparative Perspective*. New York: Halstead Press.

Pickvance, Chris (1980) "Theories of the State and Theories of Urban Crisis," *Current Perspectives in Social Theory*, 1: 31–54.

Pickvance, Chris (1984) "The Structuralist Critique in Urban Studies," pp. 31–50 in Michael Peter Smith (ed.), *Cities in Transformation*. Beverly Hills: Sage.

Pierce, Neal (1980) "Highway Cure: Rough Roads Ahead," *New Orleans Times Picayune-States Item* (December 29): 11.

Piven, Frances (1976) "The Social Structuring of Political Protest," *Politics and Society* 6(3): 297–326.

Piven, Frances Fox and Richard Cloward (1971) *Regulating the Poor*. New York: Random House.

Piven, Frances Fox and Richard Cloward (1982) *The New Class War*. New York: Pantheon.

Poltkin, Sidney (1983) "Democratic Change in the Urban Political Economy: San Antonio's Edwards Aquifer Controversy," pp. 157–174 in David R. Johnson, John A. Booth and Richard J. Harris (eds.), *The Politics of San Antonio*. Lincoln and London: University of Nebraska Press.

Pollack, Andrew (1983) "Roles of Telecommunications in Industrial Planning," *New York Times* (May 2): 30.

Polsby, Nelson W. (1963) *Community Power and Political Theory*. New Haven: Yale University Press.

Portes, Alejandro (1983) "The Informal Sector: Definition, Controversy, and Relation to National Development," *Review*, 7(1): 151–174.

Portes, Alejandro and John Walton (1981) *Labor, Class, and the International System*. New York: Academic Press.

Poulantzas, Nicos (1978) *State, Power, Socialism*. London: New Left Books.

President's Commission for a National Agenda for the Eighties (1980) *Urban America in the Eighties*. Washington, DC: US Government Printing Office.

Preteceille, E. (1977) "Equipments, Collectifs et Consumption Sociale," *International Journal of Urban and Regional Research*, 1: 101–123.

Rawls, John (1971) *A Theory of Justice*. Cambridge, MA: Belknap Press of Harvard University Press.

Rawls, Wendell (1983) "Atlanta Begins Drive to Build on Past Success as a Growth City," *New York Times* (April 28): 12.

Reich, Robert (1984) "Whatever Happened to the Welfare Ideal?" *New York Times Book Review* (January 1): 17.

Research Planning Group on Urban Social Services (1978) "The Political Management of the Urban Fiscal Crisis," *Comparative Urban Research*, 5(2,3): 71–84.

Reynolds, Morgan and Eugene Smolensky (1977) *Public Expenditures, Taxes and the Distribution of Income*. New York: Academic Press.

Reynolds, Morgan and Eugene Smolensky (1978) "The Fading Effect of Government on Inequality," *Challenge* (July/August): 32–39.

Roberts, Steven V. (1981) "Sun Belt Bias Seen in Reagan's Budget," *New York Times* (March 1): 1, 16.

Room, Graham (1979) *The Sociology of Welfare: Social Policy, Stratification, and Political Order*. New York: St Martin's Press.

Rosenbaum, David E. (1981a) "Study Shows Planned Welfare Cuts Would Hurt Poor Workers the Most," *New York Times* (March 20): 1, 11.

Rosenbaum, David E. (1981b) "Reagan Aide Concedes Proposal on Welfare Could Add Problem," *New York Times* (March 29): 1,'22.

Ryan, Cheyney C. (1981) "The Fiends of Commerce: Romantic and Marxist Criticisms of Classical Political Economy," *History of Political Economy*, 13(1): 80–94 (Spring).

Ryan, William (1981) *Equality*. New York: Pantheon Books.

Sackrey, Charles (1973) *The Political Economy of Urban Poverty*. New York: W.W. Norton.

Saks, Daniel H. (1983) *Distressed Workers in the Eighties*. Washington, DC: National Planning Association.

Salamon, Lester and John Siegfried (1977) "Economic Power and Political Influence: The Impact of Industry Structure on Public Policy," *American Political Science Review, 71*(4) (December): 1026–1043.

Sassen-Koob, Saskia (1983) "Recomposition and Peripheralization at the Core." In Marlene Dixon and Susanne Jonas (eds.), *From Immigrant Labor to Transnational Working Class.* San Francisco: Synthesis Publications.

Sassen-Koob, Saskia (1984) "The New Labor Demand in Global Cities," pp. 139–171 in Michael Peter Smith (ed.), *Cities in Transformation: Class, Capital, and the State.* Beverly Hills: Sage.

Saunders, Peter (1981) *Social Theory and the Urban Question.* London: Hutchinson.

Savas, E.S. (1974) "Municipal Monopolies vs. Competition in Delivery of Urban Services," *Urban Analysis 2*: 93–116.

Savas, E.S. (1981) "Intracity Competition Between Public and Private Service Delivery," *Public Administration Review 41*(1): 46–52 (January/February).

Savas, E.S. (1982) *Privatizing the Public Sector.* Chatam, NJ: Chatam House.

Savas, E.S. (1983) "A Positive Urban Policy for the Future," *Urban Affairs Quarterly 18*(4): 447–453 (June).

Sawers, Larry and William Tabb (eds.) (1984) *Sunbelt/Snowbelt: Urban Development and Regional Restructuring.* New York: Oxford University Press.

Saxenian, AnnaLee (1984) "The Urban Contradictions of Silicon Valley: Regional Growth and Restructuring of the Semiconductor Industry," pp. 163–197 in Larry Sawers and William Tabb (eds.) *Sunbelt/Snowbelt.* New York: Oxford University Press.

Schmidt, William (1984) "Twin Pillars of Economy Lag in South," *New York Times* (December 9): 1, 21.

Schmidt, William (1985) "Rural Southern Towns Find Manufacturing Boom Fading," *New York Times* (March 21): 1, 12.

Scott, Allen and Storper, Michael (eds.) (1986) *Production, Work, Territory: The Geographical Anatomy of Industrial Capitalism.* Boston: Allen and Unwin.

Sennett, Richard (1970) *Families Against the City: Middle Class Homes of Industrial Chicago, 1872–1890.* Cambridge, MA: Harvard University Press.

Serrin, William (1982) "Up to a Fifth of US Workers Now Rely on Part-Time Jobs," *New York Times* (August 14): 1, 22.

Serrin, William (1983a) "The New Sweatshop," *New York Times* (October 12–13): 1, 16.

Serrin, William (1983b) "Union's Stand Clouding US Steel Mill's Future," *New York Times* (December 22): 9

Seyler, H.L. (1979) "Contemporary Research Emphases in the United States," pp. 43–58 in Gene Summers and Anne Selvik (eds.), *Nonmetropolitan Industrial Growth and Community Change.* Lexington, MA: Lexington Books.

Shackleton, J.R. (1980) "Milton Friedman, Superstar?" *The Political Quarterly, 51*(3) (July-September): 349–353.

Shapira, Philip and Nancy Leigh-Preston (1984) "Urban and Rural Development in the Western United States: Emerging Conflicts and Planning Issues," *Journal of Architecture Planning Research, 1*: 37–55.

Simon, William (1978) *A Time for Truth.* New York: McGraw-Hill.

Sinfield, Adrian (1978) "Analyses in the Social Division of Welfare," *Journal of Social Policy, 7*(2) (April): 129–156.

Skidelsky, Robert (1979) "The Decline of Keynesian Politics," pp 55–87 in Colin Crouch (ed.), *State and Economy in Contemporary Capitalism.* New York: St Martin's Press.

Skocpol, Theda (1987) "America's Incomplete Welfare State: The Limits of New Deal Reforms and the Origins of the Present Crisis," pp. 35–58 in Martin Rein et al. (eds.), *Stagnation and Renewal in Social Policy.* New York: M.E. Sharpe.

Skocpol, Theda and John Inkelberry (1983) "The Political Formation of the American Welfare State in Historical and Comparative Perspective," *Comparative Social Research, 6*: 87–148.

Smith, Adam (1976) *An Inquiry into the Nature and Causes of the Wealth of Nations.* Oxford: Oxford University Press. (Originally published in 1776).

Smith, Michael Peter (1974) "Pluralism Revisited," pp. 3–32 in Michael P. Smith et al., *Politics in America: Studies in Policy Analysis.* New York: Random House.

Smith, Michael Peter (1979) *The City and Social Theory.* New York: St Martin's Press.

Smith, Michael Peter (1980a) "Critical Theory and Urban Political Theory," *Comparative Urban Research, 7*(3): 5–23.

Smith, Michael Peter (1980b) "Maintaining a Minimum," *New York Times* (December 1): 19.

Smith, Michael Peter (ed.) (1984a) *Cities in Transformation.* Urban Affairs Annual Review 26. Beverly Hills: Sage.

Smith, Michael Peter (1984b) "Urban Structure, Social Theory, and Political Power," pp. 9–27 in Michael Peter Smith (ed.), *Cities in Transformation.* Beverly Hills: Sage.

Smith, Michael Peter (1987) "The Uses of Linked Development Policies in US Cities." In Michael Parkinson et al. (eds.), *Regenerating the Cities: The UK Crisis and the American Experience.* Manchester: Manchester University Press.

Smith, Michael Peter and Hermann Borghorst (1977) "Citizen Participation in Urban Renewal in Two Federal Systems," *Problems of People's Councils, 36*: 147–187.

Smith, Michael Peter and Hermann Borghorst (1979) "Strategies of Urban Renewal Elites in the United States and the Federal Republic of Germany," *Journal of Parliamentary Affairs, 10* (June): 179–192.

Smith, Michael Peter and Dennis R. Judd (1983) "Structuralism, Elite Theory, and Urban Policy," *Comparative Urban Research, 9*(2): 28–33.

Smith, Michael Peter and Dennis R. Judd (1984) "American Cities: The Production of Ideology," pp. 173–196 in Michael Peter Smith (ed.), *Cities in Transformation: Class, Capital, and the State.* Beverly Hills: Sage.

Smith, Michael Peter and Marlene Keller (1983) "'Managed Growth' and the Politics of Uneven Development in New Orleans," pp. 126–166 in Susan S. Fainstein, Norman I. Fainstein, Richard Child Hill, Dennis Judd, and Michael Peter Smith, *Restructuring the City: The Political Economy of Urban Redevelopment.* New York: Longman.

Smith, Michael Peter and Richard Tardanico (1985) "Reactions Locales à la Crise Economique: Les Villes Americaine et la Nouvelle Division Internationale du Travail," *Anthropologie et Societés, 9*(2): 7–23.

Smith, Michael Peter and Richard Tardanico (1987) "Urban Theory Reconsidered: Production, Reproduction and Collective Action," pp. 87–110 in Michael Peter Smith and Joe R. Feagin (eds.), *The Capitalist City: Global Restructuring and Community Politics.* Oxford and New York: Basil Blackwell.

Smith, Michael Peter and Joe R. Feagin (eds.) (1987) *The Capitalist City: Global Restructuring and Community Politics.* Oxford: Basil Blackwell.

Smith, Michael Peter, Randy Ready, and Dennis R. Judd (1985) "Capital Flight, Tax Incentives and the Marginalization of American States and Localities," pp. 181–201 in Dennis R. Judd (ed.), *Public Policy Across States and Communities.* Greenwich, CT: JAI Press.

Smith, Neil and Peter Williams (eds.) (1986) *Gentrification of the City.* Boston: Allen and Unwin.

Stanbeck, Thomas M. (1979) *Understanding the Service Economy.* Baltimore: Johns Hopkins.

Stark, Fortney (1983) "Bring Fair Play to Taxing of 'Perks,'" *New York Times* (September 18): Sec. 3: 2.

Sterba, James (1975) "Booming Houston Puts its Faith in Unlimited Growth," *New York Times* (December 4): 35.

Sterba, James (1976) "Houston, as Energy Capital Sets Pace in Sunbelt Boom," *New York Times* (February 8): 1, 24.

Sternlieb, George, Robert W. Burchell and Charles M. Wilhelm (1983) "The City in a National Economic Context." Paper prepared for presentation at the Annual Conference of the Association of Collegiate Schools of Planning, San Francisco (October 21).

Stewart, Jon A. (1980) "Enterprise Zones: Tools of Urban Revitalization," *Transatlantic Perspectives* (January): 1–6.

Stone, Michael E. (1980) "Housing and the American Economy," pp. 81–116 in Pierre Clavel et al. (eds.), *Urban and Regional Planning in an Age of Austerity.* New York: Pergamon Press.

Storper, Michael (1981) "Toward a Structural Theory of Industrial Location," pp. 17–41 in J. Rees, et al. (eds.), *Industrial Location and Regional Systems.* New York: J.F. Bergin.

Subcommittee on Oversight, Committee on Ways and Means, US House of Representatives, 97th Congress, 1st Session (1981) "'Small Issue' Industrial Development Bonds." Washington, DC: US Government Printing Office.

Surrey, Stanley (1973) *Pathways to Tax Reform.* Cambridge, MA: Harvard University Press.

Swanstrom, Todd (1985) *The Crisis of Growth Politics: Kucinich and the Challenge of Urban Populism.* Philadelphia: Temple University Press.

Szelenyi, Ivan (ed.) (1984) *Cities in Recession.* Beverly Hills and London: Sage.

Tabb, William K. (1982) *The Long Default: New York City and the Urban Fiscal Crisis.* New York: Monthly Review Press.

Tarallo, Bernadette (1987) The Production of Information: An Examination of the Employment Relations of Software Engineers and Computer Programmers. Unpublished dissertation, University of California, Davis.

Tawney, Richard (1927) *The Acquisitive Society.* London: Bell.

Taylor-Gooby, Peter and Jennifer Dale (1981) *Social Theory and Social Welfare.* London: Edward Arnold.

Thurow, Lester (1980) *The Zero Sum Society.* New York: Basic Books.

Thurow, Lester C. (1982) "The Great Stagnation," *New York Times Magazine* (October 17): 32 ff.

Tiebout, C.M. (1956) "A Pure Theory of Local Expenditures," *Journal of Political Economy, 64* (October): 416–424.

Titmuss, Richard (1958) "The Social Division of Welfare." In Richard Titmuss, (ed.) *Essays on the Welfare State.* London: Allen and Unwin.

Tobin, James (1981) "Reaganomics and Economics," *New York Review of Books* (December 3): 11–14.

Tomer, John F. (1980) "Community Control and the Theory of the Firm," *Review of Social Economy, 38*(2) (October): 191–214.

Tyler, Gus (1980) "The Friedman Inventions," *Dissent* (Summer): 279–290.

Urry, J. (1981) "Localities, Regions, and Social Class," *International Journal of Urban and Regional Research, 5*(4): 455–474.

Vaughan, R.J. (1979) *State Taxation and Economic Development.* Washington, DC: The Council of State Planning Agencies.

Vidal, Avis C., Robyn S. Phillips, and H. James Brown (1984) "The Growth and Restructuring of Metropolitan Economies During the 1970s," paper presented at the Association of Collegiate Schools of Planning Twenty-Fourth Annual Conference (October 21–24).

Vidich, Arthur J. (1980) "Inflation and Social Structure: The United States in an Epoch of Declining Abundance," *Social Problems, 27*(5) (June): 636–649.

Viviano, Frank (1981) "Social Life Breaking Down in Hustling Sunbelt Cities." *San Francisco Sunday Examiner and Chronicle* (December 20): A6.

Wald, Matthew, Jr. (1980) "Welfare Means Bare Cupboards as Inflation Grows," *New York Times* (March 18): 1, B11.

Walton, John (1982) "Cities and Jobs and Politics," *Urban Affairs Quarterly, 18*(1) (September): 5–17.

Wayne, Leslie (1983) "The Corporate Tax: Uneven Unfair," *New York Times* (March 20): Section 3: 1, 26.

Weisman, Steven R. (1975) "How New York City Became a Fiscal Junkie," *New York Times Magazine* (August 17): 9.

Whitt, J.A. (1982) *Urban Elites and Mass Transportation.* Princeton, NJ: Princeton University Press.

Wiatr, Jerzey (1985) Public lecture delivered at Tulane University, New Orleans, LA (Fall).

Wilensky, Harold (1975) *The Welfare State and Equality: Structural and Ideological Roots of Public Expenditures.* Berkeley: University of California Press.

Wilensky, Harold (1976) *The 'New Corporatism,' Centralization and the Welfare State.* London and Beverly Hills: Sage.

Wolfe, Alan (1977) *The Limits of Legitimacy: Political Contradictions of Contemporary Capitalism.* New York: The Free Press.

Wolfe, Alan (1981) *America's Impasse: The Rise and Fall of the Politics of Growth.* Boston: South End Press.

Wolff, Robert Paul (1968) *The Poverty of Liberalism.* Boston: Beacon.

Wolpe, H. (1975) *Urban Politics in Nigeria.* Berkeley: University of California Press.

Yago, Glenn (1983) "Urban Policy and National Political Economy," *Urban Affairs Quarterly, 19*(1) (September): 113–132.

Zukin, Sharon (1980) "A Decade of the New Urban Sociology," *Theory and Society, 9*: 575–601.

Index